Women and society in Russia and the Soviet Union

Until the late 1960s, most western scholars studying the history, culture, social and political life and economy of the Soviet Union, paid scant attention to the participation and experience of women. The multifarious ways in which gender roles and perceptions of gender were influenced by and in turn influenced the heterogeneous cultures of the Soviet empire were largely ignored. Over the past twenty years, however, this neglect has slowly been rectified and now the study of women and gender relations has become one of the most productive fields of research into Russian and Soviet society.

This volume demonstrates the originality and diversity of this recent research. Written by leading scholars, it spans the last decades of tsarist Russia, the 1917 revolutions and the Soviet period. The essays reflect the interdisciplinary nature of women's studies and include chapters on women writers, women's work, women and politics, women as soldiers, female prostitution, popular images of women and women's experience of *perestroika*.

This study offers a fresh and interdisciplinary insight into women's experiences and the role of gender in Russia and the Soviet Union. It will be widely read by students and specialists of Russian, Soviet and women's studies.

Linda Edmondson is ESRC research fellow at the Centre for Russian and East European Studies at the University of Birmingham. She has been working for many years on the history of women in Russia and the Soviet Union and her publications include *Feminism in Russia, 1900–1917* and, as co-editor, *Civil Rights in Imperial Russia.*

Selected papers from the Fourth World Congress
for Soviet and East European Studies
Harrogate, July 1990

Edited for the
INTERNATIONAL COMMITTEE
FOR SOVIET AND EAST EUROPEAN STUDIES

General Editor
Stephen White
University of Glasgow

Women and Society in Russia and the Soviet Union

edited by

Linda Edmondson

ESRC Research Fellow, Centre for Russian and
East European Studies, University of Birmingham

CAMBRIDGE
UNIVERSITY PRESS

Published by the Press Syndicate of the University of Cambridge
The Pitt Building, Trumpington Street, Cambridge CB2 1RP
40 West 20th Street, New York, NY 10011-4211, USA
10 Stamford Road, Oakleigh, Victoria 3166, Australia

First published 1992

Printed in Great Britain at the University Press, Cambridge

A catalogue record for this book is available from the British Library

Library of Congress cataloguing in publication data

Women and society in Russia and the Soviet Union/edited by Linda
Edmondson.
   p. cm.
ISBN 0 521 41388 5
1. Women – Soviet Union – History – Congresses. 2. Women – Soviet Union –
Social conditions – Congresses. 3. Women – Soviet Union – Economic condi-
tions – Congresses. 4. Women authors – Soviet Union – Congresses. I.
Edmondson, Linda Harriet.
HQ1662. W566 1991
305.4'0947 – dc20 91-30488 CIP

ISBN 0 521 41388 5 hardback

Contents

Notes on contributors

RICHARD ABRAHAM, a former Education Fellow of Keble College, Oxford, is Head of History and Social Sciences at Graveney School in south-west London. Among his publications are *Alexander Kerensky: The First Love of the Revolution* (New York and London, 1987) and *Rosa Luxemburg: A Life for the International* (Oxford, Hamburg and New York, 1989). He is, with Lionel Kochan, co-author of *The Making of Modern Russia* (London and New York, 1983).

SUE BRIDGER is Lecturer in Russian at the University of Bradford. She is the author of *Women in the Soviet Countryside* (Cambridge, 1987) and was formerly Research Fellow on the project at Bradford funded by the Leverhulme Trust on 'Soviet Youth'. She is currently preparing a book on rural women and perestroika.

MARY BUCKLEY is Senior Lecturer in Politics at the University of Edinburgh. She is the author of *Women and Ideology in the Soviet Union* (Hemel Hempstead and Ann Arbor, 1989), co-editor of *Women, Equality and Europe* (London, 1988) and editor of *Soviet Social Scientists Talking* (London, 1986). She has edited *Perestroika and Soviet Women* (Cambridge, 1992) and is working on a book about glasnost and new social and political issues.

MARY SCHAEFFER CONROY is Associate Professor of History at the University of Colorado at Denver. She is the author of *Peter Arkad'evich Stolypin: Practical Politics in Late Tsarist Russia* (Boulder, Colorado, 1976). Since 1982 she has published a number of articles on the history of Russian medicine and pharmacy. She is currently writing a book on pharmacy, pharmacists and the pharmaceutical industry in late tsarist and early Soviet Russia.

LINDA EDMONDSON is ESRC Research Fellow at the Centre for Russian and East European Studies, University of Birmingham. She is the author of *Feminism in Russia, 1900–1917* (London, 1984) and co-editor, with Olga Crisp, of *Civil Rights in Imperial Russia* (Oxford,

1989). She is currently working on an ESRC-funded project on Women's Emancipation and Theories of Sexual Difference in Russia before 1917.

CATRIONA KELLY is Junior Research Fellow in Russian at Christ Church, University of Oxford. She is the author of *Petrushka, the Russian Carnival Puppet Theatre* (Cambridge, 1990) and of articles on Russian modernist poetry and on popular culture. She has also published several translations of fiction and poetry from the Russian, including Sergei Kaledin's *The Humble Cemetery* (London, 1990). She is currently working on a general history of Russian women's writings from 1830.

MARINA LEDKOVSKY (Astman) is Professor of Russian at Barnard College, Columbia University. Her publications include *The Other Turgenev: From Romanticism to Symbolism* (Würzburg, 1973) and *Russia Through Women's Eyes: an Anthology of Works by Women Writers Covering the Soviet Period* (Tenafly, NJ 1989). She has also written extensively on nineteenth- and twentieth-century Russian literature and culture. She is currently working with Charlotte Rosenthal and Mary Zirin on a guide to Russian women writers, for which she is preparing the post-1917 period, covering émigrés and Soviet writers.

BARBARA T. NORTON is Associate Professor of History at Widener University, Pennsylvania. She has written extensively on Russian political Masonry and the February Revolution of 1917, and she is currently working on a biography of E. D. Kuskova.

CHARLOTTE ROSENTHAL is Assistant Professor of Russian Literature and Language at the University of Southern Maine. She is the author of several articles on the Silver Age and is preparing a chapter on Silver Age prose for a book on Russian women writers, edited by Toby Clyman and Diana Greene. With Marina Ledkovsky and Mary Zirin, she is preparing a bio-critical guide to 500 Russian women writers to be published by Greenwood Press.

ELIZABETH WATERS teaches Russian and Soviet History at the Australian National University in Canberra. She has written a number of articles on social issues in the 1920s and in contemporary Russia, including prostitution, childcare and sexual equality. *Women in a Bolshevik World: Work and Family in Post-Revolutionary Russia* will be published shortly by Macmillan. She is currently working on a book on gender and Soviet society.

Preface

All the contributions to this volume were written in 1990 and revised before the disappearance of the Soviet Union. One small consequence of the final collapse of the Soviet system has been to render obsolete many place names and names of institutions that only a few months ago were still current usage. We have made some minor modifications to the texts of a number of the essays, but have decided to leave those by Sue Bridger and Mary Buckley substantially as they were. It would have been possible, if cumbersome, to have reset every 'is' as 'was' but to do so would give the impression that the conditions and debates recorded in both these chapters have disappeared along with the USSR. The problems that both these authors discuss are as pertinent to the Commonwealth of Independent States in 1992 as they were to the Soviet Union in 1990. As no one can be sure what the 'former Soviet Union' will look like a year, or five years, from now, it seems better to let these chapters stand, in effect, as eye-witness reports on the 'woman question' in the era of perestroika, and to leave it to future reporters to discover what effects the far-reaching political, economic and social changes of the coming years will have on the daily lives and aspirations of women in those lands that once comprised the Soviet Union.

February 1992

Introduction

Over the past two decades, the study of women in Russian and Soviet society has become one of the liveliest areas of Western research into Russian literature, history and the social sciences. The spark that ignited this new enthusiasm was, for many, the women's movement in the West, which burst into life in the late 1960s after a long quiescence of almost fifty years. For some of those who became involved in Russian women's studies, this new wave of feminism affirmed what they already knew; for others it had the force of a revelation; for still others it produced confusion or ambivalence and only slowly prompted them to view the world – and academia – from a new perspective. But however the new ideas were received, there is no doubt that they were responsible for generating a widespread curiosity that had never previously existed in the West about the history of Russia's female population, about Russian women writers and artists and about the current social and economic situation of women in the Soviet Union.

During this twenty-year period, however, most of the Western scholars who pursued these new concerns were living with a paradox. Many were initially attracted to the study of Russian and Soviet women because it seemed (from a Western perspective) that a degree of equality and recognition had been won by women in the Soviet Union that had not been achieved in the West. Whether or not they were working within a Marxist framework and whether or not they were sympathetic to the aspirations of Soviet socialism, they were impressed by Soviet claims not only to have legislated complete sexual equality, but also to have provided the conditions for its full realization – if not in the present, then at least in the foreseeable future.

The paradox lay in the fact that this apparent liberation was not matched by any serious interest among Soviet scholars in the processes whereby women were supposed to have achieved this state. Scholars in the Soviet Union were discouraged from writing about women, firstly by the inherited assumption (shared by the academic establishment in the West) that the subject was peripheral and even frivolous; and secondly

1

by the strait-jacket into which the history of women's liberation and the analysis of gender roles had been forced by Marxist–Leninist dogma. The Western historians, literary specialists and social scientists who sought information and enlightenment about the history of the women's movement, about women's contribution to Russian culture, about the complex problems raised by the Soviet legislation of equality and about the impact on women of the social and economic upheavals of the Soviet period, discovered that they were obliged to provide almost all the answers to their own questions.

Within the last few years this situation has begun to change. Even before the inauguration of glasnost, the bald claims made in the Stalin period and for a while thereafter, that the 'woman question' had been 'solved' in Soviet society, had been superseded by anxious concern about the seemingly harmful consequences of sexual equality for society and the Soviet family, and about the 'double burden' that women were forced to bear as a result of their liberation. As Sue Bridger and Mary Buckley discuss, in this volume, the Gorbachev era saw a very rapid development of the debate on the 'woman question' in contemporary Soviet society. Many areas that were formerly taboo were soon opened up, notably the discussion and graphic representation of sexuality, which before glasnost had been at least as heavily censored as in Britain during the 1950s. As both these contributors point out, the implications contained within much of this renewed debate are quite retrogressive, from a Western feminist viewpoint. Nevertheless, the public reopening of questions that previously were officially closed, has facilitated the reemergence of a native feminist movement and the beginnings of a serious, enquiring appraisal of women's contribution to Russia's history and culture.

It has become a cliché to state that women occupy a marginal position in the patriarchal culture and public life of Western society. Unfortunately, the cliché still contains a great deal of truth. Without question, this peripheral status led many Western researchers to assess more favourably than they would otherwise have done a society where both sexes expected to be in paid employment and where the ruling ideology (if not its implementation) was explicitly egalitarian. With few exceptions such researchers concluded, on closer scrutiny, that Soviet society in its way was as exploitative and misogynist as their own, and that the low level of material prosperity made Soviet women's lives more onerous in most respects that the lives of the majority of women in the affluent societies of the West. Once it became possible for Soviet feminists to express their opinions without fear of retribution (as occurred a decade earlier) and to engage in their own academic

research, many of the same criticisms that Western feminists had made
of their own societies were expressed by Soviet feminists of theirs. The
freedom of Soviet scholars to describe reality instead of concocted fantasy has had an enlivening effect not only on their work, but on all of us
in the West. Opportunities have grown by the month for an open
exchange of information and opinion between Soviet and Western
researchers. If it continues, the study of women and gender relations in
Russia and the states of the former Soviet Union will be transformed.

Although women remain under-represented in the sacred groves of
Western academe and the study of women is still generally accorded
marginal status, the margin has been pushed somewhat further towards
the centre in recent years. In North America, particularly, more women
are being employed by university departments, more are being appointed to influential committees and more attempts are being made to
remove the 'glass ceiling' that prevents women from being promoted to
senior positions. Women's studies courses are popular with students
(predominantly female) and increasing numbers of teachers in higher
education are recognizing gender as a legitimate category of analysis,
along with class, race, ethnicity and religion. A similar shift, if less
pronounced, has been taking place elsewhere in the West. The 1990
World Congress for Soviet and East European Studies, the source of the
contributions to this volume, was testimony to the shift. These essays
form only a percentage of the total number of papers presented whose
theme was women or gender in Russia or the Soviet Union. We may at
last have grounds for hoping that the emancipation of scholarship in
Russia – as in East-Central Europe – from the prison of conformity and
dogma, will continue to be matched by the release of Western academic
thinking from stereotyped, male-centred perceptions.

The reader of this anthology should not look for any sort of chronological narrative or thematic consistency, even though the essays are
arranged in a rough chronological order. The period covered is approximately the past century, but there is a yawning gap in the historical
coverage between 1930 and the Gorbachev era. While Charlotte Rosenthal and Marina Ledkovsky between them offer a continuous survey and
analysis of women writers from the Silver Age to our own, the volume
illustrates not only the great variety of recent research on women, but
also the huge scope still left for further research. The gulf in time
between Elizabeth Waters' chapter and Sue Bridger's is partly a consequence of the rather random choice provided by an academic meeting
like the Harrogate Congress. But it also reflects the fact that so many
vital questions were left unexamined from the moment Stalin finally
imposed his control to the moment when glasnost was formally

declared. Elizabeth Waters notes in the conclusion to her chapter that there was an official silence on the subject of prostitution for over fifty years. The same can be said of many subjects that have been taken up in the Soviet media in the last six years, as well as those that have not yet been broached. Western research, though extensive, was always constrained by the distortions and silences of Soviet scholarship before glasnost, and it is only within the past few years that scholars in the West have felt free to explore all the themes that engaged their interest.

Academic research in the West has been hemmed in by other barriers besides those erected in Moscow. It long suffered in the past from a distinct narrow-mindedness, closeted within separate and well-defended disciplines. History, literary studies and the social sciences have each tended to be so self-contained that little creative exchange was possible. Women's studies are essentially inter-disciplinary and this anthology has been designed to break down not only some of the barriers between subjects, but also the frontier-post of 1917, which for too long has neatly but unhelpfully compartmentalized the tsarist and the Soviet periods.

The selection in this volume is not by any means comprehensive. Quite apart from the gaps in subject matter and period that have already been mentioned, I must record with regret that a number of very thoughtful and imaginative papers had to be omitted, for reasons of space. I should like to thank all those who offered their papers for inclusion in this collection and to express the hope that they will publish them elsewhere in the very near future. This book is intended as just one contribution to the growing literature on women and gender relations in Russia and the Soviet Union and it is hoped that it will encourage much-needed further research in this area. Finally, I should like to thank all the contributors to the book for providing in their stimulating, well-researched and sometimes provocative essays some answers to many of the questions raised over the past two decades and, even better, for asking new questions that were never posed before.

1 'Better halves'? Representations of women in Russian urban popular entertainments, 1870–1910

Catriona Kelly

> Railway train, oh railway train!
> Brightly painted, on you run –
> Take me, take me, railway train
> To my Petersburg bit to have some fun![1]

This chapter extends an earlier study of mine, on misogyny in the Russian popular puppet show *Petrushka* (the equivalent of *Punch and Judy*). In that earlier study I argued that in the *Petrushka* show a female character was very often held up to ridicule whilst the male hero was not, that sexuality was an important element in this ridicule, and that this situation raised important problems of audience reaction which had not been properly dealt with by the three standard interpretations of *Petrushka* (vulgar Marxist class-based analysis, reading of the text as primal fertility ritual and the Bakhtinian theory of carnival).[2] The aim now is to move out from the study of the character and ramifications of one discrete popular urban tradition of the late nineteenth and early twentieth century and make some observations about the representation of women in a range of genres used for urban entertainment at that period. As before, I shall be putting considerable emphasis on the context of performance, and shall be analysing the question of the audience's reception. But I hope to take the final part of the discussion rather further, expanding a little on the possible implications of patterns in popular entertainment for wider issues of urban history at the turn of the century. Now, as then, an explicitly feminist perspective will be adopted.

The analysis of material by and about women raises some particular problems. It is fashionable to talk of the past as a difficult cultural text which requires decoding. But where this text presents women, the problem is, rather, how immediately, often distressingly, comprehensible the material seems. It may require defamiliarization (in the Formalist term) rather than decoding. To elucidate: the network of male–female power

5

relations understood by the word 'patriarchy' is susceptible to many historical variations. The political, economic and cultural dominance of men is not always identically constituted. To give one historical example: as the Soviet scholar N. L. Pushkareva has recently pointed out, the well-known restrictions on aristocratic women's movements outside the home in medieval Russia have to be understood against the background of a cultural system which also placed considerable restrictions on *men's* movements outside the home.[3]

Some of the texts which I shall look at do seem to place proscriptions on the behaviour of women which are familiar from other cultural contexts as well. As my title 'Better halves' suggests, an important aspect is the jocular presentation of marital and extra-marital relations. One central assumption is that women's sexuality is dependent on men's, another is the idea of the venal susceptibility of females to male financial largesse. In some ways this early capitalist world seems close to the late capitalist world, as is hardly surprising. But I hope to suggest that these stereotypes of female behaviour, though powerful and dominant, did not exist in isolation in the popular imagination and that the way in which they were perceived may not always have been as straightforward as first impressions might suggest.

The chapter is set out in three sections, as follows. First, there is a brief discussion on some problems of sources and methodologies. Second, there is a rather longer section dealing with the places where these genres were performed, and the composition of their audiences. Then follows a section where the genres themselves are analysed: as a preliminary, internal textual evidence is considered, and the chapter concludes with a discussion of how this material might be related to other elements in the popular culture of Russian cities.

The final part of the analysis is much the most problematic. I am aware of the objections which have been raised by historians to the pretensions of New Historicist exercises in close reading. These objections were recently given lucid exposition by Peter Burke: '[The New Historicists] do not always seem to be aware when they cross the line between evidence and speculation. At times they seem to be attempting to base conclusions about cultural or social history on little more than a close reading of a few texts.'[4] But it does seem worth trying to establish whether the selection of texts here is representative of any general trends, though the conclusions based on such a small amount of material can only be speculative. The aim must be to set up some general outlines which might be filled in later by investigation of other areas.

First, then, to the source and methodology problems – which are, in fact, quite considerable. When I told one ethnographer in Moscow recently that I was working on 'women and urban popular culture before the Revolution' her reaction was the aside: 'Who on earth gave her such a mad subject?' In a certain sense, of course, she was right: there was insanity in choosing an area so wide-ranging and so under-researched that it could be described as an undiscovered continent. It was also more than a little eccentric to select an area, which, as the remark quoted itself indicates, has suffered from a great deal of prejudice.

This prejudice is, firstly, attributable to the pro-rural bias of Russian and Soviet ethnography. It was only in the late nineteenth century that collection of urban ethnographical material began in earnest. Apart from phenomena which were sweetened by nostalgia because they seemed to be about to die out (for example, the peep show and the puppet show *Petrushka*), most of the material provoked hostile reactions even then. I shall cite some typical observations. V. Mikhulevich wrote in 1880 that only the Zaonezh'e had managed to 'preserve in purity the crystals of Russian folk fantasy'. In a characteristic synthesis of sartorial and aesthetic prejudice, he described popular urban genres as 'false and savage frock-coat–pot house poetry', saying, 'the so-called educated towndwelling member of the lower orders has dolled himself up German fashion . . . and has stuffed his vocabulary full of flowery bookish words and turns of phrase, has crammed his head with soppy romances and jolly rhyming verses – all of them, of course, in a form distorted to the point of caricature'.[5] In 1914 Aleksandr Iakub described many popular songs as 'mindless junk', saying that collections of them were 'littered with rubbish from the café chantant and the open stage'.[6] It is scarcely surprising that records of this material from before 1917 are far scantier than those of rural material, though they do exist. Mikhulevich quoted at some length from the material which he criticized, as did P. V. Shein in his late-nineteenth-century collection of songs transcribed from the oral medium, and Gleb Uspenskii in his essay on *chastushki*.[7]

Since the Revolution, suspicion of urban popular material has continued. It has been collected, but in smaller quantity than rural survivals; and between the mid-1920s and very recent times publications of it were extremely selective, since a label of 'petit-bourgeois vulgarity' and 'lumpenproletarian gypsy-ism' clung to many of the genres.[8] Recent indications are that attitudes are changing: there has, for example, recently been a major publication of narrative jokes collected in Leningrad.[9] But access to informants with first-hand knowledge of pre-revolutionary folklore is now very difficult and it is likely that much important material is gone for good.

The subject has also suffered from the blindness to gender issues which has characterized Russian culture for at least the last fifty years. A recent article in *Russkii fol'klor* pointed to the necessity of collecting urban folklore and suggesting a model questionnaire: this assumed that all informants would be men and that family traditions and most genres of folklore would be passed down in the male line.[10] However, appreciation that rural women had their own culture began in the early days of the Russian 'discovery of the people'. It provoked not only sententious reflection on 'peasant women's suffering', but also the gathering of women's own words (for example, the remarkable oral petitions made by village women against their husbands' cruelty).[11] The industry of folklore collectors in country districts also amassed material in another category, that of the presentation of women by men.[12] Hence, the paucity of material on lower-class urban women (whether in their own words or words about them), is probably as much attributable to anti-urban as to gender bias.

The relative importance of the two types of prejudice might be a matter of argument, but their combined effects are not. External records of the lives of lower-class urban women do exist; specific subcultural groups such as factory workers or prostitutes have received most attention. There has, though, been less concern to record women's actual utterances, still less folkloric texts emanating from them.[13] Any assemblage of women's own texts, therefore, tends to have an accidental character, and I have had to concern myself as much with what was said *about* women as with what was said *by* them.

As is only natural, the ideological explosiveness of these 'low' and 'vulgar' genres has also affected the methodology for their analysis. The iteration of dogma has been more common than the construction and elaboration of theories. Moreover, most studies on the culture of urban lower-class women deal, in the first instance, with political activism, and popular literary genres have been given little consideration. Two exceptions to this generalization, a book by V. Krupianskaia and N. Polishchuk, and a dissertation by Anne Bobroff, deal with material of only semi-urban origin (drawn from the Urals in the former case and the Central Industrial Region, especially the town of Kineshma, in the latter). Both studies are concerned, in the first instance, not with entertainment, but with texts tied to the seasonal 'calendar festivals' (Christmas, Shrove, Trinity Week), family festivals (marriage and funerals) and certain social rituals (fortune-telling and the departure of recruits into the army). Krupianskaia and Polishchuk have, moreover, applied what they describe as 'aesthetic' principles in selecting the folkloric material addressed, perhaps in order to facilitate their assertion that factory women enjoyed a higher 'cultural level' than did village women. Bobroff, whose spread of texts is wider and more representative, does use some material which overlaps with mine, but in many ways I find her approach unsatisfactory. She argues that popular entertainment texts, like other folklore, had one function: to condition men to bond to a peer-group of other men, women to bond to one particular man, the father of their children. This bonding was, she argues, biologically efficient in that maternal deprivation has an adverse effect on the development of all the primates (the rhesus monkey is adduced as an analogy here). But it made women politically impotent, able to protest only about issues which touched the welfare of their children.[14]

Objections could be made to the crude socio-biological reductionism of Bobroff's rhesus monkey analogy in an absolute sense; more to the point, it does not seem to suit the facts of life in the Podmoskov'e very well. Bobroff cites figures showing that the rate of mortality in Russian industrial centres between conception and adulthood was extremely high.[15] Hence, it is clear that women's conditioning could only have answered a biological imperative if that had been reduction in population numbers. Further, the arguments which she advances in order to belittle the importance of women's support groups, and deny the significance of texts in the male voice praising women or of texts in the female voice criticizing men, are not persuasive. But what is most important for my case here is that she models a society where folkloric genres were all used, irrespective of genre and context, in a pedagogical manner, and ensured a stable and cohesive set of complementary roles, which no historical process could apparently reverse. As I shall demonstrate, I think the 'pedagogical' purpose of popular entertainments is open to question. I shall argue, firstly, that the picture of social roles which they give is, though discriminatory, blurred and confused, and, secondly, that their relation to wider circumstances is contingent, problematic and fluid. Examination of this material may help to illuminate a little-known aspect of a period when, in fact, working women did occasionally become involved in protests in their own right, despite such disincentives as the family wage and a religious ethic which placed a high value on self-sacrifice.[16]

My definition of 'popular' here will be fairly general: I shall deal with genres which circulated amongst a lower-class audience: workers, small traders, artisans, domestic servants, casual labourers, prostitutes, the unemployed. The range may seem unduly wide, but there is, I feel, a need to get away from the dizzying circularity of the arguments employed by some Soviet commentators, with their rigid denomination of worker folklore versus *petit-bourgeois* folklore. The latter material is classed as vulgar because it is *petit bourgeois*, and *petit bourgeois* because it is vulgar, that is, if the commentator disapproves, it is labelled as the product of a retrograde class. It is likely that some categories of the broad group which I have outlined disapproved of entertainments: Old Believers, for example, would have seen them as the work of the devil, and the most politically self-conscious workers would also have disapproved in theory if not in practice. But there was some use of 'low' genres even by those who disapproved of them. The radical political songs which circulated amongst factory workers could never have had such success without a milieu where songs of all kinds enjoyed great popularity. Similarly, as the collection of Old Believer paintings held in the Krutitskoe Podvor'e section of the Historical Museum, Moscow, indicates, devout Old Believers drew on the secular tradition of the *lubok* print in their dissemination of religious propaganda.[17]

The places of entertainment where the genres which I shall describe were performed can be defined as 'lower-class' for the following reasons. They were all cheap, if not free: contributions might be invited according to means, or a low entrance price might be set: the range was 5 kopecks up to just over a rouble. (For comparison's sake, one might cite the 10 to 25 roubles charged for entrance to the *Bat* cabaret in Moscow in the 1900s.)[18] All the popular entertainments were accessible: the tickets were on public sale and in most cases no formal dress was required. The genres in which they all specialized were what is termed *Kleinkunst*, that is, were small scale: sentimental and comic songs, short farces, jokes and comic monologues.

There were quite a lot of places in Russian cities which satisfied these criteria of brief verbal entertainments available for low prices. To go from the most informal up, there were, firstly, the courtyards, streets, parks and other public places, where singers, musicians, puppeteers, clowns and so on gave performances. 'On Sundays the pavements [in working-class regions of Moscow] are packed with people of the lowest orders . . . and the sound of the inevitable accordion accompanies the singing of popular songs', wrote one commentator in the 1880s.[19] Secondly, there were the *traktiry*, *kabaki* and other eating and drinking houses, where it had been customary since at least the late eighteenth century for landlords to provide entertainments (gypsy choruses were much favoured), and also for patrons to invite entertainers off the street to give their shows indoors. The atmosphere of such a show was captured by Dostoevskii in *Crime and Punishment* (an account written in 1866, so a little earlier than our period):

[Raskol'nikov] found him in a tiny back room with a single window, next door to the main hall where twenty small tables were ranged and merchants, civil servants and all kinds of more humble folk [*liud*] were sitting drinking tea and listening to the hoarse bawling of a chorus. The click of billiard balls was coming from somewhere. On the table before Svidrigailov was an open bottle of champagne and a half-full glass. Besides him, there was a lad playing a small street organ and a strapping red-cheeked girl in a skirt of striped ticking. She must have been about eighteen years old, and she was singing in a rather harsh contralto voice to the organ's accompaniment, singing some lackey's song . . . Svidrigailov poured her a glass of wine and put a yellowed banknote on the table . . . Both [singer and player] had been brought in from the street.[20]

Latterly (after the turn of the century), live singing was supplemented or replaced, in the cheapest *traktiry*, by gramophone records of popular songs.[21]

By the late nineteenth century the streets and *traktiry* of Moscow and Petersburg had been joined by other venues of popular jollity: the 'manèges', riding schools become music halls, and the notorious 'café-chantants' of which contemporary commentators always spoke in tones breathless and laden with meaning. In both venues a mixed programme of songs, jokes and sketches such as was available in Western music halls was offered. Very similar were the 'cinema-miniatures', which offered film shorts as well as a live programme, and which were frequented by 'a public dressed in overcoats and often in a state of inebriation', as one variety artiste recalled disapprovingly in the Soviet period.[22]

Finally, there were the big seasonal (Shrove and Easter) funfairs given in squares and open spaces in the cities (for which the term *narodnye gulian'ia* is used in Russian), and the pleasure gardens (*uveselitel'nye sady*). These were both the oldest venues for entertainment, and in some ways the most fundamental, uniting the functions of all the others. Street singers and performers appeared at them, and there was a mixture of other shows. The small-scale entertainments at the Petersburg Easter funfair in the 1880s included 'raree-shows, jugglers' booths, cheap-jacks crying their goods'.[23] To these one might add puppet shows, and the acts by the *dedy*, clowns who stood outside roundabouts and on the outside balconies of theatres.

By the late nineteenth century the fairs and pleasure gardens also offered new venues of small-scale entertainments in the manner of café-chantants or cinema-miniatures. The open stages at the pleasure gardens presented variety shows.[24] On the fairgrounds had appeared a type of large covered roundabout, or *samokat*; here, too, variety shows were staged. Theodore Child visited one *samokat* at the Nizhnii-Novgorod fair in the 1890s, which he described as having two storeys, a large number of windows, whilst inside 'half the room was occupied with a carousel revolving on a disk sunk flush with the floor', with model horses and cars on it, and in the other half an entertainment was presented. This consisted of a Russian wind band playing alpenhorn-like instruments and a chorus singing 'lugubrious Russian songs'.[25]

The atmosphere in all these shows was informal and contact between performer and audience direct. During street and fairground shows spectators would fling open the windows to listen, applaud, join in the choruses, barrack the characters in the farces, so that 'the noise was deafening'.[26] Such audience participation also went on in the drinking-houses and café-chantants. A. Ia. Alekseev-Iakovlev records similar behaviour at Berg's café in the 1870s:

One day, when I was playing the role of the *jeune premier* Aleksandr in a vaudeville called *The Problems of Having a Tender Heart*, I had to address the actress playing the role of Katen'ka (she was a *chansonette* singer generally known by the nickname Katia the Canary) in the words, 'So, Ekaterina Ivanovna, you are innocent?' A gale of laughter rose from the stalls and there were cries of 'O-ho-ho!'[27]

'Then I sing them songs and dance like a bear or a drunken trollop [*baba*], and they laugh, yes by God they do, believe me; until they get the belly-ache', one *traktir* singer boasted.[28]

Accounts and pictures of all these types of entertainment make it clear that women were represented in the audiences and amongst the performers (they had been, indeed, since the early eighteenth century).[29] The café-chantants, and to a lesser extent the *traktiry*, were something of a special case, however, since the slur of prostitution hung over not only performers, but audience. Chekhov speaks of women in brightly coloured dresses 'like three-kopeck prints'.[30] A conferencier's song from one café-chantant programme anticipates wives' disapproval:

> Chanteuses are by the world condemned,
> But it seems unfair they should be damned,
> They're such dainty things,
> Giving skill and talent wings,
> As good food to the stomach, so they are to the head.
> Mind you, for married men things aren't that way:
> Wives should take care to keep hubby away.
> Or with passion they'll burn
> And may very well learn
> What'll soon make 'em bored with the marital bed![31]

For the two women whom Tolstoi encountered in a Khitrovka doss-house in the 1880s, 'sitting in the *traktir*' was, likewise, a euphemism for prostitution.[32]

The small-scale genres which I shall analyse were all performed, then, in conditions of some uproar and licence. All were performed dramatically: that is, they circulated in the oral tradition, though not exclusively there. Some performers might work from scripts, some from printed texts. Gramophone records and the enormously popular *pesenniki* (song books) made performances accessible outside the live arena, giving amateurs a way of learning the words, and in the case of gramophone records, also the tunes, of popular songs. So songs from the open stage or the pleasure gardens might be performed at cafés or on the streets. Accordingly, the cheap popular song-books and gramophone libretto collections are an important supplement to the scarce verbatim recordings of public entertainment material.[33] If not *created*, these songs were *re-created* in the oral milieu. The range of popular entertainment genres which I shall now present depends, therefore, not only on written records (transcriptions by philologists of performances by street entertainers) but also on printed records (a selection of a few songs from around 1500 printed in four late-nineteenth-century songbooks and three collections of gramophone libretti).

The boundaries of dating and location have been strictly observed. However, in one or two cases where no pre-revolutionary urban examples of a important genre were available, illustrations have perforce been supplied from Soviet or rural sources. This has been clearly indicated in the notes.

Most of the citations here are taken from comic genres. This is because they have attracted an even worse press than melodramatic or sentimental numbers. Iakub spoke, for example, of the 'coarse and contentless' nature of comic music hall songs; some would probably be unprintable even now in Russian official publications.[34] I have, however, given a few illustrations of the sentimental type of song as background for the main part of the discussion.

The most popular melodramatic genres for performance on streets, in pot-houses and other popular haunts were the 'romances'. The 'romances' proper were a lyric genre, often made up of rhyming four-line stanzas, sometimes with a repeating chorus. Their most favoured subject was love, frequently unhappy love. Often the unhappiness was because the beloved had died, as in the memorable number 'I lie in the grave and the damp earth drops on me', or in this song with its typical backdrop of a lilac tree:

> By the scented bough of the lilac,
> We sat near the murmuring stream,
> I fell to my knees beside her,
> Put my arm around her slender form;

The playful clouds passed above us,
And the breeze played over her face,
And her trembling hands so slender
I so long, with such passion embraced!
The funeral candles were glowing,
To the vaults came no sound from beneath,
The requiem mass they were singing,
The departed lay all decked in wreaths;
Tears of grief from my eyes descended,
I fell on her like one possessed,
And her cold dead hands so slender,
With such greed, with such passion embraced![35]

Also popular were the 'cruel romances', a term which is used to refer to
a semi-narrative genre which might also be called a 'street ballad'. The
extracts below come from two different examples. First we have a stanza
from the lachrymose tale of a Kamara muzhik who dies of exposure
after a name-day drinking bout, then a passage from a ballad narrating a
husband's gruesome double murder:

That February the twenty-ninth
Buckets of vodka and of wine
Kasian poured down his sinful throat,
Not giving his family a thought,
His dear wife and his two kiddies –
Twins they were, like as two peas.
Setting his cap in a dashing way
To his ladyfriend's house he made his way.
She'd made him a pile of pies and cakes,
Not half bad to look at, she'd got what it takes.
Her pies were good and piping hot,
And more, more, more she brought him out . . .

Though we forget, our children will not,
The story that I'm going to tell you about.
In brief, to cut the details short,
A husband's killing of his wife I report. . . .
And with his wife he soon grew cold,
And with his little daughter too.
But by and by he grew more bold,
A plan in his head began to brew.
What must be, must be, as you know:
He got the hots for the sister, so,
Like any beast so ravening wild,
He decided to skewer his wife and child.
He came to this view on the Saturday,
And on the Tuesday he got them out of the way.
The janitor helped in his wicked deed
For a sum of money that they had agreed.

And, so the neighbours wouldn't see,
They waited till night was dark as could be,
And in the cellar they dug a pit,
For to bury wife and daughter in it.
Night, it was dark, all lay asleep,
Not a soul was awake, no-one heard a peep:
They chose this time, as you may guess,
To give them a chance to clean up the mess. . . .[36]

Besides these different types of romance, there was the very specific sub-cultural genre of the *blatnaia pesnia*, or 'criminal/underworld song', often termed a 'prisoner's [*arestantskaia*] song' before the Revolution. Here the narrator, always a lawbreaker, tells of the tragedies which led to his 'going wrong':

When I was young and lived in freedom,
No sorrow and no want I knew;
My relatives they all adored me,
Happy was the family where I grew.
But wickedness my life it ruined,
And I went off the proper path,
I met a girl, became devoted,
And it nearly broke my heart.
She swore that yes she really loved me,
She swore it on her treacherous soul,
I was young and green and I believed her,
Believed that she was really mine.
And then I went to Moscow prison,
And there I served out three long years . . .[37]

Often the narrators of these songs are of unspecified gender. Where the narrator's gender *is* specified, it is, except in the criminal songs, as frequently feminine as masculine. There is some homogeneity also in the representation of behaviour: unhappy love in him is matched by unhappy love in her; both male and female infidelity are bewailed. In the street ballads, the tales of death and disaster affect both men and women, and the culprits can be of either gender. The symmetry is further illustrated by the fact that, in performance, women sang men's numbers and *vice versa*.[38]

The case of the comic genres is a good deal more complicated. Women are by no means the only subject of mockery. A song about a muzhik from Iaroslavl, for example, laughs at male dandification:

So who was I? A man from Iaroslavl,
Plain broke, not worth a penny.
But just you look where I've fetched up,
A dandy on the Nevskii!

They know just how to cut a suit,
And pad you out, them Prussians,
And if you've got the ready cash,
They'll frenchify the Russians!

If you've no hair, then buy a wig,
Shave like an Oriental man,
Your head may be *à la* muzhik,
Your mug is *à la* gentleman![39]

Mechanical and social innovations were a common subject of humour: there are peep-show texts in praise of mains drainage, car mudguards, 'wire-less telephones'.[40] Male outsiders, such as Jews, foreigners with funny accents or backward provincials, were all the butts of much popular humour.[41] But women and sexual relations were, none the less, extremely important subjects of popular comedy. These two subjects were, indeed, inseparable. It was not that women were always seen as the subject of male lubriciousness. The 'ugly old bag' was a favourite source of humour. Fairground clowns would hold up a picture of a hideous fright, 'my wife', and describe a woman so enormously fat that 'you can see her two versts away', with 'eyes like two awls' and a face 'like my shoe'.[42] But even in texts of this kind, the subject of women's sexuality was central in a negative sense: that is, the most laughable thing about these women is how unattractive they are. There was often emphasis on how ugliness and superannuation had put no brakes on sexual drive: such is the case with the 'crippled wife' and 'drunken old bag' of two peep-show texts, both of whom have made passes at much younger men:

Women one and all, look at this: a cottage in a village, what bliss; a husband who's drunk lying with empty pockets on a bunk, sleeping under the clothes and snoring through his nose. His wife is a cripple, cheeks red as an apple, she's cocking a snook at dad and spooning in the corner with a lad.

Here you are, lads, here's a drunken old bag, dressed all in rags, she's making a pass at a smart feller and asking him to go back home with her: 'come on lad, it'll be fine, let me show you a good time'. The lad eyes her up, and then 'e speaks out. 'Well, who wouldn't, says he, fancy such a beauty: hands rough and raw, hair an inch longer or more, ears like as ass's, wrinkles in masses, gob like an onion, nose like a bunion, face red as a parrot's bill, and old as the hills – or even older, maybe. Be off with you, this minute!'[43]

Given the close association between food and sex which popular texts often made (as in the Kamara muzhik's enjoyment of his ladyfriend's hot fresh pies) roundabout clowns' claims that their wives cannot cook – 'she scrapes all the dirt together and makes me a pile of pancakes like leather'[44] – might be read as a *double entendre*.

If one important source of humour in these texts is the excesses of elderly female frights, another is the tribulations of young males who attempt to interest indifferent females (for the most part not their wives) in a sexual connection. The 'stupid wife' in one of the peep show texts does not react to 'lammy della maison' when he plays footsie:

Here's another one for ye: a telephone with no wire. Or to put it in plain language, here's a picture of 'him' and 'her' at table. She's a stupid wife, and he's lammy della maison, so he stands on her tootsie under the table with hubby right by 'er, so that's what we call a telephone with no wire![45]

The husband in a song called 'The Crinoline' complains of how 'cross' this fancy new dress has made his wife:

> Crinoline, crinoline,
> I'd like to tear you apart!
> For, without you, I'd find
> My Nadezhda so kind,
> But with you, so bossy is she,
> So cross and so full of whimsy,
> Such a touch-me-not
> Of a wife I've got!
> Such a misery never was seen!
> And your hoop of steel it's been
> That has made her so stony of heart!
> Crinoline, crinoline,
> I'd like to tear you apart![46]

In a standard scene from late-nineteenth-century Petersburg versions of *Petrushka*, the puppet hero tolerates a scolding from his bride Matrena Ivanovna so that he can fondle her and pay her gross compliments.[47]

Whether in fairground genres or popular songs, the possession of material resources is often seen as a way of persuading women to comply with male sexual demands: so, in the scene just mentioned, Petrushka softens his bride with the offer of a 'bonnet and some bootees'. This connection is most evident in the *shansonetka*. In a song of blatant double meaning, one singer advertises any of the goods in her shop as available to a man who can pay cash down:

> My friends, not long ago now
> I opened a small shop:
> Trade's going well, yes and how,
> The fates have done me proud.
> I take care it's known who runs things,
> But I'm sweet to one and all,
> In commerce you can't beat that,
> You oblige, you'll have a ball!

> But I don't like to haggle,
> And credit's not my way:
> No goods without the money,
> Pay cash, or go away![48]

Another describes a bank cashier admirer who needs to keep his hand in the till on her behalf:

> I know exactly what to do with men,
> Though I'm no Venus, I do well with things:
> I do precisely what I like with them,
> They're the puppets and I pull the strings.
>   Oh, the men, how they all like me,
>   I've had so many I can't keep the slate;
>   They treat me well, they call me ducky,
>   I live damn well, I tell you straight.
>
> One cashier fancies me, the tom cat,
> He hangs around me day and night,
> Easy to see how much he likes me,
> He does the till whenever I like.
>   Oh, the men . . ., etc.[49]

For his part, the dandified muzhik from Iaroslavl decides that a wife is a commodity which he might as well acquire: 'I think I'll get myself a wife/ Who knows when I might need one?'[50]

Women, it should be noted, are not viewed as powerless in these vignettes. The *shansonetka* singers can boast of their skill in manipulating the male, and Petrushka's bride get away with spitting in the hero's eye before she gives way. But their power depends on colluding with masculine desires. Conceptions of a non-sexual role emerge only negatively, as when the roundabout clown's wife is said to be no good at housework, or when the *shansonetka* singer is reported to have escaped from a job as a servant or seamstress to go on the stage:

> That actress there, let me tell you,
> Was a housemaid just a day ago,
> Since then she's learnt a rhyme or two,
> And now she's the star of the show.[51]

Besides establishing a firm link between women and sexuality, these genres nearly always present the female sexual role as passive, where it is approved, using terms like 'kindness' to suggest complaisance. This emphasis on curtailment of women's sexual activity is underlined by structural devices. Men appeal for sympathy to other male characters on stage: so Petrushka asks his accompanist on the barrel-organ for advice on how to treat Matrena. Or the audience may be drawn in to the conflict on stage. The peep-show operator invites men in the audience to laugh at the drunken old *baba*'s approach to a young man, and approve the latter's rebuff: 'Here you are, lads . . .' Where women are addressed and drawn in, 'Women, one and all, look at this . . .' they are invited to laugh not only at the drunken husband but at his rubicund and ill-favoured wife.

As opposed to the melodramatic genres, then, the comic genres depict men and women in roles which are in some respects asymmetrical. Licence applies to men and to a lesser extent single women. It is always someone else's wife who strays; whatever their faults, the wives of narrators are chaste. The adoption of gender by comic performers seems also to have been asymmetrical. Men dressed as women in the Russian popular theatre, but there were apparently no female impersonators of men in the manner of Vesta Tilley.

So far as records allow us to determine, women spectators and women performers laughed at women's behaviour as much as men did. Benois, for example, has left a description of a group of 'housemaids, seamstresses and just plain wenches [*kakie-to devchonki*]' agog round a peep show, whilst Shein's anthology includes a disapprobatory song about a female drunk recorded from a female informant.[52] Several *chastushki* recorded in the late nineteenth and early twentieth centuries do, however, contain vigorous protests at male behaviour and statements of female autonomy:

> My dress was blue, but now the sun
> Has turned it pale and white.
> No, my beloved didn't leave me
> *I* left him. Serve him right.
>
> If they had told me what the swine
> Was going to do to me,
> I'd never have loved him at the time
> But drowned him in the sea![53]

None the less, the subject of husbands seems to have remained off-limits; lower-class women do not seem to have protested even in the oracular and abstract manner of intellectual women writers, for example, the poet Karolina Pavlova:

> Inevitably when we converse
> One subject always draws our talk:
> Too polite to name our husbands' faults
> We brand 'all husbands' as perverse.[54]

No husband stereotype, it seems, countered the wife stereotype.

It is, then, incontrovertible that the comic theatre differentiated roles.

There was a background of cynicism about all human behaviour: anything or anyone could be bought, but men did the buying more often
than women. The question at issue is whether these roles have a larger
significance, fixed patterns of behaviour once and for all. In other
words, was female subordination universal and inevitable? Here issues
become more complicated. It is important to decide how the audiences
'read' the information transmitted in the texts, that is, how they
perceived it and related it to a larger pattern of experience. It is here
that the context of performance delineated earlier in the analysis
becomes important.

If one considers the comic representations of women disseminated at
funfairs and in places of entertainment against the background of the
range of other possible views of women, rather than in isolation, important inconsistencies and incoherences emerge. The idea of disinterested
love, transcendent feeling (in the melodramas), jostles with the idea of
marriage or sexual intercourse for financial remuneration (in the com-
edies). On the one hand there is self-abnegation which levels difference,
on the other hand a self-seeking pleasure ethic to which difference is
essential. This diversity and contradiction were by no means all-
encompassing, however: by no means all the roles which were available
to women are represented here. For example, the very important issue
of parentage is largely irrelevant. Difficult as it is to believe given
current Russian views, the stereotype of woman as saintly mother-figure
does not appear in any of the popular entertainment genres.[55]

The various representations of women in popular entertainment are
contradictory when surveyed from a diachronic, as well as a synchronic,
perspective. The *shansonetki*, which suggested a possibility (however
circumscribed) of overt female sexuality, were a new genre. Russian
versions of what had originally been a French tradition had been performed since the early 1870s.[56] By the turn of the century, circulation by
means of record or song-book gave these texts, one may suppose, a
wider meaning than in their original context of paid performance for
male audiences. This new female role did not replace certain older
misogynist stereotypes, that of the 'bad housewife' and the 'scarlet
woman', which had been in circulation some centuries before.[57] But it
gave them a new emphasis. If facets of the 'bad woman' resemble those
in Daniil Zatochnik's *Epistle*, the portrait of the 'good woman' is no
longer neatly opposed, feature by feature, to that of the 'bad'. Popular
culture, unlike Russian high culture of the nineteenth century, imposed
no ethos of 'terrible perfection' on women.[58]

Since the message put over in entertainment genres was both jumbled
and partial, its pedagogical efficacy can be questioned. An important

requirement for propaganda is clarity. Equally, the context in which the texts used for popular entertainment functioned is very different to that in which the 'bonding rituals' of Bobroff's survey were performed. It was one in which norms of behaviour were suspended. Many of the texts stress their abnormal status: they contain references to the places of entertainment where they were performed, or to the idea of entertainment in a more general sense. *Shansonetki* and the equivalent genre for male singers, 'couplets', often open with a verse about song-singing:

> Evening to you, gentlemen,
> Here I am with a new song again,
> Putting all my effort in
> To give you some fun this evening . . [59]

Similar references to entertainments as such are found in the street genres too. Petrushka's bride accuses him of spending money on drinking and 'hiring musicians'.[60] Distancing procedures were also used in some texts: the participants might refer to the theatrical illusion, for example, saying 'I'll just go off-stage' or introducing another scene explicitly; ballads might open with formulae about story-telling.[61]

Rather then dealing with rituals of didactic purport, then, we are dealing with obvious fictions, travesties of reality. We have here an instance of a popular-cultural phenomenon which fits the model set up by Bertolt Brecht, where participants consciously adopt stereotypes and use them 'in quotation marks'.[62] It is worth noting that parodies of all the entertainment genres, whether sentimental or comical, were in circulation, which again suggests that disseminators and audience were capable of distancing themselves from the representations on view.[63]

That attitudes to women here were self-ironizing and unstable does not, however, mean that they were benign. Nineteenth-century Russian urban popular entertainments by no means functioned as the sort of jolly free-for-all which is often implied by the term 'carnival'; there was, rather, often an atmosphere of 'malicious and implacable violence'.[64] The aggression towards women which the comic genres licensed had unpleasant parallels in the public behaviour of working-class men towards women in cities. One of the most common manifestations of 'hooliganism' on Russian streets was crude sexual abuse directed by men at women.[65] A graphic and disturbing account of how male sexual authority might be asserted was given by Tolstoi in his Diary for 30 April 1889:

I went out to get some bread. On the way back, as I crossed the Devich'e Field, I stumbled on an appalling scene: a tall, well-built, well-dressed factory worker was demanding that a tiny little woman should either cooperate with his lewd aims as she had promised or return the money for her share of what they had drunk, that is, forty kopecks. She gave him twenty and tried to go. He boasted to the crowd surrounding them – which was on his side – that if she didn't give him the whole forty, he'd take her home for the night and rub her raw (guffaws). He started to drag her off to do the worst, then decided he'd take her over to the police and have her made to do what she'd promised. I went after him, lost hold of myself, interfered and gave him the twenty kopecks, saying, had he forgotten God and his laws. The crowd came over to my side. He was married, he said – but he had no sense of shame.[66]

The correlative was an ethic enforcing public sexual reticence on women. One set of late nineteenth-century statistics on urban women criminals indicates that one of the highest levels of conviction was for 'sexual misdemeanours', which is an indicator of social disapproval of public manifestations of sexuality as much as of the prevalence of such manifestations.[67]

The ethic of female reticence in public expressed in popular songs and street shows appears to have been an expression of wider attitudes. But so too do the uncertainty and conflict manifested in these shows. When Tolstoi objected to the scene on Devich'e Field, as described above, the crowd was swayed: 'came over to my side'; that is, two standards of behaviour were competing for recognition.

The growth in women's active participation as disseminators of popular entertainments also has some parallels in other genres performed publicly. Women workers were capable of identifying their own interests not only as members of the working class, but specifically as women.[68] They were capable of protest not only on economic, but on sexual issues; revolutionary songs which circulated in the oral milieu dealt with sexual harassment:

> Zube the foreman gives us trouble,
> Calls us in the office every day
> Shuts the door and locks it at the double,
> Then he has his wicked way.[69]

But such public protests did not include complaints against the oppressions of family life and exploitation by husbands of the kind that preoccupied bourgeois feminists at this period. There is, indeed, evidence that working-class women had little sympathy with public protests against the fabric of family life.[70]

Performed in public, popular entertainments, not surprisingly, reflected restrictions on women's public behaviour. As far as private behaviour goes, matters are less clear. One should be careful about extrapolating too much from these genres. Women in the audience watching fairground shows may not necessarily have been laughing at their own powerlessness in sexual or marital relations: they may just as well have seen these plays as reversals of reality. The facts of private sexual behaviour amongst women of the lower classes are difficult to establish, given the polemical views on sexual libertarianism held by some of the contemporary commentators from the intelligentsia who took an interest in the matter.[71] But an area where more neutral speculation is possible is that of social standing. The entertainment genres are inclined to favour unmarried young women over married older ones; in reality, one suspects, just the opposite relation obtained.[72]

In the public genres women are always presented in isolation; in private, by contrast, they seem (*pace* Bobroff) to have enjoyed some sense of solidarity and support for each other in defence against men. The worker-memoirist V. Karelina recalled, for example, that the initial hostility amongst her comrades' wives was softened when she began to act as their *confidante*.[73]

But if the entertainment genres do not necessarily reflect women's private behaviour, they do, at the very least, reflect a process by which women accepted and disseminated public representations of themselves which, for the most part, underplayed the power which they had in private. Overall, then, a binary opposition between domestic and public worlds underlay representations and reactions. There was a trade-off of spheres of influence (men's external versus women's domestic power). The evidence in popular genres suggests that a growing tradition of public female complaint about male behaviour did not include the voicing of a critical attitude to the male–female relationship in the home. There is an absence from popular genres of a sense that women's domesticity is cramping (a vital theme in writing by educated Russian women in the nineteenth century). Perhaps this absence reflects a situation which had never been questioned. But, since the years after 1870 were a period in which very rapid changes were taking place, and one when the binary opposition private/public must have come under considerable threat, given the enforcedly public nature of many working-class families' domestic arrangements in the late nineteenth century, it is more likely that women held on to their domestic role as something reassuring, something that offered them, even, a degree of autonomy and personal space. Whether one chooses to see this attachment as self-affirmation or self-deception,[74] it was more a compromise with immediate circumstances than the inevitable result of tradition since time immemorial.[75] In this matter, as in much else, there was a marked contrast between the urban popular culture of this period and the settled, binarily organized proscriptions reflected in traditional village culture on the one hand, and Old Russian written culture on the other.[76]

Notes

1. Z. I. Vlasova and A. A. Gorelov, *Chastushka v zapisiakh sovetskogo vremeni* (Moscow–Leningrad, 1965), no. 5386. (Recorded in the 1920s.)
2. Catriona Kelly, 'A stick with two ends: *Petrushka* as a case-study of misogyny in popular culture', in Jane Costlow, Stephanie Sandler and Judith Vowles (eds), *Bodies, Stories and Images: Representations of Sexuality in Russian Culture* (in preparation).
3. N. L. Pushkareva, *Zhenshchiny drevnei Rusi* (Moscow, 1989), p. 96. I do not think the interests of women's history are best served by the crude ahistorical reductionism of, for example, Joanna Hubbs' recent gallop through half a dozen millennia in *Mother Russia* (Bloomington, IN, 1989). But I hope to avoid the converse danger – pusillanimous relativism – too.
4. Peter Burke, 'Open the curtains and see the puppets play', *London Review of Books*, 5 Jan. 1989, pp. 18–19.
5. V. Mikhulevich, 'Izvrashchenie narodnogo pesnetvorchestva', *Istoricheskii vestnik*, vol. 3 (1880), pp. 753, 756, 751.
6. Aleksandr Iakub, 'Sovremennye narodnye pesenniki', *Izvestiia otdeleniia russkogo iazyka i slovesnosti Imperatorskoi akademii nauk*, no. 1 (1914), p. 91.
7. P. V. Shein, *Velikoruss v svoikh pesniakh, obriadakh, obychaiakh, verovaniiakh, skazkakh, legendakh i t.p.* (St Petersburg, 1891); Gleb Uspenskii, 'Novye narodnye pesni: iz derevenskikh zametok', *Polnoe sobranie sochinenii*, vol. 12 (Moscow, 1953), pp. 39–56.
8. For attacks on *petit-bourgeois* folklore see M. Reisner, 'Bogema i kul'turnaia revoliutsiia', *Pechat' i revoliutsiia* no. 5 (1928), pp. 81–96; P. Sobolev, 'Sovetskii fabrichno-gorodskoi fol'klor', *Pechat' i revoliutsiia* no. 6, (1929), pp. 89–98; Iurii Sokolov, *Russkii fol'klor*, pt 4 (Moscow, 1932). The history of such attacks is summarized in G. S. Smith, *Songs to Seven Strings* (Bloomington, IN, 1984), pp. 58–96, and in the introduction to O. B, Alekseeva, *Ustnaia poeziia russkikh rabochikh: dorevoliutsionnyi period* (Leningrad, 1971) – which itself demonstrates the persistence of hostility to the category *petit-bourgeois*.
9. Ia. Lur'e, 'Sovremennyi leningradskii fol'klor', *Uchebnyi material po istorii literatury: zhanry slovesnogo teksta: anekdot* (Tallinn, 1989), pp. 118–51.
10. B. P. Krugliashova, 'Russkii fol'klor v sovremennom gorode: metodika sobiraniia, zhanrovyi sostav', *Russkii fol'klor*, vol. 23 (1985), pp. 88–94.
11. Ia. Ludmer, 'Bab'i stony', *Iuridicheskii vestnik*, no. 11 (1884), pp. 446–67 (pt 1); no. 12 (1884), pp. 658–75 (pt 2).
12. See for example N. Amerigo, *Zhenshchina v russkikh poslovitsakh* (Moscow, 1908); E. F. Budde, *Polozhenie russkoi zhenshchiny po bytovym pesniam* (Voronezh 1883); M. Maksimov, *Koe-chto o zhenshchinakh: sbornik poslovits, izrechenii, shutok* (Moscow, 1910).
13. The memoirs of women workers are an exception to the general silence of sources on working-class women's lives, and, for all their emphasis on political activism, are often illuminating on other matters as well. The

revelation that picnics and parties were used as cover for illegal meetings illustrates, for example, what regular occurrences such events must have been. See A. G. Boldyreva in E. A. Korol'chuk, *V nachale puti: vospominaniia peterburgskikh rabochikh, 1872–1897 gg.* (Leningrad, 1975), p. 263.

14. V. P. Krupianskaia and N. S. Polishchuk, *Kul'tura i byt rabochikh gornozavodskogo Urala kontsa XIX – nachala XX veka* (Moscow, 1971); Anne Bobroff 'Working women, bonding patterns and the politics of daily life' (PhD Thesis, University of Michigan, 1982). For a summary see her 'Russian working women: sexuality in bonding patterns and the politics of daily life', in Ann Snitow, Christine Stansell and Sharon Thompson (eds), *Powers of Desire: the Politics of Sexuality* (New York, 1983), pp. 206–27.

15. Bobroff, 'Working women', p. 141.

16. No vows are made in the Orthodox wedding service, but prayers and readings stress the need for self-sacrifice or even self-martyrdom. The Troparia sung at the Crowning speak of 'holy Martyrs, ye who have bravely striven, and have been crowned', *The Sacrament of Holy Matrimony: The Greek Text with a Rendering in English* (London, 1929), p. 28. The first reading is taken from St Paul's Epistle to the Ephesians, chapter 5 (the familiar passage exhorting wives to obey their husbands), ibid., p. 20. A decline in agricultural ritual seems to have gone with urbanization (see note 76 below). There may have been a corresponding decline in the peasant rituals associated with marriage, and hence an increase in the prominence of Orthodox marriage practice in popular culture.

17. Some such paintings are reproduced in Alla Sytova, *The Lubok* (Leningrad, 1984), pp. 116–23.

18. Harold B. Segel, *Turn of the Century Cabaret: Paris, Barcelona, Berlin, Moscow, St Petersburg, Vienna, Munich* (New York, 1987), p. 263.

19. D. A. Pokrovskii, 'Ocherki Moskvy', *Istoricheskii vestnik*, vol. 53 (1893), p. 116; see also N. S. Anushkin (ed.), *Ushedshaia Moskva: vospominaniia sovremennikov o Moskve vtoroi poloviny XIX veka* (Moscow, 1964), pp. 151, 339–42; P. Boborykin, 'Sovremennaia Moskva', in *Moskva i moskovskaia promyshlennaia oblast'* (St Petersburg, 1899), p. 281; M. Baranov, 'Malen'kie oborvantsy: iz zhizni zabroshennykh detei: ocherk', *Severnyi vestnik* no. 11, (1888), pp. 1–29.

20. Fedor Dostoevskii, *Prestuplenie i nakazanie*, pt 6, ch. 3, in *Polnoe sobranie sochinenii v 30 tomakh*, vol. 6 (Moscow, 1973), pp. 355–6.

21. Maurice Baring, *Mainsprings of Russia* (London, 1915), p. 169. Gramophone records were manufactured by the British-owned Gramophone Company at their factory in Riga from 1901; the recording engineer Fred Gaisberd made several trips to Russia from 1900 to 1914, during which he made a large number of recordings. Gramophones cost up to 600 roubles, but cheap models were available at 80 roubles apiece. They were massively popular in Russia: by 1912 the turnover of the two foreign companies operating there was more than 20 million roubles p.a., and by 1915 the six factories in the empire were producing about 20 million records a year. See J. R. Bennett, *A Catalogue of Vocal Recordings from the Catalogue of the Gramophone Company Ltd* Blandford, 1977); J. N. Moore,

Voice in Time: The Gramophone of Fred Gaisberd (London, 1976); entries under 'Grammofon' in *Novyi entsiklopedicheskii slovar'*, izd. Brokgauza i Efrona, vol. 14 (St Petersburg, 1914), cols. 696–6. and *Bol'shaia sovetskaia entsiklopediia*, vol. 7 (Moscow, 1972), p. 244. In cheap *traktiry*, gramophones seem to have replaced the mechanical organs, or orchestrions, which are mentioned in many earlier accounts of visits to taverns.

22. *Langenscheidts Sachwörterbuch: Land und Leute in Russland* (St Petersburg, c. 1910), p. 86; Anton Chekhov, 'Salon de Varieté', in *Polnoe sobranie sochinenii i pisem v 30 tomakh*, vol. 1 (Moscow, 1974), pp. 90–4; Moore, *Voice in Time*, pp. 66–7; E. M. Uvarova, *Estradnyi teatr: miniatiury, obozreniia, miuzik-kholly 1917–1945 gg.* (Moscow, 1983), p. 13.

23. John Baddeley, *Russia in the 'Eighties* (London, 1921), p. 216. On street-singers see G. Vasilich, 'Ulitsy i liudi sovremennoi Moskvy', *Moskva v ee proshlom i nastoiashchem*, vol. 12 (1912), p. 11; on other acts A. M. Konechnyi, 'Peterburgskie narodnye gulian'ia na maslenoi i paskhal'noi nedeliakh', in N V. Iukhneva (ed.), *Peterburg i guberniia: istoriko-etnograficheskie issledovaniia* (Leningrad, 1989), pp. 21–52; Catriona Kelly, *Petrushka: The Russian Carnival Puppet Theatre* (Cambridge, 1990), pp. 18–58.

24. There were two open stages at the *Aquarium* gardens in Petersburg, one English visitor recorded in the 1890s, J. Cartwell Ridley, *Things Seen in Russia* (Newcastle-upon-Tyne, 1893), p. 94; cf. W. Barnes Steveni, *Petrograd* (London, 1915), pp. 182–6. The capital had the highest share of the 110 public gardens in the Russian Empire, according to a survey of 1896, 'Smes'', *Istoricheskii vestnik* vol. 63 (1896), p. 736. On the pleasure gardens in Moscow, see P. I. Shchukin, 'Iz vospominanii', *Shchukinskii sbornik* vol. 10 (Moscow, 1912), p. 140; Anushkin, *Ushedshaia Moskva*, p. 149; *Vseobshchii putevoditel' po Moskve* (Moscow, 1910), pp. 59–61.

25. Theodore Child *et al.*, *The Tsar and His People* (New York, 1891), p. 234; cf. Konechnyi, 'Peterburgskie narodnye gulian'ia', p. 43.

26. Baddeley, *Russia*, p. 216; see also Anushkin, *Ushedshaia Moskva*, pp. 151, 339, 362.

27. A. Ia. Alekseev-Iakovlev, 'Vospominaniia'. GPB, f. 1130, arkh. A. P. Gershuni, no. 317. Publication, with annotations, in preparation as N. A. Rumiantseva and A. M. Konechnyi, 'Peterburgskii balagannyi master A. Ia. Alekseev-Iakovlev'. I would like to acknowledge A. M. Konechnyi's kindness in showing me the manuscript of this publication.

28. E. Liatskii, 'Skomoroshina nashikh dnei', *Istoricheskii vestnik*, vol. 78 (1899), p. 469.

29. Information on women spectators in the eighteenth century – they were sometimes arrested when drunk – can be found in L. M. Starikova's 1987 publication of material from police archives, 'Teatral'no-zrelishchnaia zhizn' Moskvy v seredine XVIII veka', *Pamiatniki kul'tury: novye otkrytiia. Ezhegodnik 1986* (Moscow, 1987), pp. 133–88. On women performers see Starikova, 'Novye dokumenty o deiatel'nosti ital'ianskoi truppy v Rossii v 30-e XVIII veka v russkom liubitel'skom teatre etogo perioda', *Pamiatniki kul'tury: novye otkrytiia. Ezhegodnik 1988* (Moscow, 1989), pp. 67–95, and

Sergei Ignatov's excellent short history of the early Russian theatre, *Nachalo russkogo teatra i teatr petrovskoi epokhi* (Moscow, 1920).

30. Chekhov, 'Salonde Varieté', p. 90.
31. *Polnyi sbornik libretto dlia gramofona* (see note 33), vol. 5 (c. 1906), p. 131.
32. L. N. Tolstoi, 'Tak chto zhe nam delat'', *Polnoe sobranie sochinenii* vol. 25 (Moscow, 1937), p. 209.
33. The general observations about popular entertainments below are based on the following sources. 1. Orally transmitted material: V. S. Bakhtin, *Chastushka* (Moscow–Leningrad, 1966); A. M. Konechnyi, 'Raek v sisteme peterburgskoi narodnoi kul'tury', *Russkii fol'klor*, 25 (1989), pp. 123–38; Eugenie Lineff, *The Peasant Songs of Great Russia, as They Are in the Folk's Harmonization*, pt 1 (St Petersburg, 1906); A. F. Nekrylova and N. I. Savushkina, *Fol'klornyi teatr* (Moscow, 1988); Shein, *Velikoruss*; Uspenskii, 'Novye narodnye pesni'; Vlasova and Gorelov, *Chastushka*. 2. Popular printed editions: *Novyi polnyi pesennik: sbornik izbrannykh pesen russkikh, malorossiiskikh, tsyganskikh, zhidovskikh i tatarskikh romansov, iumoristicheskikh i satiricheskikh stikhotvorenii, arii i kupletov* (Moscow, 1869); *Polnyi russkii pesennik: 1000 pesen* [1] (Moscow, 1893); *Polnyi russkii pesennik bolee 600 pesen russkikh i tsyganskikh* (Moscow, 1893); *Polnyi russkii pesennik: 1000 pesen* ([2]: a different compilation from [1] above) (Moscow, 1893); *Polnyi sbornik libretto dlia grammofona* vols 2–5 (St Petersburg, c. 1904–6) (a series published by the Gramophone Company in Russia to accompany its records). The evidence for *transmission* between the two sources is as follows. Mikhulevich, 'Izvrashchenie narodnogo pesnetvorchestva', gives full details on the reproduction of high literary texts in songbooks; he also indicates that by the late nineteenth century many songs from the popular theatre appeared in these widely circulated volumes. There is overlap, too, between song collections taken down orally by philologists and songbooks. Shein, *Velikoruss*, nos 982–3, 975, 921 all appear in Sytin's 1893 collections; a *shansonetka*-like song appears in Sytin's *Polnyi russkii pesennik: 1000 pesen*. The gramophone libretti reproduce certain songs also found in street texts, e.g. 'Pogib ia mal'chishka', *Polnyi sbornik libretto*, vol. 2, p. 197, is quoted in the version of *Petrushka* recorded by V. Doroshevich, *Sakhalin* (St Petersburg, 1901), p. 131. There are also more indirect kinds of cross-fertilization: the stereotype of the 'Iaroslavl muzhik' was dramatized in the *Petrushka* shows, where the hero was represented as an arrival from Iaroslavl leading the life of a Petersburg dandy.
34. Iakub, 'Sovremennye narodnye pesenniki', p. 83.
35. *Polnyi sbornik libretto*, vol. 2, p. 188.
36. *Polnyi russkii pesennik: 1000 pesen* [1], p. 1; Sokolov, *Russkii fol'klor*, p. 66 (Recorded in the 1920s).
37. *Polnyi sbornik libretto* vol. 2, p. 189.
38. The romance quoted in the text is for a man, but similar romances for women are common; Ibid., vol. 5, p. 251 is a man's song, 'Ia by umeret' zhelal', in a recording by the famous contralto Varia Panina; 'Bednaia mat'', ibid., vol. 2, p. 44, is rendered by a baritone 'mother'.

28   *Catriona Kelly*

39. *Polnyi russkii pesennik: 1000 pesen* [1], p. 11.
40. Konechnyi, 'Raek', pp. 135, 138.
41. See for example *Polnyi sbornik libretto*, vol. 2, pp. 192, 230.
42. Nekrylova and Savushkina, *Fol'klornyi teatr*, pp. 396–7.
43. Konechnyi, 'Raek', p. 135.
44. Nekrylova and Savushkina, *Fol'klornyi teatr*, p. 397.
45. Konechnyi, 'Raek', p. 135.
46. *Noveishii pesennik*, p. 336.
47. Nekrylova and Savushkina, *Fol'klornyi teatr*, pp. 286–7.
48. *Polnyi sbornik libretto*, vol. 5, p. 148.
49. Ibid., vol. 3, p. 36.
50. *Polnyi russkii pesennik: 1000 pesen* [1], p. 11.
51. *Polnyi sbornik libretto* vol. 2, p. 33.
52. Aleksandr Benua [=Alexandre Benois], *Moi vospominaniia*, vol. 1 (Moscow, 1981), p. 217; Shein, *Velikoruss*, no. 676.
53. Bakhtin, *Chastushka*, no. 578 (first published by Eleonskaia in 1914); Uspenskii, 'Novye narodnye pesni', p. 47. Both of these were recorded in villages, but, whatever the origins of the *chastushka*, which are disputed, it was on the way to becoming *the* central genre of urban popular song by the late nineteenth century.
54. Karolina Pavlova, *Polnoe sobranie stikhotvorenii* (Moscow–Leningrad, 1964), p. 312.
55. The mother veneration cult of popular Russian life is enormously strong. I was told by a working-class Russian friend that girls should not take part in the Epiphany ritual of breaking the ice of rivers in order to swim, because they were 'future mothers'. He was absolutely serious; indeed, such beliefs are so little a laughing matter that they have more to do with Orthodox veneration of the Mother of God than with the flippancy of the popular entertainment genres. It might be added that there is no direct evidence in these genres, either, for the supposed popular hostility to prostitution on which Bolshevik post-revolutionary propaganda drew (see for example Aleksandra Kollontai's story 'Sisters' in *The Love of Worker Bees*); see also Elizabeth Waters' contribution to this volume (editor's note).
56. Anushkin, *Ushedshaia Moskva*, p. 151; A.F.B., 'Teatr Opera-Buff i frant-suzskie pevtsy v Peterburge', *Peterburgskii listok,* 2 Mar. 1878, p. 3.
57. The stereotype of the 'bad housewife' and the 'scarlet woman' both had been in circulation since the Middle Ages: they appear in Daniil Zatochnik's 'Epistle' and in many other medieval Russian sources (See Pushkareva, *Zhenshchina*, pp. 100–2).
58. See Barbara Heldt, *Terrible Perfection* (Bloomington, IN, 1987), where this is the term used for the coercive ideology of female self-sacrifice and gen-teelism incumbent on women from the Russian gentry and bourgeoisie. That hierarchical societies may place more restrictions on upper-class than on lower-class women has been convincingly argued by Jacklyn Cock in her study of black South African servants, *Maids and Madams* (London, 1989).
59. *Polnyi sbornik libretto* vol. 5, p. 129; cf. vol. 2, pp. 218, 233, 259. 261, 264; vol. 5, p. 150.
60. Nekrylova and Savushkina, *Fol'klornyi teatr*, pp. 286–7.

61. Ibid., p. 419; for the ballad formula Sokolov, *Russkii fol'klor*, p. 66 (also quoted above).

62. Bertolt Brecht, *Gesammelte Werke*, vol. 8 (Frankfurt am Main, 1967), p. 504.

63. On parodies see Ia. I. Gudoshnikov, *Ocherki russkoi literaturnoi pesni XVIII–XIX vv.* (Voronezh, 1972), p. 145, where a parody of the well-known 'cruel romance' 'Spriatalsia mesiats za tuchu' is given: 'Kogda ty byvaesh' so mnoiu / Togda ia byvaiu s toboi / Kogda ia byvaiu s toboiu / Togda ty byvaesh' so mnoi.' Parodies of the *shansonetka* appear in all the volumes of *Polnyi sbornik libretto*; its fourth volume also contains a parody of the 'criminal song' entitled 'Khuligan'. The self-conscious and parodistic tendency in the popular theatre was perhaps not as marked as it was in the elite cabaret, but 'metatheatre' was not a feature proper only to the latter (*pace* a recent article by A. M. Konechnyi, V. Ia. Morderer, A. E. Parnis and R. D. Timenchik, 'Artisticheskoe kabare "Prival komediantov" ', *Pamiatniki kul'tury. Novye otkrytiia. Ezhegodnik 1988* (Moscow, 1989), p. 100).

64. Terry Eagleton, 'Bakhtin, Schopenhauer, Kundera', in Ken Hirschkop and David Shepherd (eds), *Bakhtin and Cultural Theory* (Manchester and New York, 1989), p. 185.

65. Bobroff, 'Working women', p. 247; Joan Neuberger, 'Stories of the street; hooliganism in the Saint Petersburg popular press', *Slavic Review*, vol. 48, no. 2 (Summer 1989), p. 183.

66. L. N. Tolstoi, 'Dnevnik 1889 goda', *Polnoe sobranie sochinenii* vol. 50 (Moscow, 1952), p. 77.

67. I. Foinitskii, 'Zhenshchina-prestupnitsa', *Severnyi vestnik*, vol. 2 (1893), p. 138; cf. A. Zhbankov, 'Polovaya prestupnost' ', *Sovremennyi mir*, no. 7 (1909), p. 56.

68. S. A. Smith, 'Workers and civil rights 1899–1917', in Olga Crisp and Linda Edmondson (eds), *Civil Rights in Imperial Russia* (Oxford, 1989), p. 164.

69. A. I. Astakhova and P. G. Shiriaeva, 'Staraia rabochaia pesnia', *Sovetskaia etnografiia*, nos 1–2 (1934) p. 201 (recorded in the 1930s).

70. Richard Stites, *The Women's Liberation Movement in Russia: Feminism, Nihilism and Bolshevism 1860–1930* (Princeton, 1978), pp. 302–3.

71. To intellectual observers, Russian working-class women seemed extremely free in their sexual behaviour, at least before marriage, see M. and O. 'Tsifry i fakty iz perepisi Sankt Peterburga v 1900 godu', *Russkaia mysl'*, no. 11 (1902), p. 92; cf. Aleksandra Kollontai's *Novaia moral' i rabochii klass* (Moscow, 1919), on the absence of hypocrisy and traditions of disinterested comradeship in the proletarian marriage. But such observations were often made as part of an attack on the sexual ethics of the bourgeois marriage, in which the emphasis is on the fact that proleterian marital or extra-marital relations offer an alternative to the double standards of bourgeois practices. A rather less libertarian picture emerges from the first-hand accounts cited by Bobroff, 'Working women', which make it clear that unwanted pregnancies were a very great fear amongst working women (see e.g. pp. 127, 142).

72. It is not clear how far the traditional peasant family structure, with its

30   *Catriona Kelly*

subordination of younger to older women, survived amongst Russian working-class women in major cities. But whatever their family status, at work Russian working-class women would have been exposed to an age-related hierarchy. There are in any case problems in establishing how 'realistic' popular entertainment texts are. They combine topical references with distancing techniques. Direct reversals of real-life pattern are very common. There is hence a danger that the analyst may fall into the double bind of admitting that popular phenomena are perceived by their audience as trivial, yet arguing that this is somehow not the whole story. For example, Kate Purcell's recent study of fortune-telling amongst British women factory workers argues that reading magazine horoscopes, perceived as an entertainment by women workers, is in fact an indication of their intellectually underprivileged status *vis-à-vis* their male colleagues, who prefer the less 'fatalistic' pursuit of betting, *More in Hope than Anticipation: Fatalism and Fortune-Telling Amongst Women Factory Workers*, Studies of Sexual Politics no. 20 (Manchester, 1989).

73. V. Karelina in Korol'chuk, *V nachale*, p. 284.

74. Received opinion has tended to sentimentalize the condition of Russian lower-class women; they have been seen as either pathetic victims or marmorean heroines. The demography of the Russian urban lower-class population at the turn of the century (there was a high number of single women, and greater migrancy amongst men than women) must have made a degree of independence essential for women, since in many cases it was they on whom family welfare rested. But the conditions of enforced self-reliance in which they lived by no means resembled a feminist utopia of self-determination.

75. Erosion of the prohibitions on women in the public domain is suggested by the fact that the female *khuligan* begins to appear in the *blatnaia pesnia* during the 1920s. The famous song 'Murka' describes a female thief so cunning and resourceful 'that even the meanest cons were scared of her', Iakov Vaiskopf (comp.), *Blatnaia lira* (Jerusalem, 1981), p. 22: reference kindly supplied by Gerry Smith.

76. The division of labour in the traditional Russian village was supported by a range of festivals, rites and folklore genres which were work-attached. The patron saints of chicken-rearing were Cosmos and Damian, and these were accounted women's saints, as was St Paraskeva Piatnitsa, a spinning saint whose name was used as a special woman's oath. Various secular rituals, such as the burning of 'Kostroma', a straw doll, and the placating of the 'hen god', a stone with a hole in it, were also the exclusive practice of women. Whether peculiar to women or to men, these rites reflected shared assumptions. Many women's rites were connected with fertility beliefs; men's rites, festivals and folklore genres also linked women and fertility, see B. A. Uspenskii, *Filologicheskie razyskaniia v oblasti slavianskikh drevnostei: relikty iazychestva v vostochnoslavianskom kul'te Nikolaia Mirlikiiskogo* (Moscow, 1982), esp. pp. 151–5. In the city, agricultural rituals, where they survived, seem to have been adopted by both genders (Semik, the seventh Thursday after Easter, was a girls' festival in the country, but a mixed one in towns even early in the nineteenth century:

Noveishii i liubopytneishii ukazatel' Moskvy, ili Al'manakh dlya priezzhaiushchikh v siiu Stolitsu, vol. 1 (Moscow, 1829), p. 66). About saints' cults it is harder to say. There were churches dedicated to SS Cosmos and Damian and St Paraskeva in Moscow, according to G. Le Cointe de Lareau, *Description de Moscou, contenant tout . . .*, vol. 1 (Moscow, 1835), pp. 338–43), but these were relatively few in number (seven and two respectively), and located in the centre rather than in working-class areas. The saint who appears to have had wider currency is St Nicholas the Miracle-Worker (thirty-nine churches situated all over Moscow). But without further research on religious practices and naming patterns in Russian cities, it is hard to say. The binary model of traditional rural culture (itself no longer so 'traditional' by the late nineteenth century) is introduced here as a method of defining urban culture by what it was *not*.

2   The Silver Age: highpoint for women?

Charlotte Rosenthal

The 'Golden Age' is a literary historical term used to designate the Pushkin period and the writing of poetry by men. The term 'Silver Age' designates the period of modernism, but also refers to the achievement of male poets. However, the Silver Age period was more of a Golden Age for women writers, especially for female lyric poets. In any case, the Silver Age was definitely a period of transition during which women became professionals in all areas of literary activity – in poetry, prose, drama, literary criticism, as well as in the area of popular literature. If at the beginning of the period there were no major female poets, by 1910 there were several. In 1909 Annenskii noted this wealth of female poets as a unique contribution of the modernist movement: 'Female lyric poetry is one of the achievements of that cultural effort which modernism will bequeath to history'.[1] By the end of the period, there was firmly established a female poetic tradition that has remained a vital stream in modern Russian literature both in the Soviet Union and abroad.

To explain this transition, one must consider aesthetic, historical, philosophical and economic factors. Historically women's status was changing, as Russian society itself was being restructured by the forces of industrialization and urbanization.[2] Economically, a new market for popular commercial fiction gave women writers the possibility of earning a living by writing 'women's novels'.[3] Philosophically, part of the intelligentsia turned away from any form of determinism or obligation, whether biological, social, historical or even moral. The catchword was 'freedom'. As Liubov' Gurevich, the publisher and co-editor of *Severnyi vestnik*, put it: 'I professed freedom of the spirit unhampered by any sort of pledge of allegiance.'[4] Freedom also meant rebellion against social convention. Here Nietzsche's call to 'write new values on new tablets',[5] provoked a powerful response among women. Finally, in the realm of aesthetics and literary history, the modernist movement proved to be especially beneficial to women.

Literature in Russia bifurcated into the realist and modernist camps, though there was a degree of overlap and mutual influence between them. Women writers were found in both, but the greatest achievements were made by those associated with modernism. This was in part because of modernism's preference for lyric poetry, a genre in which Russian women were able to excel, and a thematics that, in all genres, de-emphasized man as social animal, and defined fulfilment within the individual personality and life of the spirit – again a preference that proved more congenial to women's experiential background[6] and powers of observation. Again, under Nietzsche's influence, the modernists' elevation of art to the status of a secular religion, to a justification of existence, and their emphasis on the power of individual creativity[7] encouraged women to take the risk of society's opprobrium by stepping outside their traditional roles of wife and mother. By endowing art with such a metaphysical status, the modernists elevated a sphere that had hitherto been justified only in terms of its social utilitarian function. In the 1860s the intelligentsia's values of duty and self-sacrifice had led many women not to art, but to political and civic activities in which they subordinated an exploration of personal identity and personal needs. Many of these women, while they disdained marriage and family, also despised art.[8] In the nineties, art also became an attractive path. While some women continued to work for political causes, many others joined the cause of Art. In some cases women pursued both paths, sometimes thereby experiencing a conflict of loyalties.[9] Finally, the Silver Age created or discovered an array of female models of inspiration, success, or recognition, which became the basis for women's substantial participation in the cultural world by the early twentieth century.

This chapter explores this last factor, the one that gave women with literary ambitions the confidence not only to write – they had been doing so avidly for over a century – but to address a larger audience, to publish in places where their work would be noticed, and to seek out recognition and critical response, in short, to take themselves seriously as writers. I am using the concept of model here in a triple sense: (1) a literary model, someone to emulate, a predecessor who has solved certain kinds of literary problems unique to women writers; (2) a model of literary success evidenced by critical recognition, imitation, or prominence brought about by large-scale publication, receipt of awards and so on; (3) a model in a more symbolic sense, a female figure of inspiration. It is the contention of this chapter that by the early twentieth century, female writers had before them such models in all three senses and it was partly owing to the existence of such models that this generation gave birth to so many outstanding women writers.

The importance to a woman writer of knowing about the existence of predecessors – women who wrote and who were read and recognized –

cannot be overemphasized. The difference it makes has been well explained by Dale Spender in discussing English women's tradition:

While the catalogues, the library shelves, the book-shops, the reviews, the courses of study, all help to suggest that women are without a literary tradition, the belief in female inferiority is surely sustained. And it erodes women's confidence; it undermines the woman writer; it produces doubts. If women were indeed without a great literary tradition, much could be said for the advisability of inventing one, for the positive influence it could provide for women and women's literary endeavours. Such is the power of tradition.[10]

The American writer Alice Walker has expressed well the need that women writers have for literary models: 'one of my first tasks was simply to determine whether they had existed. After this, I could breathe easier.'[11] While Walker set about looking for earlier black women writers, a similar process was taking place in Russia. What Walker discovered about her predecessors – that most of them were out of print, abandoned, discredited, maligned and nearly lost[12] – was also applicable to Russian women writers of the eighteenth and nineteenth centuries. A series of 'discoveries' and 'rediscoveries' took place which returned Russian women writers to literary history. The motives for these 're-discoveries' were varied: a part of a large sense of retrospectivism and a general need to 'sum up' the achievements of Russian culture at the end of the century,[13] including the publication of bibliographic and bio-graphic works on earlier women writers,[14] the publication and reissuing of women's works and articles about them in such journals as *Russkii arkhiv*, *Russkaia starina*, *Istoricheskii vestnik*, and *Mir bozhii*.[15]

The establishment of a lineage of writing by women in the Russian literary tradition had great significance for Russian women writers in the Silver Age. It helped them – equipped as they were with their particular education, experience, horizons, upbringing and steeped in a literary tradition produced largely by men, evaluated by men, and controlled by men – to contend with a male tradition.

In addition to the establishment of a heritage of writing by women, the end of the nineteenth century witnessed the emergence of several powerful models of female literary creativity. The first type that we shall look at was perhaps more influential as a psychological and symbolic source of inspiration than as a literary model. This type was best exem-plified by Mariia Bashkirtseva (1860–84), the expatriate Russian artist who became famous for her diary, written in French, that was published upon her death at the age of 24.[16] Portions of it were translated into Russian and published in 1887. Here we must disagree with Mirsky who declares in his *History of Russian Literature* that 'its importance has probably been overrated, and in any case it stands entirely outside the line of development of Russian literature'.[17] This is not the case. In 1888 the future editor and publisher of *Severnyi vestnik*, Liubov' Gurevich wrote an extensive laudatory article on Bashkirtseva for *Russkoe bogatstvo*,[18] defending her from accusations of egotism and the inability to love. (Gurevich had visited Bashkirtseva's grave and studio in Paris, calling the latter a 'world of art and thought'.) A few months later this same journal published a poem by O. N. Chiumina, 'Pamiati Marii Bashkirtsevoi' in which she too lauds Bashkirtseva's 'thirst for art'. This was the beginning of Bashkirtseva's career in her homeland.

A Russian translation of Bashkirtseva's diary was published in 1889. This was followed by another translation which appeared in 1892 in *Severnyi vestnik*[19] and then as a separate book in 1893, with a second edition in 1894. Versions of the diary were published also in 1902, 1904, 1910 (in 30,000 copies), 1911 and 1916. Besides Gurevich's article, book reviews of the diary and a monograph on Bashkirtseva published in 1905,[20] Zinaida Vengerova mentions Bashkirtseva's diary in an introduction to her translation of Annie Besant's 'Confession' in 1895, calling it 'the starting point of those complex literary and aesthetic movements which have been given the label "Decadence"', and included a section on Bashkirtseva in her article 'La Femme russe' for a French journal in 1897.[21] Vengerova views Bashkirtseva as the very essence of the 'new woman': she rebelled against social, religious and moral conventions, devoted herself to aesthetic endeavours, and tried to live the life of a free personality. It was these very qualities, coupled with the success of her writing and the recognition that it brought her, which made Bashkirtseva such a model of inspiration.[22]

One obviously inspired Russian woman writer was Marina Tsvetaeva. Her sister Anastasiia reports in her *Vospominaniia* about an ecstatic encounter in 1910 with the artist Levi who knew Bashkirtseva personally. Meeting with someone who knew their idol firsthand transports the sisters: 'We left for home as though touched by her hand, and couldn't get back to our own lives right away.'[23] Marina had already been corresponding with Bashkirtseva's mother who had sent Tsvetaeva several photographs of the artist. The same year she dedicated *Evening Album*, her first volume of poetry, to Bashkirtseva's memory. In 1913 she announced that her third collection would be entitled 'Mariia Bashkirtseva'. This is not surprising. By then Bashkirtseva had become a 'model of female creativity'.[24] And much more than that. Here was a very talented woman who had devoted her life to art, who had become internationally famous through her writing, whose diary reveals a strong-willed, relentlessly self-analytic, ambitious, very intelligent and sexually curious woman, who also happened to have been beautiful and who died at the age of twenty-four. Not least of all, in writing her diary with such daring honesty, and at the same time, with an eye to potential readers, she made herself into a legend, touched by notoriety. She was an emblematic figure who no doubt inspired other women to live an unconventional life devoted to art.

In 1914, in an article for Vengerov's *Russkaia literatura XX veka*, Valerii Briusov named three Russian women poets who should be a source of national pride.[25] One, Karolina Pavlova, had died twenty years before in Germany. The other two had begun publishing in the late 1880s and changed Russian literary history for women by establishing themselves as models of achievement and recognition, if not success. Over the course of the next fifteen years, their writing, particularly their lyric poetry, provided a wide range of possible themes, images, linguistic strategies and poetic personae, along with a formal competence – even perfection – that future female poets could build on. The two were Mirra Lokhvitskaia (1869–1905) and Zinaida Gippius (1869–1945).

While as poets and personalities the two represented almost opposite extremes, they had some curious experiences in common. Both were daughters of lawyers; both were surrounded by artistic sisters, both attained a degree of popularity based on a personal charisma tinged with notoriety, both initially had some trouble getting their poetry published, and for both the 'thick journal' *Severnyi vestnik* played an important role in their acceptance by the 'high-brow' literary world. But the similarities end here.

The more popular of the two was Lokhvitskaia. She was also the less formally experimental and her solutions to the problems faced by a female poet writing in a male tradition, though new and daring in their day, were more acceptable than those of Gippius. Thematically, Lokhvitskaia's range also was more traditional: her most prominent theme is love, both as earthly passion and as ideal.[26] Yet, by the end of her short life, she had expanded her thematic range, reached a certain level of formal competence, created a variety of female images and a poetic persona that is comfortable with her femininity and her poetic calling.

Formally at times she achieved perfection. Critics have noted the musicality of her verse. This quality has resulted in many of her poems being set to music. In addition she wrote in a wide variety of metres, often using the somewhat less common trochee, dactyl and anapest. Aside from lyrics, she wrote narrative *poemy* and verse dramas, neither of which genres has been much discussed.[27] While there is much repetition and convention in her images and epithets – certain flowers and colours appear rather frequently – she was quite creative in her rhetorical devices: she effectively employs the imperative and conditional moods and repetitions of various kinds.

For her female images she borrowed from the Bible and Christian tradition (Lilith, Hagar, St Catherine), Greek myth (Aphrodite, Sappho), folk belief and folklore, contemporary opera (Bizet), and the figure of the poetess herself. These images are decidedly feminine. She wrote about motherhood; for example, in the poem 'Umei stradat'' (1895) she advises women to be practised in the art of silence, and to know how to love and to suffer. In a later poem entitled 'Skazki i zhizn'' she contrasts the happy endings of three fairy tales about women and the unhappy lot that they would meet in 'real life'. She also has a group of non-Russian *femmes fatales*: (Dzhamile: an enchantress from the Sahara desert in 'Charodeika', Lilith, Dzhemali and Madelaine (in the play *In Nomine Domini*). The female figures are often depicted as passively awaiting their lovers, especially in the narrative poems, but they are described in detail, and the narrative often unfolds from their point of view. Other female personae, especially that of the poetess, are often assertive, self-confident, sensual, sometimes coy and bantering. In the last two volumes of her work (1904, 1908) we find a greater thematic range. Together with her familiar themes, we find here poems about motherhood side by side with poems of entrapment.

Lokhvitskaia was both a literary model and a model of success. In formally competent poetry, she expanded the thematic range for women and introduced an array of female images. Her personae's lack of modesty on the one hand, and their overt sensuality on the other, provoked a great deal of commentary. Although her fellow male poets also created a stir with their allegedly 'pornographic' verse, Lokhvitskaia's work caused a greater stir. Critics such as A. I. Pokrovskii complained about her ignorance of 'purely feminine modesty'.[28] Her personae's sensuality widened the thematic range of women's love poetry. Her image of the female poet – a totally feminine figure who views herself on equal terms with her fellow male poets and as a member of a close fraternity – stated once and for all that one could be both feminine and a serious poet.[29]

By the mid-1890s, Lokhvitskaia was already well known, and by the beginning of the twentieth century she was sufficiently popular to have been the butt of numerous parodies.[30] The popularity of her work can be attested by the fact that between 1896 and 1904 she published five volumes of poetry and that the first two volumes were republished in second editions in 1900. No doubt, some of this popularity was based on her notoriety as an authoress of outspokenly sensual verse. One critic even claimed that '22 out of 25 readers would never have held the poet's verses in their hands, but her name would have been very well known to them from hearsay'.[31] Her popularity was also furthered by her own personal charisma. She frequently read her work at public gatherings and these appearances were accompanied by 'noisy success'. Bunin described her charm – a lovely voice, a glimmer in her eyes, and a lively, bantering manner.[32] Photographs of her show a beautiful woman, with dark eyes and an abundant head of hair (which she mentions in her poetry).

Lokhvitskaia was not only popular, she was also recognized critically, winning two Pushkin Prizes from the Imperial Academy of Sciences, once in 1896 and one posthumously in 1905. We know for certain that she was an early influence on Cherubina de Gabriak according to the latter's autobiography.[33] And one scholar has suggested a possible linkage to Akhmatova: 'the reputation won by Lokhvitskaia's intense, intimate, and feminine love lyrics perhaps broke ground for such major figures as Anna Akhmatova'.[34] Several of her poems in which the female persona is thinking of her lover, or a poem such as the twelve-line 'Pustoi sluchainyi razgovor' (1894), in its feminine point of view and its movement from external exchange to the woman's inner response, suggest this possibility.

The second figure in our poetic triumvirate is Zinaida Gippius, in many ways the polar opposite of Lokhvitskaia, so that taken together the options they presented to women poets covered a wide range. Gippius was the far more radical both in her person and in her poetic practice. Therefore she had less direct influence on other women. Despite a haphazard education, she made the most of the cultural contacts she gained through an early marriage to Dmitrii Merezhkovskii. She was eventually able to publish her poetry regularly in *Severnyi vestnik* in the 1890s, even when it had become far more iconoclastic. Like Lokhvitskaia, she had garnered some fame by the turn of the century, and also, like Lokhvitskaia, her fame was partly based on her personal presence and notoriety, especially on her unconventional behaviour and eccentric dress.[35] Gippius was to make a personal and professional assault on perceived biologically determined differences between males and females.

Both women in their poems used personae that are hardly demure, but Lokhvitskaia's persona is much more of a participant in her verse, while Gippius' often is distant and impersonal. Unlike Lokhvitskaia, she used male pseudonyms – usually for literary criticism and philosophical essays – and masculine and androgynous personae in her poetry.[36] Gippius undoubtedly realized that in the Russian literary tradition, masculine personae represented the 'neutral' form: feminine personae were marked and would arouse expectations in a reader, which she found restrictive.[37] Both thematically and formally Gippius' poetry diverged from the kind that women were supposed to write. Her poetry tends to be abstract and intellectual. She wrote philosophical and political poetry which women were not supposed to do. The negative response to her poetry often stemmed from critics' expectations about what is proper subject matter for women's poetry. Even sympathetic critics sometimes betray these expectations. Here again we cite Mirsky:

The most salient feature in all her writing is intellectual power and wit, things rare in a woman. In fact there is very little that is feminine in Mme. Hippius, except a tendency to be oversubtle and a certain willfulness – the capriciousness of a brilliant and spoiled coquette. This last quality gives a peculiarly piquant flavor to her work, which is, on the whole, intense and serious.[38]

Gippius understood that male poets had a much wider range from which to speak than female poets, and aesthetically, philosophically and psychologically, she wanted the greatest possible freedom from which to write. This necessitated certain radical divergences from the female poetic tradition. One can find a range of solutions in her poetry. One of them is to leave the gender of the persona unspecified in a poem that includes either a masculine or feminine addressee. Gippius accomplishes that in part by avoiding the past tense and other grammatical categories which in Russian are marked for gender.[39] This is certainly different from Lokhvitskaia's decidedly 'feminine' voice.

There are many other differences. Whereas in the early poetry of Lokhvitskaia, we are presented with a variety of female images including the *femme fatale*, there is little of this in Gippius' poetry,[40] and the later Gippius presented an androgynous ideal. Whereas Lokhvitskaia wrote poems on motherhood and depicted female figures accompanied by children in her poetry, Gippius did not.[41] Lokhvitskaia's poetry is far more sensual, visual and concrete. Their differences show up most clearly when one compares their poems on the same theme: in Lokhvitskaia's 'V nashi dni' (1898) and Gippius' 'Chto est' grekh?' (1902), the speakers condemn the mediocrity of moderation and halfheartedness which characterizes their times. They even share the root for dreaming, *mechta*, and the use of the prefix for half, *polu-*. Yet Gippius' poem is much more abstract and intellectual, and builds, like many of her poems, to a logical crescendo, capped by an axiomatic final line. This line refers to a 'mother', but as with many of her feminine images, this one too is a personified abstraction. Another major difference is Gippius' formal innovations. These were mainly in the area of metrics, especially the use of *dol'niki* and blank verse. Her metrical experiments were picked up by Blok and others to the point where they became a regular feature of twentieth-century Russian poetry.[42]

As with Lokhvitskaia, Gippius received positive reviews from those sympathetic to modernism. Anti-modernist critics sometimes went to extremes in condemning her. She was especially appreciated by her fellow poets – Bal'mont, Bunin, Briusov, Annenskii, Blok and Belyi.[43] But she did not garner the wider recognition that Lokhvitskaia did or equal her in popularity. This fact was bemoaned by Marietta Shaginian who, in 1912, published a book on Gippius, *O blazhenstve imushchego: poeziia Z. N. Gippius*. Shaginian states that the purpose of her book is to impart to readers an appreciation of the serious religious thought that forms the basis of Gippius' poetry.

It is difficult to assess Gippius' direct importance for other women poets. She was clearly an influence on several women personally: Poliksena Solov'eva, Liudmila Vil'kina and Marietta Shaginian. As a literary model, Gippius' importance can be seen in Shaginian's first book of poetry, *Pervye vstrechi* and Kuz'mina-Karavaeva's *Skifskie cherepki*.[44] Other women poets like Solov'eva and Vil'kina followed Gippius' use of masculine personae. Her play with gender categories and idealization of the androgyne is later to be found in Tsvetaeva, but we cannot speak here for certain of direct influence. One has to consider Gippius' influence in broader terms: in her poetry she broke new ground for women thematically, in her exploration of gender categories, and formally by showing that women poets could be innovators whose practice would then become part of the mainstream of modern Russian poetry which subsequent poets like Akhmatova and Tsvetaeva would inherit.

The third female poet mentioned by Briusov is Karolina Pavlova. While it is not quite the case that she had been completely forgotten in her homeland by the time she died in 1893, the last collection of her work had been published in 1863.[45] She was 'rediscovered' as part of the general retrospectivism noted above, especially by poets interested in their Russian predecessors. There ensued a series of positive evaluations of her work by Bal'mont, Belyi, Briusov and others. *Vesy* in 1904 announced a forthcoming appreciation of her work, calling her 'one of the most remarkable Russian poets'.[46] Bal'mont praised her in his collection of essays *Gornye vershiny* (1904) for having created 'several poems marked by an unwomanly (*nezhenskii*) power'. Andrei Belyi ranked her along with Lermontov and others in his study of iambic tetrametre, and had frequent recourse to examples from her poetry in his book *Simvolizm*.[47] Briusov used an epigraph from her for his *Zerkalo tenei* and, in his introduction to her collected works published in 1915, he called her one of the best Russian poets.[48] One of the most positive discussions of her work was written by Sergei Ernst for *Russkii bibliofil* in 1916.[49] Singling out her religious poetry for special praise, he also notes her prose, her 'remarkable novel' *Dvoinaia zhizn'* in particular, her 'modernist' rhymes and admirable use of metre.

With the approval of such male authorities, it is not surprising to find that Pavlova appealed to women poets of the early twentieth century. After all, she was an outstanding example of a singular dedication to a poetic calling, was insistent on perfecting the formal aspect of her craft, and, in a number of poems dealt with the consolation to be found in the inner world of the spirit and the imagination. Hers is a case in which we have some written evidence by women poets themselves of her importance. Thus, Cherubina de Gabriak writes in her autobiography of Pavlova's importance to her and quotes from Pavlova's poem containing the line about her 'sacred craft' (*remeslo*). This occurs in the same place in which she cites Lokhvitskaia's early influence: 'Mirra had a very big influence on me – in childhood (ages 13–15). I considered her an inaccessible ideal and trembled when reading her poems. And later on, in my second period, Karolina appeared. . . . They are both so close to me, both so infinitely inaccessible.'[50] Unfortunately de Gabriak does not elaborate on these statements. One can find in her earlier poetry echoes of Lokhvitskaia's thematics – concerned as they both were with love – and both frequently writing lyrics with a female speaker addressing a male alter. They also share an interest in the Middle Ages. In addition, one can see connections in the concentration on visual imagery, especially on light and colours, flower symbolism, and the mention of concrete objects, e.g. the female speaker's hair. In de Gabriak's later poetry, besides Pavlova's devotion to her 'sacred craft', there are echoes of the latter's religious poetry, the expression of agonizing loneliness, and the existence of a double life. In the introduction to de Gabriak's 'Autobiography', Vladimir Glotser points out her influence on both Tsvetaeva and Akhmatova: Tsvetaeva herself had noted the closeness of Akhmatova's imagery to de Gabriak's and of her own metrical practice to de Gabriak's.[51] Pavlova was also an inspiration for Sofiia Parnok, as indicated by a poem devoted to Pavlova in 1915. Barbara Heldt has noted this link between the two poets: 'This poem is a call to a sister-self across the years, with a rhetorical, echoing answer. . . . The fact that Pavlova had been a poet is important to the speaker here.'[52] Parnok had introduced Tsvetaeva to Pavlova in 1914. The two used quotations from Pavlova in poems addressed to one another. Tsvetaeva called her 1921 collection of poetry *Remeslo*, an echo of Pavlova's poem on her sacred craft, and originally intended to use it as an epigraph.[53] This is one example of the fact that in the early twentieth century, Russian women had finally established for themselves a recognition of a female literary heritage that reached across generations. As one scholar has put it: 'at long last, as illustrated with metaliterary reference by Cvetaeva to her predecessor Pavlova, women writers have come to recognize themselves as writing within a continuum, a continuum often directly opposed to the myths that restrict their literary lives no less than they do their social mobility'.[54]

There is other evidence. The poet Nadezhda L'vova, writing about women poets in 1913, calls the twentieth century 'the women's century', the century when women finally awoke to their creative potential. She goes on to say that to add up the number of Russian women poets at the present time would not be an easy task. 'Women have entered poetry', she declares.[55] This is not to say that women poets had yet been accepted as equal in stature. There is much evidence to the contrary, including L'vova's own article. For example, Vadim Shershenevich writing on 'Futurism and women' in 1914 declares: 'It's funny, of course, but we don't have art by women. Art by women is a synonym for imitation.'[56] But while critics might express negative expectations of women poets, within the same article they might also indicate that the female poetic heritage was firmly enough established. One often encounters mention of the influence of one woman on another. For example, the book reviewer for *Utrenniki* in 1922, reviewing Vera Inber's third book of poetry, *Brennye slova*, sees here the influence of Akhmatova, Moravskaia and Lesnaia.[57]

While Russian women poets finally felt themselves writing within a continuum of their own which provided them with both literary example and psychological support, this does not appear to be the case for women prose writers. This is despite what Skabichevskii refers to as a 'flood' of women's prose fiction as early as 1899 and his certainty that the nineteenth century would go down in history as the century of women's prose fiction.[58] One cannot find the same kind of statement about the impact of women's prose writing on Russian literature that one finds about their impact on poetry. For example, Gippius received far more positive commentary about her poetic practice than she did about her prose. And while her poetry was undoubtedly innovative, her prose was not.

Women prose writers appear to have faced obstacles which they found more difficult to overcome than women poets. One of these obstacles may have been the very popularity and success of women's autobiography. The prominence of women's autobiography and 'pseudo'-autobiography in the Silver Age is striking. This preference needs to be explained. Perhaps it was an expression of a lack of self-confidence in the creation of prose fiction and a comfort with the kind of writing that women had always practised at home and had had success in publishing: diary-writing, memoirs and letters. Perhaps it was also an expression of an intense interest in self-definition and the exploration of women's nature. The success of Bashkirtseva's diary may have been instructive. While the practice of this kind of writing did develop in some cases into a form of narrative fiction,[59] it did not appear to have led to the establishment of a continuum in women's prose fiction that we have claimed for women's poetry.

Notes

1. 'One', *Apollon*, no. 3 (Dec. 1909), p. 5.
2. In this 'era of transition', the issue of sex roles became a major concern. See Bernice Glatzer Rosenthal (ed.), *Nietzsche in Russia* (Princeton, 1986), p. 41. The so-called 'woman question' once more became a central focus of attention. Its prominence is indicated by the appearance of new women's organizations, greater educational opportunities for women and by a plethora of books, pamphlets and articles on the subject of women and their roles. This spurt of interest was noted by two different Russian authors in the nineties. M. V. Sevliakov prefaced his *Woman, Life and Love (Pro and Contra)* (1891) thus: 'The topic of woman at the present time is the most engaging of all topics, and European literature has been enriched by a large number of all manner of books and brochures with extensive treatments of all these fashionable themes.' A certain V. P. indicates a similar situation in *Woman and Her Role in Life*: 'At the present time there has been quite a lot of discussion about woman's nature, importance and position in human society.' A number of books, focused on the psychology, anthropology and physiology of women, were translated into Russian and a number of special periodicals aimed at a female audience made their appearance in this period including *Sovremennaia zhenshchina*, *Damskii mir* and *Zhurnal dlia zhenshchin*.
3. See Jeffrey Brooks on the great expansion of book publishing in *When Russian Learned to Read* (Princeton, 1985), especially pp. 60–1.
4. Liubov' Gurevich, 'Istoriia "Severnogo vestnika"', in S. A. Vengerov (ed.), *Russkaia literatura XX veka (1890–1910)*, 2 vols (Moscow, 1914–16), vol. 1, p. 246. See also Ann Marie Lane, 'Nietzsche in Russian thought', (PhD dissertation, University of Wisconsin, 1976), p.11.
5. Bernice G. Rosenthal, 'Nietzsche in Russia: the case of Merezhkovsky', *Slavic Review* (Sept. 1974), p. 429.
6. For example, women were still 'largely excluded' from professional circles and could not be 'practising lawyers, professors in universities, or elected representatives of zemstvo assemblies'. See Linda Harriet Edmondson, *Feminism in Russia, 1900–1917* (Stanford, 1984), pp. 27–8.

7. See Edith W. Clowes, 'A philosophy "For All and None": the early reception of Friedrich Nietzsche's thought in Russian literature, 1892–1912' (PhD dissertation, Yale University, 1981), pp. 5, 192.
8. Irina Paperno, *Chernyshevsky and the Age of Realism* (Stanford, 1988), p. 18.
9. Some examples of the latter group include Sof'ia Dubnova, Liubov' Gurevich, and, of course, Aleksandra Kollontai.
10. Dale Spender, 'Women and literary history', in Catherine Belsey and Jane Moore (eds), *The Feminist Reader: Essays in Gender and the Politics of Literary Criticism* (New York, 1989), pp. 32–3.
11. Alice Walker, 'Saving the life that is your own: the importance of models in the artist's life', in Mary Eagleton (ed.) *Feminist Literary Theory, A Reader* (Oxford, 1986), p. 28.
12. Ibid.
13. William Richardson, *'Zolotoe Runo' and Russian Modernism, 1905–1910* (Ann Arbor, 1986), pp. 28–9.
14. Such as N. N. Golitsyn's *Bibliograficheskii slovar' russkikh pisatel'nits* (St Petersburg, 1889); S. I. Ponomarev, *Nashi pisatel'nitsy* (St Petersburg, 1891); P. Vladimirov, *Pervye russkie pisatel'nitsy XVIII veka* (Kiev, 1892), and the 25-volume *Russkii biograficheskii slovar'* (St Petersburg–Petrograd, 1896–1918).
15. Just one example, among many, is M. K. Tsebrikova's article 'Ocherk zhizni N. D. Khvoshchinskoi-Zaionchkovskoi (V. Krestovskogo-psevdonima)', *Mir bozhii*, no. 12 (1897), pp. 1–40.
16. The great popularity of Bashkirtseva's diary may have encouraged other women to write diaries, autobiographies and fictionalized autobiographies with a third-person narrator. These forms were all very popular. Examples from the 1890s and early twentieth century include N. A. Lukhmanova's *20 let nazad* (also called *Devochki*, first published in 1893 in *Russkoe bogatstvo* as 'Institutskie zapiski'). The book edition was published six times between 1894 and 1912. *Institutka*, its sequel, was published in 1904. M. V. Krestovskaia's epistolary novel, which she claimed to be based on actual letters, remained unfinished. 'Zhenskaia zhizn' (povest' v pis'makh)', *Severnyi vestnik*, nos 11–12 (1894) and no. 1 (1895). V. N. Tsekhovskaia (who wrote under the pseudonym of O. N. Ol'nem) published what is likely a fictionalized autobiography entitled 'Na poroge zhizni (Stranichki iz biografii dvukh sovremennits)', *Russkoe bogatstvo*, no. 4 (1900) pp. 65–92. Another very popular diary was E. A. D'iakonova's, published in two volumes in 1904–5 and republished three more times by 1912. Finally there are Verbitskaia's autobiographies, *Moemu chitateliu* (1908, 2nd edn 1911), *Detstvo, gody ucheniia* (1911), *Iunost', grezy* (1911).
17. D. S. Mirsky, *A History of Russian Literature*, (ed.) Francis J. Whitfield (New York, 1966), p. 340.
18. 'M. K. Bashkirtseva (Biografiko-psikhologicheskii etiud', *Russkoe bogatstvo*, no. 2 (1888), pp. 73–122.
19. *Severnyi vestnik*, nos 5–12 (1892).
20. The first published translation was by K. Plavinskii, *Iz dnevnika Marii Bashkirtsevoi* (St Petersburg, 1889). Other editions: *Dnevnik*, Liubov' Gurevich (trans.) (St Petersburg, 1893; 2nd edn 1894); *Neizdannyi dnevnik i*

perepiska s Giui-de-Mopassanom, M. Gel'rot (trans. and ed.) (Yalta, 1904); three editions of the translation supervised by Gurevich were published by Vol'f in St Petersburg in 1902, 1910 and 1916. The 1910 edition was published in 30,000 copies. The fact that it was republished in 1916 indicates its popularity. The remaining unpublished section of the diary appeared as a free supplement to the journal *Za sem' dnei: Novyi dnevnik, neizdannaia chast' (1873–1876 gg.)* R. Markovich (trans.) (St Petersburg, 1911). The monograph was by Gerro, *Mariia Bashkirtseva: Kritiko-biograficheskii ocherk* (Moscow, 1905). This author is less laudatory than Gurevich. While the author defends Bashkirtseva from the charge of 'egotism', he or she dwells on Bashkirtseva's separation from her homeland and her lack of the female experience of marriage and motherhood. An indication of Bashkirtseva's importance to Russian women is given by the artist A. P. Ostroumova-Lebedeva. She reports that she went to visit Bashkirtseva's grave, just as Gurevich had done earlier. See *Avtobiograficheskie zapiski 1900–16*, 3 vols (Leningrad, 1935), vol. 1, pp. 184–247. It is interesting to note that once more Bashkirtseva is receiving attention in her native land. The publishing house 'Molodaia gvardiia' announced a new edition of the diary in 100,000 copies for 1990 (yet to appear); the journal *Detskaia literatura* published sections of it in nos 4–8 in 1989.

21. Zinaida Vengerova, 'Predislovie' to her translation of Annie Besant's 'Confession', *Severnyi vestnik*, no. 1 (Jan. 1895) p. 215; *Revue des revues*, (Sept. 1897), pp. 489–99.

22. Her work also appealed to some Silver Age male writers. Briusov recorded his response to her diary – a strong identification with her – in 1892. Khlebnikov considered the diary a unique phenomenon in world culture. See the entry under 'Bashkirtseva' in *Russkie pisateli, 1800–1917, biograficheskii slovar'*, vol. 1 (Moscow, 1989) p. 188.

23. Anastasiia Tsvetaeva, *Vospominaniia*, 3rd edn (Moscow, 1983), pp. 331–2.

24. Jane Taubman, *A Life Through Poetry: Marina Tsvetaeva's Lyric Diary* (Columbus, OH, 1989), p. 43.

25. 'Z. N. Gippius', *Russkaia literatura XX veka (1890–1910)*, vol. 1, p. 188.

26. Both provide a means for escape into an ideal realm. For a detailed discussion of Lokhvitskaia's thematics, see R. Christine Greedan, 'Mirra Lokhvitskaia's "Duality" as a "Romantic Conflict" and its reflection in her poetry' (PhD dissertation, University of Pittsburgh, 1982), pp. viii–xi, 25–8.

27. For example, in her last verse drama 'In Nomine Domini' (1902), published in her fifth volume of poetry in 1904, Lokhvitskaia develops two interesting female figures: Madelaine, who is caught in a conflict between religious duty and her own sensuality – a conflict which she never really resolves – and Louise, a religious zealot who is motivated by envy and all-too-ready to employ violence in the name of God.

28. Greedan, 'Lokhvitskaia's "Duality" ', fn. 116 cited on p. 19.

29. See such poems as 'Moim sobrat'iam' (1897), 'Ia ne znaiu, zachem uprekaiut menia' (between 1896 and 1898), and 'Sopernitse' (between 1896 and 1898).

30. See L. K. Dolgopolov and L. A. Nikolaeva (comps) *Poety 1880–1890kh godov* (Leningrad, 1972), pp. 502 and 604.

31. Greedan, 'Lokhvitskaia's "Duality" ', p. 17.

32. Dolgopolov and Nikolaeva, *Poety*, p. 603.
33. Elizaveta Vasil'eva (Cherubina de Gabriak), 'Dve veshchi v mire dlia menia vsegda byli samymi sviatymi: stikhi i liubov', *Novyi mir*, no. 12 (Dec. 1988), p. 139.
34. Greedan, 'Lokhvitskaia's "Duality"', p. 145.
35. See Olga Matich, 'The religious poetry of Zinaida Gippius' (PhD dissertation, University of California at Los Angeles, 1969), pp. 15–21. A. A. Izmailov also comments on her striking appearance and clothing in *Pestrye znamena: literaturnye portrety bezvremen'ia* (Moscow, 1913), p. 150.
36. A number of reasons have been offered for this practice, aesthetic, philosophical and psychological. David Schaffer discusses this issue at some length in his PhD dissertation, 'The short stories of Zinaida Gippius: decadent or symbolist?' (University of Wisconsin at Madison, 1979), pp. 16–23. Antonina Gove looks at the whole issue of gender in Gippius' poetry in her article 'Gender as a poetic feature in the verse of Zinaida Gippius', in *American Contributions to the Eighth International Congress of Slavists*, 2 vols (Columbus, OH, 1978), vol. 2, pp. 379–407.
37. In one of her earlier stories, 'Nebesnye slova' (1906), Gippius' first-person male narrator takes aim at one of these expectations – that women write only about love: 'Psychology – and love . . . True, you might think that it's a woman who wrote these notes, or even an inveterate Don Juan . . . There are such types. In my time they could be met particularly among poets.' Excerpt from: Temira Pachmuss (trans.) *Selected Works of Zinaida Hippius* (Urbana, 1972), p. 54. Also see Sarah Pratt's discussion of gender shifts in Russian poetry in 'The obverse of self: gender shifts in poems by Tjutcev and Axmatova', and Daniel Rancour-Laferriere (ed.), *Russian Literature and Psychoanalysis* (Amsterdam, 1989), pp. 225–7 and 242, n. 4.
38. Mirsky, *History*, p. 440.
39. Gove found that in her sample the gender of the persona was unspecified in 51.2 per cent of them. See 'Gender as a poetic feature', p. 381.
40. An exception is the poem 'Grizel'da' (1895).
41. These differences could have had an autobiographical basis: Lokhvitskaia had several children, whereas Gippius had none. Some critics even claim that Gippius was devoid of maternal feelings. See Schaffer, 'Short stories', pp. 19–20.
42. For a discussion of Gippius' formal innovations, see Matich, 'Religious poetry', p. 13; Simon Karlinsky, 'Introduction' to *A Difficult Soul: Zinaida Gippius* by Vladimir Zlobin (Berkeley, 1980), p. 6. Karlinsky also points out her innovatory use of assonance rhymes.
43. See a summary of these opinions in Matich, 'Religious poetry', pp. 52–5; Temira Pachmuss, 'Zinaida Hippius and Andrey Bely: a story of their relationship', in Boris Christa (ed.), *Andrey Bely Centenary Papers* (Amsterdam, 1980), p. 58; Annenskii, 'One', pp. 8–12; Valerii Briusov, 'Z. N. Gippius', in *Russkaia literatura XX veka (1890–1910)*, vol. 1, pp. 178–188.
44. Marietta Shaginian, *Pervye vstrechi* (Moscow, 1909) and Elizaveta Iur'evna Kuz'mina-Karavaeva (later known as 'Mat' Mariia'), *Skifskie cherepki* (St Petersburg, 1912).

45. Upon her death, five Russian newspapers ran obituary notices about her, several articles on her appeared in the 1890s, and she was anthologized in such collections as A. N. Sal'nikov's *Russkie poety za 100 let v portretakh, biografiiakh i obraztsakh* (1901).

46. *Vesy*, no. 1 (1904), p. 83.

47. Andrei Belyi, *Simvolizm* (Moscow, 1910), pp. 358–60, 628.

48. Karolina Karlovna Pavlova, *Sobranie sochinenii*, Valerii Briusov (ed.), 2 vols (Moscow, 1915), vol. 1, p. viii.

49. 'Karolina Pavlova i gr. Evdokiia Rastopchina', *Russkii bibliofil*, no. 6 (1916), pp. 7–35.

50. Elizaveta Vasil'eva (Cherubina de Gabriak), 'Dve veshchi', pp. 139–40.

51. See ibid., p. 137; Tsvetaeva's observation occurs in her essay on Voloshin, 'Zhivoe o zhivom', which can be found in *Izbrannaia proza v dvukh tomakh* (New York, 1979), vol. 2, p. 30.

52. Heldt, citing a later poem, 'Otryvok', that mentions Pavlova again, indicates that it was Pavlova's life of exile and isolation that may have been as important to Parnok as the fact that Pavlova was both a woman and a poet. See *Terrible Perfection* (Bloomington, 1987), pp. 118–19.

53. Simon Karlinsky, *Marina Tsvetaeva: The Woman, Her World, and Her Poetry* (Cambridge, 1986), p. 107.

54. Diane Nemec-Ignashev, review of Barbara Heldt's *Terrible Perfection*, *Slavic and East European Journal*, vol. 23, no. 2 (Summer 1989), p. 302.

55. Nadezhda Grigor'evna L'vova, 'Kholod utra (neskol'ko slov o zhenskom tvorchestve)', *Zhatva*, no. 5 (1914), p. 249.

56. Vadim Shershenevich, 'Futurizm i zhenshchina', *Sovremennaia zhenshchina*, no. 1 (27 Mar. 1914), p. 3.

57. Anonymous review, *Utrenniki*, no. 2 (1922), p. 152.

58. A. Skabichevskii, 'Tekushchaia literatura', *Syn otechestva*, no. 224 (1899).

59. In addition to the examples given in note 16, we can cite: Nadezhda Sanzhar', *Zapiski Anny* (St Petersburg, 1910) and Anastasiia Tsvetaeva, *Dym, dym i dym* (Moscow, 1916). In a foreward to Sanzhar', the publisher even encourages the public to read the book as an autobiography (p. iii).

3 Women pharmacists in Russia before World War I: women's emancipation, feminism, professionalization, nationalism, and class conflict

Mary Schaeffer Conroy

The number of women pharmacists in nineteenth- and early twentieth-century Russia was minuscule – well under 1,000 by the First World War in a pharmacist population of some 10,000 and a general population of over 125,000,000. Nevertheless, an examination of women pharmacists in pre-Soviet Russia provides interesting information on significant socio-economic and political trends and developments and, additionally, serves as an indicator of the strength and vitality of female emancipation in the Russia of that era. Women pharmacists reflected the socio-economic, national and political diversity of late imperial Russia. Some became successful entrepreneurs, members of the pharmaceutical aristocracy, and worked for pharmaceutical professionalization. Others identified with the proletariat, becoming labour organizers, participants in strikes and Marxists of Menshevik hue. Still others withdrew to the sanctuary of the research laboratory. To a greater degree than their male colleagues, women pharmacists represented non-Russian minorities – Jews, Poles and Germans – but they exhibited an 'imperial' outlook at least until mid-First World War. All women pharmacists strove for their own emancipation and some extended a helping hand to their sisters. But their commitment to feminism and equal rights for women in general was subordinate to securing their own personal advancement and to their various political ideologies.

Women had been allowed to practise as pharmacists (*aptekari*) in *women*'s medical facilities from 1871.[1] They had been able also to own pharmacies.[2] In 1901, of 3,518 pharmacies in the Russian Empire, wives of pharmacists owned 110 in European Russia and 20 in Asiatic Russia.[3] But they were allowed to become pharmacists with right of general practice only in 1888. This made pharmacy one of the last medically related fields in Russia accessible to women[4] and put Russia behind the United States,[5] Canada,[6] Great Britain,[7] the Netherlands,[8] and

Belgium[9] but in advance of Germany,[10] Austria-Hungary,[11] the Scandinavian countries,[12] Spain,[13] and France.[14]

Sometime after 1871 women petitioned the Ministry of Internal Affairs to allow them to become pharmacists with right of general practice.[15] In 1882, Tsar Alexander III, despite having a conservative reputation and closing most courses for women physicians in that year, approved the request and instructed government agencies to work out procedures.[16] But only in 1888 – testifying to both the thoroughness and dilatoriness of the tsarist government – did the Medical Department of the Ministry of Internal Affairs issue a circular announcing that women could become pharmacy students (*ucheniki*) and take exams for the title 'assistant pharmacist' (*aptekarskii pomoshchnik*) and *provizor*. By 1902, women were eligible for the highest degree of *Magistr* of Pharmacy.[17] Finnish women were allowed to practise pharmacy in 1902.[18]

Male pharmacists reacted both positively and negatively to the admission of women to their fraternity. At the Second Congress of Pharmacists in 1888, noted pharmacologist A. B. Tikhomirov opposed women in the field.[19] Conversely, other pharmacists immediately took on female apprentices[20] and, in 1892, A. M. Semenov published a pamphlet supporting women pharmacists.[21] In 1889 the physician V. S. Bogoslovskii stressed that women pharmacists would be competent and were needed because of the great increase in pharmacies, particularly rural pharmacies, between 1878 and 1886.[22] Finally, even reluctant male pharmacists were forced to acquiesce to female colleagues because of the depletion of qualified male pharmacists.[23] While the number of male pharmacy students continued to rise in the last years of the nineteenth century – in 1896 there were 1,160 students compared to 1,488 in 1899 – the number of male assistant pharmacists declined from 2,584 in 1897 to 2,171 in 1899.[24]

Pharmacy was in the throes of professionalization in late nineteenth- and early twentieth-century Russia. Therefore, women entering this field could expect to share burdens as well as rewards. It took three years' apprenticeship and a stiff examination to become an assistant pharmacist. Three more years' apprenticeship, two years' university courses, and a second demanding examination were required to become a *provizor*. Many assistant pharmacists never progressed to this stage. Work days in turn-of-the-century Russian pharmacies were frequently long and salaries often low. Pharmacists faced night duty several times per month, difficulty in purchasing pharmacies, and competition from new, unregulated *aptekarskie magaziny* or 'drug stores', which at 5,700 in the early twentieth century outnumbered the 3,500 pharmacies.[25]

Thus, pharmacy in late imperial Russia was a field in flux; the minuses as well as the pluses for women were particularly evident in the arena of pharmaceutical education. Women entered pharmacy on an equal footing with men, but in so doing they struggled with the same excessive apprenticeship and inadequate formal instruction which impeded their male colleagues and which reformers urged pharmacy to shed in order to adapt to the rapid scientific and technological advancements of the era.

Educational requirements for women entering pharmacy were identical to those for men – completion of the equivalent of four years of the eight-year *gimnaziia*. After passing a Latin language examination women certified as governesses could become pharmacy students.[26] Indeed, women enjoyed a slight advantage over male candidates by the first decade of the twentieth century; whereas in the 1890s there were three times as many boys 'in school' as girls,[27] by 1910 there were 958 girls' *gimnazii* compared to 657 boys' *gimnazii* and in 1912 303,690 female *gimnaziia* students compared to 142,935 male *gimnaziia* students.[28] In 1899 both women and men pharmacy students who had finished the full eight years of the *gimnaziia* were allowed to reduce their period of initial apprenticeship from three to two years.[29] In 1900 women graduates of church schools were allowed to become pharmacy students if they took examinations in supplementary subjects.[30]

An apparently confining proviso in the circular of 1888, which forbade pharmacists who hired female apprentices to hire males[31] was intended to protect women, since pharmacy students often boarded in the pharmacy.[32] In any case it was rescinded in 1892, although women were to live outside the pharmacy and work in daytime if males were employed simultaneously.[33] The circular of 1888 also stipulated that women obtain private pharmaceutical instruction[34] but, in fact, circumstances forced many men to do this as well. Although preparatory courses for the assistant pharmacist examination were offered at universities or in large cities, men typically studied on their own or with tutors during their apprenticeship. Thus, both men and women lacked adequate formal instruction for the assistant pharmacist exam.

Women moving to the level of *provizor* or fully-fledged pharmacist[35] initially were more disadvantaged than men. This title required three more years' apprenticeship in the *apteka*, then two years' university education.[36] The university was inaccessible to many male pharmacists; those who attended were labelled auditors and denied access to laboratories if places were scarce. However, Russian universities did not admit women at all until 1906, and then only for two years. Consequently, the Imperial Military Medical Academy authorized private instruction for the first two women who took the *provizor*'s exam in 1898.[37]

Nevertheless, the circular of 1888, which admitted women to pharmacy, intended the establishment of their formal instruction and courses to prepare women for the assistant pharmacist and *provizor* examinations gradually appeared. The Women's Medical Institute, which opened in St Petersburg in 1897, was empowered by its statute to prepare women 'for pharmaceutical activity'.[38] In 1899 the St Petersburg 'Municipal Barrack Hospital in Memory of S. N. Botkin' began to offer courses to prepare women for the degree of *provizor*.[39] In Moscow in 1898 the Society of Russian Doctors received permission from the Ministry of Internal Affairs to open special pharmaceutical courses to prepare women for the degrees of assistant pharmacist and *provizor*.[40] By 1902, the Iurev-Dorpat Pharmaceutical Institute in Estland was open to women.[41] In the same year, Antonina Lesnevskaia, one of the first women pharmacists, established a pharmacy school in Petersburg to prepare women assistants and *provizory*. Special pharmaceutical courses appeared in other cities,[42] although the opening of pharmaceutical courses by the Society of Women Doctors in Warsaw was apparently deferred indefinitely because of lack of a suitable place.[43] The Russian government also honoured foreign degrees.[44] In 1898 a Russian woman, Luisa Tendler, received a doctorate from the New York College of Pharmacy.[45] Thus, by the early twentieth century a modicum of university-level education was available to women aspiring to the degree of *provizor*.[46] By February 1905, women were admitted to laboratories at Novorossiisk University in Odessa.[47]

A small band of women immediately entered the field. According to a Soviet historian, Anna Mikhailovna Makarova passed the exam for assistant pharmacist at Kiev University, 11 March 1892. Antonina Lesnevskaia became a pharmacy student in 1889; the Soviet historian cites her and Z. (Zinaida) I. Akker as the first to receive the title *provizor* in 1897,[48] although the contemporary *Farmatsevticheskii zhurnal* announced that Stanislavna Frantsevna Doviaglo was the first woman to pass the exam for degree of *provizor* and noted that the Ministry of Public Enlightenment had permitted two other women to take the *provizor*'s examination.[49] The two, who did so in the fall of 1898, were A. I. Levitan and A. P. Gal'perin-Vogava.[50] Antonina Lesnevskaia was the first to take the examination for the degree Master (*Magistr*) of Pharmacy at the Military Medical Academy in 1900. However, Ol'ga Evgen'evna Gabrilovich was the first actually to receive the *Magistr* degree. She took the examination at Moscow University in 1904 and defended her thesis at the Military Medical Academy in

December 1906. Apparently, she was the second woman to receive a learned degree in a Russian educational institution, a woman having received the degree Doctor of Medicine in 1876.[51]

Although figures vary, because of inexact terminology, the number of women pharmacy students, assistant pharmacists and *provizory* increased slowly but steadily in the last two decades of the nineteenth century indicating women's attraction to pharmacy as a career. According to the 1897 Russian census there were 8,723 pharmacists in the Empire, excluding apprentices; 245 pharmacists were women.[52] In 1902 a German pharmacy journal mentioned 500 women 'assistants' in Russian pharmacies.[53] In contrast, an 1898 article in *Farmatsevticheskii zhurnal* alluded to about 100 student pharmacists and 29 women pharmacists (26 assistant pharmacists and 3 *provizory*) in Russia.[54] A 1901 article in *Farmatsevt* provided a breakdown on women pharmacists in the last years of the twentieth century. In 1896, according to this source, 60 women students were apprenticing in all the pharmacies in the Empire, in 1897 the number 'had increased insignificantly' to 62, but the next year, 1898, witnessed a leap to 101 women students.[55] For women assistant pharmacists this article gave figures of 13 in 1895, 22 in 1896, 28 in 1897, and 47 in 1898.[56] In 1902, a *Dotsent* at the Iurev-Dorpat Pharmaceutical Institute, J. Schindelmeiser, provided nearly identical statistics adding 123 women student pharmacists and 56 assistant pharmacists in 1900.[57] In 1902 five women pharmacists were working in the Caucasus.[58]

Women physicians outnumbered women pharmacists, an understandable phenomenon, in view of the fact that the latter profession had at least a ten-year lead. There were over 470 Russian women medical students in 1878 and almost 1,400 by 1903.[59] The number of women pharmacists was also meagre when compared to the number of men pharmacists. By 1905 official statistics reported a total of 6,800 pharmacists and 4,600 pharmacy students.[60] Nevertheless, the ratio of women pharmacists to men pharmacists in early twentieth-century Russia was comparable with that in the United States. In 1870 there were 34 women out of 17,335 'Traders and dealers in medicine' in the United States; in 1900 American women constituted 1,178 'Traders and dealers in medicine' compared with 56,168 men in the same category.[61]

Women entered pharmacy for a variety of reasons – emulation of their fathers, desire for intellectual fulfillment, economic security, social advancement, physical mobility and the fact that there were openings in pharmacy.

Two early pharmacists, Lesnevskaia and Gabrilovich had physician fathers.[62] Lesnevskaia dreamed of assisting her father who practised in a

Volga town. She was also determined to have a career and believed pharmacy would be interesting.[63] Eva Broido, who later became a Menshevik, asserted that she entered pharmacy because of 'an unquenchable desire for learning but also for escape . . . from the depressing, inactive life at home and in our little town . . .'[64] Further, Broido's family, comfortably well-off when she was a small child, suffered a reversal of fortune when she was ten, which stimulated her to strive for economic security.[65] Whereas women physicians were predominantly Orthodox, and thus, by implication Russian, pharmacy was a magnet for minority women in the Empire.[66] These included Stanislavna Doviaglo who passed the *provizor*'s examination at Moscow University in 1897,[67] Antonina Lesnevskaia,[68] her sister Zhosefa (Josepha) Boleslavna, who received the *provizor* degree in 1910, and the Polish woman *provizor* Florentina Florian Stankevich, friend of Antonina Lesnevskaia, who managed the latter's pharmacy from 1908.[69] Ol'ga Gabrilovich and Eva Broido were Jewish, as were 13 of 18 women studying pharmacy at the Iurev-Dorpat Pharmaceutical Institute in 1902. Two of the latter were Poles, one was a Baltic German and one was Russian.[70] By 1910, there were 85 women *provizory*, 58 of whom were Jewish and 7 Polish; only 16 were Russian.[71]

However, these women studied and served as pharmacists in Russian, not border cities, and it appeared that their goals were assimilation and financial advancement, rather than the promotion of national interests. Relatives of the Lesnevskaia sisters had participated in the Polish uprising of 1830 and were exiled to Siberia.[72] But like many other cosmopolitan Poles[73] the Polish sympathies of Antonina and Zhosefa Lesnevskaia, Florentina Stankevich and Doviaglo were in low profile, at least until World War I.[74] Doviaglo worked in Antonina's Petersburg pharmacy during 1904; she became active in the Polish School Society only in 1918.[75] Antonina established her women's *apteka* adjacent to the neoclassical Roman Catholic St Catherine's Church, in a building, according to one source, owned by the Polish Benevolent Society.[76] (The society had been founded in Petersburg in 1884.)[77] Lesnevskaia also published a Polish-language pamphlet on women pharmacists in Warsaw in 1908 entitled *Nowa dziedzina pracy kobiet*.[78] But her other writings were in Russian and Lesnevskaia did not appear to participate regularly in Polish functions in St Petersburg. Between 1905 and 1909 *Kraj*, the journal which detailed the Polish activities in various Russian cities of the Empire, mentioned three times that Polish meetings were held in the building which housed Lesnevskaia's *apteka*, but cited her directly only once in contrast to prolific mention of other Poles in Petersburg.[79]

Similarly, Eva Broido desired to 'escape from the Pale'; she took exams at Kazan University and served for a time in a pharmacy in Petersburg.[80] Ol'ga Gabrilovich also was Jewish[81] but had been born in Petersburg[82] and studied at Moscow University and the Military Medical Academy in Petersburg, where she was part of the pharmaceutical elite.[83]

Another factor propelling women into pharmacy was simply availability of positions. The number of pharmacies continued to expand – there were 3,518 in 1901 and 4,804 in 1910.[84] Conscription of male pharmacists during the Russo-Japanese War of 1904–05 accentuated the reduction in numbers of male assistant pharmacists evident at the turn of the century. World War I created further openings for women, causing the *Peterburgskaia gazeta* to comment in 1916 that the 'insufficiency of male pharmacists in recent times significantly increased the number of women pharmacists'.[85]

It must be noted that mature women, as well as teen-age girls were willing to commit themselves to a period of three to six years' apprenticeship, one or two demanding examinations, special courses and a considerable outlay of money to become pharmacists. The 18 women students at the Iurev-Dorpat Pharmacy Institute ranged in age from 22 to over 40 years. One student had graduated from a trade school in Berlin; another had graduated from a conservatory in Leipzig.[86] The first class of 24 students at Lesnevskaia's Petersburg pharmacy school ranged in age from 16 to 26. All the women in the school, as well as six on a waiting list, had completed secondary education. This meant that their families had paid the tuition fees which amounted to half the total support of girls' schools,[87] and that the women or their families were willing to pay the 300 roubles' tuition for the two-year course at Lesnevskaia's school.[88]

Historians have emphasized the difficulties of Eva Broido and Antonina Lesnevskaia,[89] but the women's own reminiscences provide a different picture. In general, while Eva Broido considered life with her first husband 'three years in private hell',[90] her recollections of her work as a pharmacist exude ebullience. As an apprentice, hours were long (9 am until 9 pm and often until 10 or 11) and pay low (8 roubles per month plus lunch and dinner). But she enjoyed happy times with her male and female colleagues, had no trouble passing her examinations and quickly found jobs, one of them in a big chemist's shop in Petersburg where the full board and 35 roubles per month made her 'feel a Croesus'.[91]

Antonina Lesnevskaia met some obstacles in her pharmacy career which were gender related. The wife of one mentor was jealous and

Lesnevskaia had to teach his children[92] (a fate which also befell other women apprentices);[93] to some inquiries for positions she was asked to send her photograph and received marriage proposals.[94] But other problems were common to male pharmacists as well. Lesnevskaia's family and friends disapproved of her finishing a long education to stand behind a counter rolling pills, preparing powders and pouring castor oil.[95] She was readily accepted as an apprentice numerous times but in two instances was dissatisfied with her training and left of her own accord.[96] Her pay was low and living conditions uncomfortable.[97] Fortunately several principals, with whom she developed camaraderie, gave her good training.[98] Studying for the assistant pharmacist exam in Petersburg, Lesnevskaia, the only woman in a class of forty, became friends with her classmates.[99] She met no difficulty in getting permission to take or in passing the assistant pharmacist, *provizor*, and *magistr* exams, although by the time she prepared for the last exam she was weary.[100] At all stages government officials and professors were helpful.[101] She also had no problems in finding assistant pharmacist positions,[102] although in one case she became exhausted from fourteen-hour working days.[103]

The experiences of other women aspiring to become pharmacists varied. In 1904, Bertha Aizenshtadt asserted that women pharmacists encountered special prejudice. However, she also criticized the apprentice system which prevented adequate training for males as well as females entering pharmacy.[104] In early 1905 Anna Roget, from the Ural region, described low pay for the student pharmacist (5 roubles per month) and the burden of caring for the *apteka* owner's child (at 4 roubles per month).[105] But, in contrast, in 1904 Liubov' Lavrova optimistically noted that more women were entering pharmacy each year and with higher qualifications than men, since most completed *gimnaziia* or secondary school. She also recommended eliminating the apprentice system.[106]

The feminist commitment of women pharmacists also varied. Antonina Lesnevskaia was sympathetic to aspiring women pharmacists. In 1898 after receiving her *provizor* degree, Lesnevskaia invited her 'sisters' to write to her for advice on becoming pharmacists and practising pharmacy.[107] In 1900, she spoke about organizing a society of women pharmacists.[108] In 1901 she established a clearing house for women pharmacy students and assistants seeking positions, inviting them, on the one hand, and doctors and pharmacists needing employees, on the other, to contact her.[109]

However, Lesnevskaia was not solely or even predominantly a feminist. She recognized that excessive apprenticeship and lack of educational opportunity was a flaw in turn-of-the-century Russian pharmacy affecting men as well as women, and all her public utterances put women pharmacists' problems in a general context.

In 1904, for example, in a report to the Third Congress of Technologists, she emphasized the difficulties women faced in becoming pharmacists. She claimed it was hard for women to begin apprenticeship and complete additional practical work in pharmacies. Most pharmacists wanted cheap labour; pharmacy apprentices and assistants worked fourteen-hour days. Women were often hidden from the public; fifteen women in one Moscow pharmacy worked behind opaque glass. On the other hand, Lesnevskaia also admitted that men had trouble acquiring the formal education required for the assistant pharmacist exam; they could hear university lectures only as auditors and not fully-fledged students. In fact, the thrust of this report was that pharmacy education as a whole needed overhauling. Nevertheless, ignoring the university level courses available to women, she claimed that women were more disadvantaged than men in acquiring formal pharmacy education because they were not admitted to the universities at all. She confirmed that professors at the Military Medical Academy had cooperated with the first women to prepare for the *provizor* exam but this was not repeated for successive women. Some women took formal courses but many struggled to prepare for the exam for three to six months without laboratories.[110]

Lesnevskaia similarly emphasized both women's problems in becoming pharmacists and inadequate education for all entry-level pharmacists in her address to the First All-Russian Women's Congress, held in Petersburg in December 1908. She admitted that women pharmacy students were often forced to double as governesses and were rarely paid. But she also related that professors at the Military Medical Academy had greatly helped her and the other first women pharmacists, she decried poor educational facilities for male pharmacy students and assistant pharmacists, and affirmed that once women had their degree they received the same pay as men.[111] In 1912 Lesnevskaia again balanced women pharmacists' problems with those of male pharmacists. She asserted that women had difficulty getting pharmacists to accept them as students, sometimes having to pay as much as 100 roubles to the proprietor. Additionally, Lesnevskaia emphasized that because pharmacists feared that women would drive away customers, they often had to work out of the public eye – in late night shifts and as *fasovshchiki* or cleaners of the pharmacy vessels and implements – or were allowed only to sell medicaments, artists' wares and the like over the counter. However, she also admitted that women students were more easily accepted in small pharmacies and got more hands-on experience there. Furthermore, she claimed that more and more often, pharmacies located in the capitals of Petersburg and Moscow, while shunning women pharmacy students, invited women to positions of assistant pharmacist and *provizor*. Some *aptekari* had begun to send their daughters to special pharmacy courses before putting them to work in their pharmacies.[112]

Lesnevskaia attempted to solve both the problem of women's pharmacy education and that of inadequate early pharmacy education with her 'First Women's Pharmacy' and Women's Pharmacy Institute. She established the former in 1901 and the latter in 1902 in St Petersburg.

Lesnevskaia intended her women's pharmacy to provide capital for her school and also to serve as a training facility. Both were to enable women to acquire quality pharmaceutical education. But, in addition, Lesnevskaia hoped the school and institute would serve as prototypes for upgrading pharmacy education in general.[113]

She petitioned the Medical Department of the Ministry of Internal Affairs to open a women's pharmacy in 1898, just after she received her *provizor* degree, a requirement for operating a 'normal pharmacy'. Her petition generated opposition within the pharmaceutical community. At least three letters to the editor were published in the major pharmacy journals. One relayed supposed complaints from a former male student. The other two lamented that women would be forced to spend long days at menial labour, such as cutting the labels or *signatury*, required for medicaments, filling capsules and so on.

Lesnevskaia's reaction to these criticisms, both personal and general, revealed the strong personality and also the political savvy that enabled her to achieve her goals. She vehemently assailed the criticism of her teaching ability, dismissing her opponent Levitov's statements as 'lies'. She stoutly insisted that she had twenty-four students, not eight as Levitov had stated, and that her income from them was 700 roubles not a paltry 240 as he had claimed. She asserted that her students had done very well at their exams and that not one of them had complained about her.[114] She rebutted the general question of women's suitability for pharmacy by noting that male pharmacy students also were forced to perform mundane tasks. The solution was not to prevent women from becoming apprentices but to reform the apprentice system. She advocated shortening the work day in private pharmacies.[115]

But Lesnevskaia also took care to cultivate the pharmaceutical community and undoubtedly this strategy, coupled with her indomitable drive, accounted for much of her success. At the Third All-Russian

Pharmaceutical Congress in 1899 she 'expressed her heartfelt . . . hope in the name of all women pharmacists that with general comradeship we would resolve effectively all problems for the general good of science and our society. Women pharmacists have entrusted me to express to all the honourable members the hope that the congress will be success-ful'.[116] This got her high marks from the journal *Farmatsevt* which described the opening of her First Women's Pharmacy, emphasizing that Lesnevskaia was known to many readers for her energetic support of the proposal to raise the issue of women's pharmacy education at the third All Russian Pharmaceutical Congress. The anonymous author believed that this had earned her 'the sympathy of her comrades'.[117]

Lesnevskaia was the first woman in Russia to receive a concession for a new pharmacy.[118] Although a contemporary observer claimed that Lesnevskaia obtained permission to open her pharmacy only after 'diffi-cult battles with the Russian authorities',[119] the author also noted that the Minister of Internal Affairs personally intervened and waived the ordinary rules for establishing new normal pharmacies when he permit-ted Lesnevskaia to open her pharmacy.[120]

Lesnevskaia's First Women's Pharmacy (Pervaia zhenskaia apteka) opened with fanfare on 5 June 1901, with many notables in attendance.[121] The pharmacy was situated in a choice section of Petersburg at 32 Nevskii Prospekt, near the city duma, Gostinnyi Dvor, the Passage women's store, the Singer Sewing Machine Building, and Our Lady of Kazan Cathedral. According to a 1902 account the First Women's Pharmacy had an elegant layout – all white and gold – which cost 22,000 roubles. Like all normal pharmacies, whose floor plans the government dictated, the pharmacy had a cash register, a section for over-the-counter items, a prescription area, a 'nicely furnished waiting room', and a laboratory. Laboratory equipment was state-of-the-art, including a steam apparatus from Wolff and Sons.[122] Women between 16 and 26 were employed, exclusively. Contemporary photographs portrayed them, attired in white smocks, attentively inspecting lavishly stocked shelves and apparatus.[123]

In her 1901 autobiography, Lesnevskaia blamed both *aptekari* and working pharmacists (*sluzhashchie*) for the class conflict that was rending the pharmaceutical *soslovie*.[124] She herself was a progressive pharmacy owner. She instituted double shifts and a 7-hour work day.[125] The women pharmacists she employed handled the night shift but, according to a contemporary observer, no improprieties had occurred during the first six months of operation. Lesnevskaia also provided a lodging house where, according to the contemporary observer, 'incoming girls from the provinces, who without shelter would have been exposed to the dangers of the capital, can find food, lodging and supervision'.[126]

Lesnevskaia acknowleged that Russia was in the avant-garde with this first all-women's pharmacy.[127] The Russian and international press acclaimed her as a pioneer. Reaction from pharmacists and society in general was mixed. Some members of the Society of Russian Pharmacists and Physicians were sympathetic. The public were both curious and sceptical. In some cases patrons took prescriptions filled at the women's pharmacy to neighbouring pharmacies, claiming that the original medicine was too weak. Some people were convinced there were male pharmacists working behind the scenes who actually prepared the medicine. Others believed the female pharmacy students were sisters of mercy because they wore white uniforms. During the first year a summer theatre performance satirized the Women's Pharmacy; as a result young drunkards came to the pharmacy at night for the purpose of harassment.[128]

In her autobiography, Lesnevskaia claimed that, in contrast to the many men who helped her and Akker, a female patron was ineffectual.[129] Likewise, she told the representatives to the First All-Russian Women's Congress that most often *women* exhibited hostility towards or lack of confidence in her Women's Pharmacy. In one case a physician asked that a prescription for a seriously sick infant be filled at the Women's Pharmacy since it was closest; the mother insisted that the prescription be filled at a pharmacy managed by males. In other instances women bought sundries such as glycerine and cold creams at the Women's Pharmacy but refused to have their prescriptions filled there.[130]

Nevertheless, the First Women's Pharmacy stayed in business at least until 1916.[131] Woman-*Provizor* Zinaida I. Akker was the first manager; she was followed by one Bulatova and in 1908 by Florentina Stankevich.[132] In 1916 two *provizory*, ten assistant pharmacists and two students staffed the pharmacy.[133]

Immediately after opening her *apteka*, Lesnevskaia petitioned the Medical Council to open a women's pharmacy institute.[134] The school opened in September 1902, although Lesnevskaia did not receive final permission until July 1903.[135] Entrance requirements were higher than normal – completion of the full eight years of the female *gimnaziia*.[136] Thirty young women applied for the first class, although there was space for only twenty-four to be accepted.[137] The curriculum, which was two years or four semesters in length, appeared to provide excellent preparation for pharmacy. Lesnevskaia considered it nearly equal to the full university course demanded for *provizor*; certainly it was more thorough than the six- to eight-week courses she claimed most pharmacists took with *provizory* in university cities in order to pass the assistant pharmacy exam.[138] Liubov' Lavrova, one of the successful graduates, claimed in 1904 that the course at Lesnevskaia's school 'included all that was necessary for a *provizor* degree (in other words equal to the first two years of university)' and 'all the subjects of the first two courses of the Woman's Medical Institute with wider requirements in chemistry and pharmaceutical sciences'.[139] It also is interesting to note that the course in Lesnevskaia's women's pharmacy school was very similar to that advocated for new Soviet pharmacy schools by I. Levenshtein, Director of the State Pharmacy Administration in November 1921.[140] The curriculum in Lesnevskaia's school was as in the table below.

	Subject	Hours per week
First year	chemistry	3
	zoology	2
	physics	2
	botany+practical application	2
	mathematics	1
Second year	organic chemistry	2
	analytical chemistry	2
	pharmaceutical chemistry	2
	pharmacognosy	1
	mineralogy and geology	2
	hygiene	1
	pharmacology	1
	physics	2
	jurisprudence	1/2

All chemistry courses included laboratory work with quantitative and qualitative analysis and use of microscopes where appropriate. One contemporary photograph recorded such a class – twenty-four serious women seated in a rococo room adorned with a portrait of Tsarina Alexandra, waiting expectantly for a male chemistry professor, standing before a table laden with vessels and apparatus, to begin his lecture. The curriculum of Lesnevskaia's school also included practicums in preparation of prescriptions and first aid. In the first year students performed practical work for three to four hours weekly in a special pharmacy connected with the school. During the fourteen-week summer vacation students were required to work at least six weeks in a zemstvo, village or general pharmacy. During their second year students worked four hours per day in the Women's Pharmacy. Students finishing the course were then eligible to take the exam for assistant pharmacist.[141]

The government granted graduates of Lesnevskaia's school preferential treatment in admitting them to the assistant pharmacist examinations given by the Military Medical Academy in Petersburg. Normally the Academy allowed only three-fifths of the pharmacy students who applied each semester to take the examination; the remainder had to work not less than one year in Petersburg pharmacies – obviously a disappointment, if not an outright hardship. Authorities waived this limitation for Lesnevskaia's students. In the fall of 1904, *Farmatsevticheskii vestnik* noted that 'in the last semester it was possible to allow more than three-fifths . . . deviating from the rule in order to examine eighteen students from the First Women's Pharmacy of A. B. Lesnevskaia for the title Assistant Pharmacist'.[142]

The happy symbiosis between Lesnevskaia and the pharmacy establishment prevailed until the collapse of the tsarist government. However, solidarity between Lesnevskaia and her pharmacist 'sisters' was strained during the revolutionary years of 1905 and 1906. Two clashes erupted; apparently, they resulted less from class antagonisms, about which socialist feminists harangued,[143] than conflict between individual and group interests.

A few women pharmacists exhibited radical tendencies. Eva Broido became a revolutionary, married a fellow revolutionary, and was exiled to Siberia. There she periodically worked as a pharmacist, once in a municipal dispensary in Iakutsk.[144] Some women pharmacists participated in strikes in 1905. By 1914 two women pharmacists became officers in a Menshevik-oriented pharmacy society. But most prominent women pharmacists entered the establishment. Stanislavna Doviaglo managed her own pharmacy in Livonia from 1897 to 1900. Antonina Lesnevskaia became an *aptekar'* or pharmacy owner; Zinaida Akker and Florentina Stankevich ran her *apteka*; Zhosefa Lesnevskaia worked in it. Ol'ga Gabrilovich, Liubov' Lavrova, and L. A. Kovaleva, whose work is reviewed below, became noted pharmacologists.

These women, unlike some other outstanding feminists,[145] did not support political movements, suffragist or otherwise; on the contrary, during 1905 Antonina Lesnevskaia's solidarity with the pharmacy establishment and concern for the solvency of her *apteka* and proprietary pharmacy school superseded her commitment to feminism.

Late in 1904 all still was well; pharmacy journals carried announcements that applications to Lesnevskaia's school for the spring term should be sent before 15 December.[146] But, despite the fact that Lesnevskaia's pharmacy was run on progressive lines, strikes which broke out in St Petersburg pharmacies in September 1905 finally engulfed her pharmacy.[147] That the women in Lesnevskaia's First Women's Pharmacy joined the strike is one of the strongest proofs that agitators rather than real grievances had fanned if not fomented some strikes, for the chief demands had already been met at Lesnevskaia's pharmacy.

Although a purported letter from Lesnevskaia, in which she expressed sympathy with the strike, was read to a meeting of pharmacists in Petersburg on 3 November, on 9 November she gave notice to her women pharmacists that they would be fired unless they stopped striking. Additionally, she forbade them to participate either in further strikes or even in meetings of *sluzhashchie* pharmacists.[148] When the strikers resisted, Lesnevskaia proposed to the students in her pharmacy school that they take over the responsibilities of the striking pharmacists. The students refused and Lesnevskaia retaliated by declaring the school closed until 1 September 1906. The students, in turn, protested, noting that having paid 150 roubles per year they were entitled to the courses. However, Lesnevskaia refused to revoke her decision and the students threatened a lawsuit.[149]

Following on the heels of this imbroglio, in 1906, Lesnevskaia met formidable economic competition from a women's group, the 'Society for the Preservation of Women's Health'. The Society opened a 'Second Women's Pharmacy' in Petersburg. The Society initially contributed 20,000 roubles to the *apteka* and sold 700 shares at 50 roubles each to raise the total 35,000 roubles estimated as necessary for establishing the pharmacy.[150]

A few years later, Lesnevskaia mended her fences with feminists. In 1908 she participated in the All-Russian Women's Congress, as described above, and in April 1909 hosted a meeting of the women's section of the Petersburg Polish *kolo* which was establishing training courses for practical work, such as furriery, for the winter season.[151]

Despite disruption in 1905, Lesnevskaia's school was a success. By 1913, 387 women had attended her school[152] and 199 had graduated, one (Liubov' Lavrova) dying an untimely death in 1908.[153] Fourteen graduates went on to take the *provizor*'s exam.[154] Two of those receiving *provizor* degrees, N. F. Kasperovich and Zhosefa Lesnevskaia, Antonina's sister, remained as assistants in Lesnevskaia's pharmacy school.[155] In the 1908 First All-Russian Women's Congress, Lesnevskaia asserted that thirty-nine of those who had graduated from her school by that time worked in St Petersburg pharmacies – predominantly in city pharmacies and those owned by societies; three worked in private pharmacies. The majority of graduates had received places in the provinces.[156] In 1912 Lesnevskaia reported a reverse trend – nearly 100 of the 198 living graduates worked in St Petersburg. Many of those graduates who had become *provizory* managed zemstvo and railroad pharmacies or those owned by societies.[157] Two students of Lesnevskaia's school, Liubov' Nikolaevna Lavrova and L. A. Kovaleva, discussed below, did research at the Institute of Experimental Medicine.[158]

The Russian government publicly acknowledged Lesnevskaia's contribution to pharmacy education. In 1912 the Ministry of Internal Affairs and the Ministry of Public Enlightenment publicly recognized her school as the exclusive institution for training women pharmacists; the ministries planned to upgrade the school to a scientific institute of pharmacy in 1913.[159]

The response of Lesnevskaia's male colleagues to her activities was mixed. Some generously applauded her educational experiments; others ignored her. Among the former was V. V. Rumiantsev who praised Lesnevskaia's school in 1912.[160] Among the latter were T. I. Lonachevskii-Petruniak, professor at St Vladimir University in Kiev, who did not mention Lesnevskaia's school in his 1905 plea for pharmacy institutes,[161] and an influential Petersburg pharmacist, Aleksandr Semenovich Ginzburg, who, in fact, appeared adversarial either out of personal frustration or out of simple competitiveness. Ginzburg ignored Lesnevskaia's school in his twelve-page pamphlet of 1913, on pharmaceutical education in Russia.[162]

While A. N. Shvarts forbade women to attend university in 1908,[163] Lesnevskaia's school and an emerging network of medical facilities for women[164] began to bear fruit in the first decade of the twentieth century. A handful of women *magistr* pharmacists made scientific contributions. Ol'ga Evgen'evna Gabrilovich, contemporary of Lesnevskaia, wrote her Master of Pharmacy thesis on 'The cause of so-called intoxicating bread', performing the chemical experiments for thc thcsis in the laboratory of A. Ia. Danilevskii, at the Military Medical Academy.[165] Danilevskii termed her work the 'first to find a simple method of separating healthy flour from harmful'.[166]

Gabrilovich's thesis responded to a disease which occurred a few hours after eating rye bread. The symptoms of the disease included throat ache, dizziness, deterioration of vision and vomiting, and it attacked animals as well as humans. Since these symptoms were similar to those resulting from drinking too much vodka, the bread had been nicknamed 'intoxicating bread'.[167] This disease occurred in dry regions during rainy years[168] but was distinct from ergotism.[169]

The disease caused by 'drunken bread' had had serious repercussions in Belozersk, the southern Ukraine, Novgorod *guberniia*, Vologda and other areas. In order to combat the disease, several district zemstvo executive committees had requested that the St Petersburg Society for Preservation of Public Health investigate both rye kernels and flour.[170] In 1905 the Russian Society for the Preservation of Public Health sponsored research on the problem and the Medical Academy offered a prize for papers on the subject.[171]

Through laborious chemical experiments and tests for both kernels and flour on frogs, Gabrilovich concluded that the most likely cause of the disease was the fungus *Fusarium roseum link*, a glucoside whose nitrous content was formed at the expense of protein in the rye kernel, thus depriving the rye of nutrition.[172] In the course of her experiments she noted the coexistence of penicillin and bacteria in her petri dishes, but unfortunately did not note penicillin's effect on bacteria.[173]

At Gabrilovich's dissertation defence in the Military Medical Academy on 21 December 1906, the audience applauded[174] and the pharmaceutical press hailed her thesis as 'especially important, being the first case of a major independent work of a woman pharmacist in Russia to have attained the degree of Master of Pharmacy, and because of the major significance of the topic in the contemporary life of our peasantry'.[175]

Liubov' Nikolaevna Lavrova, a product of Lesnevskaia's women's pharmacy school, did seminal research on a method of preventing arterio-sclerosis caused by massive injections of adrenalin. This research resulted from the therapeutics of the time. Scientists had isolated adrenalin in the early twentieth century and injected massive amounts into patients to combat enlarged, obtrusive red veins, particularly those on the face. For example, in 1909 a Kharkov physician, E. A. Rothmann, informed the British medical journal *The Lancet* that he had successfully injected adrenalin, one of the strongest 'vaso-constrictors', into two patients in 1907 to cure the condition known as 'red nose' or 'erythematous taches'.[176] Unfortunately, this treatment frequently also enlarged the walls of the blood vessels and affected the heart, with fatal results.[177]

During 1906 Lavrova conducted numerous experiments on rabbits and dogs and concluded that iodine and iodine salts were the substances which could successfully counter vascular changes leading to the arterio-sclerosis which resulted from massive injections of adrenalin.[178] Her work was published early in 1908.[179] In November 1908, *The Lancet* announced that a German scientist, Dr Mansfield, had successfully conducted experiments showing that one grain of cholin subcutaneously injected prevented serious disease of the aorta in rabbits which had been injected with two and a half grains of adrenalin.[180] Allowing for a time lag in the German researcher's reporting and publication it appears that Lavrova's experiments preceded his. Unfortunately she died in 1908.

L. A. Kovaleva graduated from Lesnevskaia's school in 1908. She then did research in the Institute of Experimental Medicine, receiving her *provizor* degree in 1912. Kovaleva published two articles. One, published in 1912, reported her research on the effect of the 'growth substance' lecithin – on the oxidization processes of animals.[181]

In the years immediately preceding World War I women pharmacists did not achieve complete equality with men but their position was respectable. Women pharmacists continued to be heavily outnumbered by men. By 1910 there were 85 *zhenshchiny-provizory* as compared with 4,724 male *provizory*. Women *provizory*, therefore, amounted to only 1.8 per cent of the total. The majority of these women received their degrees at Moscow and Kharkov universities between 1907 and 1910.[182] There were only a handful of women masters of pharmacy; the *Russkii meditsinskii spisok* or Register of Medical Practitioners for 1916 recorded only three.[183] But on the credit side of the ledger, women *provizory* owned three rural and five normal or fully stocked pharmacies in their own right and almost one-third of women *provizory* managed normal pharmacies. The majority of women pharmacists were single.[184]

With regard to salaries, women's positions varied. Lesnevskaia had reported to the First All-Russian Women's Congress in 1908 that women pharmacists' pay was commensurate with men's. She asserted that women assistant pharmacists or *aptekarskie pomoshchnitsy* received between 50 and 90 roubles per month – 600 to 1,080 per year; the salaries of women *provizory* ranged from 100 to 150 roubles per month – 1,200 to 1,800 per year.[185] Independent data supported her contention, for in 1913, *provizory* at an average pharmacy in a provincial city received 1,200 roubles per year, senior assistant pharmacists received 800 roubles, and junior assistant pharmacists received 720 roubles.[186] Undoubtedly there had been some inflation between 1908 and 1913. In 1914 in the First City Pharmacy in Tomsk, women pharmacists did not occupy high positions but their pay was equivalent to that of their male counterparts. For example, both the female laboratory technician and the two male pharmacists-receptionists received 80 roubles per month. The only apparent inequality was that the female had worked longer at the pharmacy. But the pay of the female assistant pharmacist at 60 roubles per month exceeded that of the male assistant pharmacist at 50 roubles.[187]

On the other hand, *Farmatsevticheskii zhurnal* claimed in 1916 that the average pay for women pharmacists was less than that for men.

According to the journal the average *provizor*'s income was 141 roubles per month, women *provizory* received on the average only 86 roubles; men assistant pharmacists' salaries averaged 98 roubles per month, women assistant pharmacists', 77; male students' pay on the average was 48 roubles per month, female students' 34.[188]

Although some pharmacies had introduced double shifts as early as 1904,[189] double shifts and 7-hour days were fairly common in large cities by 1910 and women pharmacists undoubtedly benefited.[190] The woman assistant pharmacist at the Tomsk City Pharmacy worked the same hours and fulfilled the same responsibilities as her male associates. The pharmacy personnel, excluding the manager, laboratory technician, cashiers and menials or cleaning help, worked 6-hour shifts, alternating between day and evening shifts. In addition, all pharmacists, including students, had night duty every five days; the female assistant pharmacist then worked twenty-four hours straight alongside male students.[191]

Despite these hopeful signs, trouble seemed to be brewing by the spring of 1914. There were hints of a recurrence of the 1905 clashes between 'establishment' women pharmacists like Antonina Lesnevskaia and her socialist sisters, who were prominent in a Menshevik oriented pharmacy union. Indeed, in 1919, all that Antonina Lesnevskaia had worked for would be wrested from her.[192] But on the eve of these upheavals pharmacy provided an interesting and obtainable career for *determined* women. Women were able to enter pharmacy and were accepted on fairly equal terms with men, because pharmaceutical practice was in a transitional phase. Women choosing pharmacy had to share with their male colleagues various problems and the drive for professionalization. This, in turn, presented women with opportunities which a few seized, making contributions to pharmacy, pharmacology and the advancement of women in Russia.

Notes

1. 'O zhenshchinakh-farmatsevtakh; Vysochaishee povelenie 14 ianvaria 1871 g.', *Sbornik zakonopolozhenii dlia farmatsevtov, soderzhatelei aptek i drogistov* (comp.) P. N. Bulatov (St Petersburg, 1897), p. 81.
2. R. B., 'Die erste Frauen-Apoteke', *Apothekenbilder von Nah und Fern* (Vienna, 1901), pt 2, p. 3.
3. Toropov, D. M. 'Dvizhenie i rost aptechnogo dela v Imperii za poslednee desiatiletie (1901–1910 g.g.)', *Vestnik obshchestvennoi gigieny, sudebnoi i prakticheskoi meditsiny*, no. 9 (1911), p. 1293.
4. Women were trained for midwifery from the mid-eighteenth century,

studied medicine, albeit irregularly, from the 1860s, became paramedics or *fel'dshery* from the 1870s, and comprised two-thirds of the students in the first proprietory dental school which opened in 1881. They continued to comprise a half to three-quarters of the students in the nine or so other proprietary dental schools successively founded in Russia. For information on women in other medical specialities see Jeanette E. Tuve, *The First Russian Women Physicians* (Newtonville, MA, 1984); Richard Stites, *The Women's Liberation Movement in Russia* (Princeton, 1978), pp. 31, 84; Samuel Ramer, 'Who was the Russian fel'dsher?', *Bulletin of the History of Medicine*, vol. 50 (1976), p. 216; 'Khronika i smes'', *Zubovrachebnyi vestnik*, vol. 1, no. 2 (1885), p. 231 and author's MS on women dentists in tsarist Russia.

5. Women practised pharmacy in America from the 1770s but became licensed pharmacists only in the post Civil-War period. For women pharmacists in the United States see Emma Gary Wallace, 'Women in pharmacy', *The Pharmaceutical Era*, vol. 45, no. 1 (January, 1912), p. 102; Glenn Sonnedecker, 'Women as pharmacy students in 19th-century America', *Veröffentlichungen der Internationalen Gesellschaft für Geschichte der Pharmazie*, vol. 40 (Stuttgart, 1973), pp. 136–7; 'Mrs Anna B. Hummel, pharmacist', *The New York Times*, 22 June 1896, p. 3, col. 3; and Teresa Catherine Gallagher, 'From family helpmeet to independent professional: women in American pharmacy, 1870–1940', *Pharmacy in History*, vol. 31, no. 2 (1989), pp. 60–77.

6. Canadian women in Ontario began to be licensed between 1868 and 1871. Ernest W. Stieb, *et al.*, 'Women in Ontario pharmacy, 1867–1927', *Pharmacy in History*, vol. 28, no. 3 (1986), pp. 125–34.

7. Elizabeth Garret received an apothecary licence in 1865; two women had passed pharmaceutical examinations by 1868 when the Pharmacy Act officially admitted women to examinations in Great Britain. However, women were not allowed to prepare for examinations at the lectures or in the laboratory of the British Pharmaceutical Society until 1872. Esther Pohl Lovejoy, *Women Doctors of the World* (New York, 1957), p. 141; W. J. Uglow Woolcock, 'Historical sketch of the Pharmaceutical Society of Great Britain: XXI-women pharmacists; examination regulations', *The Pharmaceutical Journal*, vol. 75, no. 22 (1906), p. 364.

8. Women were admitted to the practice of pharmacy in the Netherlands in 1872; by 1892 fifteen Dutch women had received pharmaceutical diplomas. Sonnedecker, 'Women as pharmacy students', p. 135. In 1898 there were 840 female 'assistant' apothecaries in Holland and 540 male apothecaries. Martha M. James, 'That a woman makes as good a pharmacist as a man, providing they have equal advantage', *Proceedings of the Wisconsin Pharmaceutical Association* (1898), p. 36.

9. Seventeen Belgian women passed pharmaceutical examinations between 1881 and 1891. Sonnedecker, 'Women as pharmacy students', p. 135.

10. V. Vekhter, 'Zhenshchiny v apteke', *Farmatsevticheskii vestnik* (hereafter cited *FV*), vol. 4, no. 32 (1900), p. 580.

11. The Austrian government permitted women to audit university medical courses in 1896 and to become physicians and pharmacists in 1900. Anon.,

'Uspekhi zhenshchin na vrachebnom i farmatsevticheskom poprishchakh', *FV*, vol. 4, no. 37 (1900), p. 664. To manage pharmacies independently women needed specific approval from the Ministry of Internal Affairs. Hungarian women in the Dual Monarchy were allowed to practise pharmacy 'a few years earlier'. R. B., 'Die erste Frauen-Apoteke', Apothekenbilder von Nah und Fern (Vienna, 1901), pt 2, p. 1. The Austrian government permitted women in Austrian-occupied Croatia to enter pharmacy in 1901, ibid.

12. Swedish women were allowed to study and practise pharmacy in 1891; the first Norwegian women passed the qualifying examination in 1894. Sonnedecker, 'Women as pharmacy students', p. 135.

13. Spanish women were permitted to study pharmacy in 1892, ibid.

14. In France in 1900 20 women (19 French and 1 foreign) were studying pharmacy in universities; 129 women (29 French) were studying medicine. Anon., 'Khronika', *FV*, vol. 4, no. 7 (1900), p. 137.

15. 'O dopushchenii lits zhenskogo pola postupat' v apteki dlia obucheniia (Circular of the MVD, Medical Department, 19 May 1888, no. 1886', *Sbornik zakonopolozhenii*, p. 82. No dates were cited for the arrival of the women's petition at the Ministry of Internal Affairs.

16. J. Schindelmeiser, 'Nichtamtlicher Teil, weibliche Pharmazeuten im Russland', *Apotheker-Zeitung*, no. 74 (1902), p. 636 and 'O dopushchenii lits zhenskogo pola', *Sbornik zakonopolozhenii*, p. 82.

17. *Ispytaniia na zvaniia i stepeni lekaria, zubnogo vracha, povival'noi babki, provizora, aptekarskogo pomoshchnika i apterkarskogo uchenika. Svod uzakonenii, razporiazhenii, postanovlenii i raz''iasnenii Pravitel'stva, pravila, trebovaniia, instruktsii, programmy dlia ekzamenatorov i eksamenuiushchikhsia* (comp.) I. Malinovskii (St Petersburg, 1907), p. 215 [no. 46]. The degree *Magistr* required four years university education, a qualifying examination and thesis.

18. 'Khronika', *FV*, vol. 5, no. 48 (1902), p. 579. Russian women were allowed to study medicine (though not pharmacy) at the University of Helsinki in the 1870s. Tuve, *Russian Women Physicians*, p. 34.

19. A. M. Semenov, *Zaslugu zhenshchin na vrachebno-farmatsevticheskom poprishche* (Moscow, 1892), pp. 5–6.

20. See stories of Eva Broido and Antonina Lesnevskaia in text, below.

21. Semenov, *Zaslugu zhenshchin*, pp. 5–6, 9–10, 27, 29–45.

22. V. S. Bogoslovskii, *O predstoiashchei farmatsevticheskoi deiatel'nosti zhenshchin i neobkhodimosti ustroistva zhenskogo farmatsevticheskogo instituta* (Moscow, 1889), pp. 4, 6, 7–8, 9.

23. Schindelmeiser, 'Nichtamtlicher Teil: Weibliche', p. 636.

24. In 1897 there were 1,162 pharmacy students and in 1898, 1,208. In 1898 there were 2,391 assistant pharmacists. Data cited in Vs. Mosal'skii, 'Neskol'ko slov o zhenskom trude v aptekakh', *Farmatsevt*, vol. 9, no. 28 (1901), p. 891.

25. For more on education and conditions in nineteenth- and early twentieth-century Russian pharmacies see Mary Schaeffer Conroy, 'Pharmacy in pre-Soviet Russia', *Pharmacy in History*, vol. 27, no. 3 (1985), pp. 121–5; Rodionova, *Ocherki istorii professional'nogo dvizheniia meditsinskikh*

rabotnikov (Moscow, 1962), pp. 27–31; Jonathan Sanders, 'Drugs and revolution: Moscow pharmacists in the First Russian Revolution', *The Russian Review*, vol. 44 (1985), pp. 351–77.

26. 'O dopushchenii lits zhenskogo pola', p. 82 and *Ispytaniia na zvaniia i stepeni*, p. 231 [no. 83]. In 1881 there were 103 girls' secondary schools – 76 girls' *gimnazii* under the Ministry of Public Enlightenment and 27 comparable schools of the Empress Maria. Patrick L. Alston, *Education and the State in Tsarist Russia* (Stanford, 1969), p. 70.
27. Stites, *Women's Liberation Movement*, p. 166.
28. Alston, *Education and the State*, pp. 70, 204, 289, 286.
29. *Ispytaniia*, p. 223 [no. 68].
30. These were Latin, German, French, history, geometry and algebra. Anon, 'Voprosy i otvety', *FV*, vol. 4, no. 1 (1900), p. 15.
31. 'O dopushchenii', p. 82.
32. According to a survey of 1900, 89.7 per cent of pharmacists were compelled to board in the pharmacy; this was called the *pansion* system. See Sanders, 'Drugs and revolution', p. 357.
33. 'O razreshenii litsam zhenskogo pola zanimat'sia v aptekakh v kachestve aptekarskikh uchenits odnovremenno s litsami muzhskogo pola' (Circular Med. Dept. 24 Feb. 1892, no. 1906) *Sbornik zakonopolozhenii*, pp. 82–3. Also *Ispytaniia*, p. 225.
34. 'O dopushchenii', p. 82.
35. Pharmacists with this title were permitted to manage 'normal' or fully stocked *apteki*.
36. The required courses included botany, zoology, chemistry and physics. See Conroy, 'Pharmacy in pre-Soviet Russia', p. 123.
37. 'Akusherskie, fel'dsherskie, zubovrachebnye i farmatsevticheskie kursy – Zhenshchiny-Farmatsevty', in P. N. Ariian, *Pervyi zhenskii kalendar'* (St Petersburg, 1899), p. 154.
38. *Ispytaniia*, 215 [no. 46 (10)].
39. 'Zhenshchiny-Farmatsevty', *Pervyi zhenskii kalendar'*, p. 154.
40. R. T. S., untitled (editorial), *Farmatsevticheskii zhurnal* (hereafter cited *FZh*), vol. 20, no. 1 (1898), p. 8 and Anon., 'Melkie soobshcheniia', no. 44, ibid., p. 627. The rooms in which the courses were to be held were fully equipped with labs and necessary apparatus.
41. Schindelmeiser, 'Nichtamtlicher Teil: Weibliche', p. 636.
42. Ibid., p. 636. Schindelmeiser did not enumerate the cities. James McClelland considers the women's courses equivalent to those in universities. McClelland, 'Diversification in Russian–Soviet education', in Konrad H. Jarausch (ed.), *The Transformation of Higher Learning 1860–1930* (Chicago, 1983), p. 184.
43. 'Khronika', *FV*, vol. 5, no. 43 (1902), p. 522.
44. Anon, 'Uspekhi zhenshchin', p. 664.
45. Announcement in *FZh*, vol. 20, no. 28 (1898), p. 397.
46. By 1906 the State Council ruled that the Women's Medical Institute in St Petersburg could give the assistant pharmacist and *provizor* exams, heretofore held in the Military Medical School in Petersburg and universities in other areas. *Ispytaniia*, 215 [no. 46].

47. 'Khronika', *Farmatsevt*, vol. 13, no. 8 (1905), p. 237.
48. A. M. Sidorkov, 'Vozniknovenie i razvitie zhenskogo farmatsevticheskogo obrazovaniia v Rossii', *Aptechnoe delo*, vol. 6, no. 4 (1957), p. 60. See also, Antonina Lesnevskaia, *Po neprotorennoi doroge* (St Petersburg, 1901 – reprinted 1914), pp. 3, 22, 39.
49. 'Khronika', *FZh*, vol. 20, no. 3 (1898), p. 41.
50. Anon. Untitled, *FZh*, vol. 20, no. 41 (1898), p. 584.
51. S. Iu. Borisovskaia, 'Iz istorii nauchnoi farmatsevticheskoi deiatel'nosti zhenshchin', *Farmatsiia*, no. 3 (1947), p. 32; also Sidorkov, 'Vozniknovenie i razvitie', pp. 60, 61. The first woman to receive a learned degree, according to Sidorkov, was V. A. Rudneva-Kashevarova.
52. Sanders, 'Drugs and revolution', p. 357. Purportedly, there were 21 female pharmacists (and 756 male pharmacists) in St Petersburg in 1900 and 43 female pharmacists (and 729 male pharmacists) in Moscow in 1902. Ibid.
53. R. B., 'Die erste Frauen-Apotheke', p. 3.
54. 'Khronika', *FZh*, vol. 20, no. 1 (1898), p. 14.
55. Mosal'skii, 'Neskol'ko slov o zhenskom trude v aptekakh', pp. 859.
56. Ibid., p. 892.
57. In 1895 there were 77 women student pharmacists; in 1896, 72; in 1897, 60; in 1898, 62; in 1899, 101; and in 1900, 123. The corresponding numbers for women assistant pharmacists were 13, 22, 28, 47, 41 and 56. Schindelmeiser, 'Weibliche', p. 636.
58. Anon., 'Sovremennoe polozhenie uslovii farmatsevticheskogo truda v Zakavkaze', *FV*, vol. 5, no. 25 (1902), p. 298.
59. Tuve, *Russian Women Physicians*, pp. 67–8, 111. This also was the case in the United States. In 1889–90, 884 American women were studying medicine as compared with 60 studying pharmacy; in 1899–1900, 1,456 American women were enrolled in medical school as compared with 196 in pharmacy school. Wallace, 'Women in pharmacy', pp. 17, 20; Sonnedecker, 'Women as pharmacy students', p. 139.
60. Upravlenie glavnogo vrachebnogo inspektora, *Otchet o sostoianii narodnogo zdraviia i organizatsii vrachebnoi pomoshchi v Rossii za 1905 god* (St Petersburg, 1907), pp. 123–6.
61. Wallace, 'Women in pharmacy', pp. 17, 20; Sonnedecker, 'Women as pharmacy students', p. 139; 1990 census in Anon, 'Women in pharmacy', *The Druggists Circular*, vol. 51 (January, 1907), p. 151.
62. O. E. Gabrilovich, *Deistvuiushchee nachalo 'p'ianogo khleba'* (St Petersburg, 1906), p. 59.
63. Lesnevskaia, *Po neprotorennoi doroge*, pp. 3, 5–6.
64. Cited in Sanders, 'Drugs and revolution', p. 357. According to Sanders, Eva Broido commented that this desire for personal fulfillment was the result of 'the oppressive shtetl environment'. Ibid.
65. Eva Broido, *Memoirs of a Revolutionary* (trans., ed. Vera Broido) (London, 1967), p. 4 and *passim*.
66. This was also true for male pharmacists, to a lesser degree. Of 4,724 total *provizory* in 1911, 32.7 per cent were Jewish, 29.4 per cent were Polish,

12.9 per cent were German, and 13.2 per cent were Russian. Toropov, 'Dvizhenie', p. 1303.

67. Miroslawa Pabis-Braunstein, 'The first Polish women pharmacists', *Pharmacy in History*, vol. 31, no. 1 (1989), pp. 12–13, 15.

68. Ibid., p. 15.

69. A. B. Lesnevskaia, 'Zhenshchiny-farmatsevty', *Trudy I-go Vserossiiskogo zhenskogo s″ezda. 10–16 dek 1908g* (St Petersburg, 1909), p. 688. Also *Rossiiskii meditsinskii spisok na 1916 god* (Petrograd, 1916), p. 104 and Pabis-Braunstein, 'The first Polish women pharmacists', p. 15.

70. Schindelmeiser, 'Weibliche', p. 636.

71. Toropov, 'Dvizhenie i rost', p. 1304. Of 85 women *provizory* in 1910, Estonians, Germans, Belorussians, and Latvians claimed only one each. While nearly two-thirds of women *provizory* were Jews, less than a third of men (32.7 per cent) were. Ibid.

72. These were the Cheliuta branch of the family. Reminiscences of Madame Cheliuta and Dr Jerzy Lesniewski, Antonina's nephew, Warsaw, March 1990.

73. Antonina's father practised in a Volga town. A grandmother of Madame Cheliuta, Antonina's relative, graduated from the Women's *Gimnaziia* of the Empress Maria in Saratov; this family also had a dacha in Finland. Antonina Lesnevskaia's younger brother, Boleslav, possessed religious documents from the Roman Catholic Consistory in Tver; he graduated from the Iaroslavl Kadet Corps school and served in a Viatka regiment in 1917. *Gimnaziia* certificate in the possession of Madame Cheliuta, Warsaw; Boleslav's documents in the possession of Dr Jerzy Lesniewski, Warsaw; both examined by the author, March 1990.

74. According to Pabis-Braunstein, during the war Antonina Lesnevskaia became an ardent patriot, who hid Polish prisoners of war in her pharmacy and aided the cause of Polish independence. 'The first Polish women pharmacists', p. 15. See also Wojciech Roeske, *Antonina Lesniewska, 1866–1937* (Warsaw, 1970), pp. 20–1. This charge has to be investigated more thoroughly.

75. Pabis-Braunstein, 'The first Polish women pharmacists', p. 15.

76. Roeske, *Antonina Lesniewska, 1866–1937*, p. 14. *Farmatsevt* ('Otkrytie v S. Peterburge pervoi zhenskoi apteki'), vol. 9, no 23 (1901), p. 727 stated that the building which housed the pharmacy belonged to St Catherine's Catholic church. R. B., 'Die erste Frauen-Apotheke', p. 3 stated that the *apteka* was housed in the 'Catholic church building'.

77. In 1909 the Polish Benevolent Society, which had branches in various cities of the Empire, celebrated its twenty-fifth anniversary in Petersburg. *Kraj*, no. 17 (1909), p. 9.

78. A. Lesniewska, *Nowa Dziedzina pracy kobiet. W związku z reformą zawodu farmaceutycznego* (Warsaw, 1908), located in the University of Warsaw library.

79. *Kraj*, no. 17 (1905), p. 22; no. 10 (1909), p. 10; no. 14 (1909), p. 12; no. 17 (1909), p. 9.

80. Quote cited in Sanders, 'Drugs and revolution', p. 357.

81. Gabrilovich, *Deistvuiushchee nachalo 'p'ianogo khleba'*, 'Curriculum vitae', p. 59.
82. Sidorkov, 'Vozniknovenie i razvitie zhenskogo farmatsevticheskogo obrazovaniia v Rossii', p. 61.
83. In contrast to the high percentage of minority women in pharmacy, a much smaller percentage of minority women enrolled in the practical, more obviously 'feminine' courses established in Moscow by Privy Councillor Novikov and his wife. Between 1888 and 1912, only 395 Catholic and 152 Jewish women (compared to 7,513 Orthodox women) took advantage of these classes in sewing, cooking, housekeeping, drawing, stenography and the like. *Kratkii ocherk deiatel'nosti Obshchestva rasprostraneniia mezhdu obrazovannymi zhenshchinami prakticheskikh znanii* (Moscow, 1912), p. 23.
84. Toropov, 'Dvizhenie i rost', pp. 1278–9.
85. Cited in Borisovskaia, 'Iz istorii nauchnoi farmatsevticheskoi deiatel'nosti zhenshchin', p. 31.
86. Schindelmeiser, 'Weibliche,' p. 636.
87. Alston, *Education and the State*, p. 285.
88. R. B., 'Die erste Frauen-Apotheke', pp. 3–4.
89. For example, Jonathan Sanders ('Drugs and revolution', p. 357) remarks of Eva Broido that: 'Legislation and practice did not bar women from pharmacy work. However, the apprenticeship system, frequent night duty, the close quarters of the boarding system offered too many opportunities for sexual harassment to make pharmacy an attractive career. Furthermore, curtailment of opportunities for women's higher education precluded them from advancing into the *provizor* rank.' Similarly Richard Stites has claimed that 'Lesnevskaia has left us a depressing account of her wanderings and her efforts to study and practice pharmacy in the face of every sort of unpleasant obstacle.' *Women's Liberation Movement*, p. 175.
90. Broido, *Memoirs of a Revolutionary*, p. 11.
91. Ibid., pp. 6–14.
92. In all fairness to her 'principal', Lesnevskaia had advertised in pharmacy journals that she had qualifications as a governess' (*domashniaia uchitel'nitsa*). *Po neprotorennoi doroge*, p. 6.
93. In 1902, 'a few' of the eighteen female students at the Iurev Pharmaceutical Institute also had to tutor the children of their principal. Schindelmeiser, 'Weibliche', p. 636.
94. Lesnevskaia, *Po neprotorennoi doroge*, p. 28.
95. Ibid., pp. 3–4.
96. For example, her second 'principal' had told her his *apteka* was fully stocked and had 'normal' status required for pharmacy apprentices, but this was not true; moreover the pharmacy was small and dirty. Ibid., pp. 7–13.
97. At one point flies and heat forced her to camp outdoors. Ibid., pp. 3–14.
98. Ibid., pp. 14–18, 29–30.
99. Ibid., pp. 19–22.
100. Ibid., p. 13.
101. For example, a government official helped her retrieve her papers from her

second principal. Ibid., p. 13. The Master of Pharmacy who helped her prepare for the assistant exam again helped prepare her for the *provizor* exam. p. 34.

102. Ibid., p. 28.
103. Ibid., pp. 28–40. Also, Lesnevskaia, 'Zhenshiny-farmatsevty', p. 684.
104. Bertha Aizenshtadt, 'Koe-chto o polozhenii zhenshchiny v apteke', *FV*, vol. 8, no. 44 (1904), pp. 698–9.
105. 'Ne pora li prekratit' neobosnovannuiu bran' aptekarei v pechati?' *Farmatsevt*, vol. 13, no. 5 (1905), pp. 144–7. An *aptekar'* refuted her accusations, 'Pis'mo v redaktsiiu', ibid., no. 29, pp. 910–12.
106. L. Lavrova, 'K reforme farmatsevticheskogo obrazovaniia', *FV*, vol. 8, no. 49 (1904), p. 971.
107. Lesnevskaia, 'Pis'ma v redaktsiiu', *FZh*, vol. 20, no. 45 (1898), p. 643.
108. Lesnevskaia, *FV*, vol. 4, no. 48 (1900), p. 856.
109. Lesnevskaia, 'V redaktsiiu,' Ibid., vol. 5, no. 3 (1901), p. 50 and no. 12, p. 192. Also A. Lesnevskaia, 'Pis'mo v redaktsiiu', *Farmatsevt*, vol. 9, no. 5 (1901), p. 144.
110. A. B. Lesnevskaia, 'Bytovoi otdel. Doklad tret'emu s'ezdu Russkikh deiatelei po tekhnicheskomu i professional'nomu obrazovaniiu v Rossii, "O farmatsevticheskom obrazovanii zhenshchin"', *FV*, vol. 8, no. 1 (1904), pp. 56–7.
111. Lesnevskaia, 'Zhenshchiny-farmatsevty', pp. 683–7.
112. A. B. Lesnevskaia, *K voprosu o reforme farmatsevticheskogo obrazovaniia v Rossii* (1912), p. 4–5.
113. Lesnevskaia, 'O farmatsevticheskom obrazovanii', p. 57.
114. A. Lesnevskaia, 'Pis'mo v redaktsiiu', *Farmatsevt*, vol. 10, no. 1 (1902), p. 11.
115. A. Lesnevskaia, 'Pis'ma v redaktsiiu,' *FV*, vol. 4, no. 50 (1900), pp. 894–5; and 'Pis'ma v redaktsiiu,' *FV*, vol. 5, no. 1 (1902), p. 11; and 'Pis'ma v redaktsiiu', no. 23, *FV*, p. 278, also 'Pis'mo v redaktsiiu', *Farmatsevt*, vol. 10, no. 1 (1902), pp. 10–12.
116. 'III Vserossiiskii farmatsevticheskii s"ezd', *Farmatsevt*, vol. 8, no. 3 (1900), p. 78.
117. 'Otkrytie v S-Peterburge pervoi zhenskoi apteki,' Ibid., vol. 9, no. 23 (1901), pp. 728–9.
118. The Russian government allowed women to manage rural *apteki* from 1892. 'O dopushchenii zhenshchin k upravleniiu scl'skimi aptekami', p. 83.
119. R. B., 'Die erste Frauen-Apotheke', p. 4.
120. Ibid.
121. 'Otkrytie v S.-Peterburge pervoi zhenskoi apteki', *Farmatsevt*, pp. 727–8.
122. R. B., 'Die erste Frauen-Apotheke', p. 3.
123. *Ibid.*, pp. 3–4.
124. Lesnevskaia criticized *aptekari* for regarding working pharmacists as cheap labour. She criticized working pharmacists for their carelessness and lack of attention to the owners' property, *Po neprotorennoi doroge*, p. 21.
125. A. M. Prokof'ev, 'Pisma v redaktsiiu,' *FV*, vol. 4, no. 46 (1900) p. 817; also, N.I. Afanas'ev, *Sovremenniki. Al'bom biografii* (St Petersburg,

1910), vol. 2, cited in a letter from R. Arbuzov, Assistant Director of the Military Medical Academy, Leningrad, 18 Nov. 1987, no. 25–131–331 to Dr Teodor Kikta, Director of the Museum of Pharmacy, Warsaw, p. 1.

126. R. B., 'Die erste Frauen-Apoteke', pp. 3–4.
127. Lesnevskaia, 'O farmatsevticheskom obrazovanii', p. 58.
128. Lesnevskaia, 'Zhenshchiny-farmatsevty', pp. 687–8.
129. Lesnevskaia, *Po neprotorennoi doroge*, pp. 37–8.
130. Lesnevskaia, 'Zhenshchiny-farmatsevty', p. 688.
131. *Rossiiskii meditsinskii spisok na 1916 god*, p. 104.
132. Lesnevskaia, 'Zhenshchiny-farmatsevty', p. 688.
133. *Rossiiskii meditsinskii spisok na 1916 god*, p. 104.
134. 'Protokol zasedanii konferentsii Imperatorskoi Voenno-meditsinskoi akademii za 1901–1902 uch. god', cited in letter of Arbuzov to Dr Teodor Kikta, 18 Nov., 1987, p. 1, Warsaw Pharmacy Museum.
135. For comparison with the United States of that era see Eunice Bonow Bardell, 'America's only School of Pharmacy for Women', *Pharmacy in History*, vol. 26, no. 3 (1984), pp. 127–33.
136. Lesnevskaia, 'Zhenshchiny-farmatsevty,' p. 688; Lesnevskaia, *K voprosu o reforme farmatsevticheskogo obrazovaniia v Rossii*, p. 13.
137. Sidorkov, 'Vozniknovenie i razvitie', p. 60; R. B., 'Die erste Frauen-Apoteke', pp. 3–4.
138. Lesnevskaia, *K. voprosu o reforme*, pp. 5, 14. Lesnevskaia claimed that in these short courses pharmacy students basically concentrated on topics to be covered on the examination.
139. Lavrova, 'K reforme farmatsevticheskogo obrazovaniia', p. 972.
140. I. Levenshtein, *Materialy po farmatsevticheskomu obrazovaniiu* (Moscow, 1922), pp. 3–6, 7 and *passim*.
141. Sidorkov, 'Vozniknovenie i razvitie', pp. 60–1. Also, A. Lesnevskaia, *K voprosu o reforme*, p. 14. Lesnevskaia believed the ideal course in a pharmacy institute should be three years in length. Ibid., pp. 11–12.
142. 'Ekzamen v voenno-meditsinskoi Akademii', *FV*, vol. 7, no. 36 (1904), p. 571.
143. See Linda Harriet Edmondson, *Feminism in Russia, 1900–1917* (London, 1984), pp. 87–101.
144. Broido, *Memoirs of a Revolutionary*, p. 34.
145. See Edmondson, *Feminism in Russia, passim*.
146. *FV*, vol. 7, no. 46 (1904), p. 930.
147. Sanders, 'Drugs and revolution', pp. 370–1.
148. *Nasha zhizn'*, as cited in 'Khronika', *Farmatsevt*, vol. 13, nos. 41–2 (1905), pp. 1240–1.
149. 'Khronika', *Farmatsevt*, vol. 14, no. 3 (1906), p. 78.
150. Ibid., no. 10 (1906), pp. 283–4 and no. 26, p. 757.
151. 'Z naszej kolonyi', *Kraj*, no. 14 (1909), p. 12.
152. S. Iu Borisovskaia, 'Iz istorii nauchnoi farmatsevticheskoi deiatel'nosti zhenshchin', *Farmatsiia*, vol. 3 (1947), p. 32.
153. Lesnevskaia, *K voprosu o reforme*, pp. 14–15.
154. Sidorkov, 'Vozniknovenie i razvitie, p. 61.
155. Lesnevskaia, *K. voprosu o reforme*, p. 14. Zhosefa or Josepha Boleslavna

Lesnevskaia received her *provizor* degree in St Petersburg 1910. *Rossiiskii meditsinskii spisok na 1916 god*, p. 121.

156. Lesnevskaia, 'Zhenshchiny-farmatsevty', p. 689.
157. Lesnevskaia, *K voprosu o reforme*, p. 14.
158. The Russian government established the Institute of Experimental Medicine in 1892. It was a premier institution which attracted world attention when I. P. Pavlov, who conducted research on the neurophysiology of digestion, received a Nobel Prize in 1904. The journal of the institute was the renowned *Archives of Biological Sciences*, published in Russian and French. Alexander Vucinich, *Empire of Knowledge. The Academy of Sciences of the USSR (1917–1970)* (Berkeley, 1984). pp. 66–7.
159. Pabis-Braunstein, 'The first Polish women pharmacists', p. 14 and Wojciech Roeske, *Women of Polish Pharmacy* (Warsaw, 1976), p. 18.
160. Rumiantsev noted that women could now enter the pharmacy division of thePsycho-Neurological Institute in Petersburg to prepare for the *provizor* examination. V. V. Rumiantsev, *Zhenskoe farmatsevticheskoe obrazovanie* (Moscow, 1912), pp. 3–12.
161. I. Lonachevskii-Petruniak, *Vopros ob obrazovanii russkikh farmatsevtov* (St Petersburg, 1905), pp. 7, 13, 20, *passim*.
162. Instead he mentioned that a pharmacy section was due to be instituted at the Women's Medical Courses in Petersburg, where he taught. A. S. Ginzburg, *K. voprosu ob obshchem i spetsial'nom obrazovanii farmatsevtov* (St Petersburg, 1913), pp. 7–9.
163. E. P. Braunshtein, *K. istorii zhenskogo meditsinskogo obrazovaniia* (Kharkov, 1911), p. 14.
164. The City government in Odessa began organizing a women's medical institute, which finally opened in the fall of 1910. *Otkrytie vysshikh zhenskikh meditsinskikh kursov v g. Odesse* (Odessa, 1911), pp.& 18–28. The Kharkov Medical Society founded an autonomous women's medical institute; in 1911 there were 980 students. E. P. Braunshtein, *K. istorii zhenskogo meditsinskogo obrazovaniia* (Kharkov, 1911), pp. 1, 14.
165. O. E. Gabrilovich, *Deistvuiushchee nachalo 'p'ianogo khleba.' (Materialy dlia ustanovki sposoba vydeleniia ego iz muki i ego khimicheskikh svoistv ... Dissertatsiia na stepeni magistra farmatsii* (St Petersburg, 1906), cover and p. 5.
166. A. Abramson, 'K zashchite dissertatsii O. E. Gabrilovicha', *Farmatsevt*, vol. 15, no. 1 (1907), p. 9.
167. Gabrilovich, *Deistvuiushchee*, p. 3.
168. Ibid., p. 4.
169. For a study of the effects of ergotism on population see Mary Kilbourne Matossian, 'Climate, crops, and natural increase in rural Russia, 1861–1913', *Slavic Review*, vol. 45, no. 3 (1986), pp. 457–69.
170. Gabrilovich, *Deistvuiushchee*, pp. 4–5. Also, I. R. Zakharevich, 'Belozerskii krai', *Farmatsevt*, vol. 13, no. 20 (1905), pp. 629–30. The Russian Society for the Preservation of Public Health originated in St Petersburg in 1878. There were branches in nineteen other cities by the end of the nineteenth century.
171. *Farmatsevt*, vol. 13, no. 2 (1905), p. 44 and no. 14, ibid., p. 433.

172. Gabrilovich, *Deistvuiushchee*, pp. 7–58.
173. Ibid., pp. 18–19.
174. Abramson, 'K zashchite,' p. 9.
175. 'Khronika,' *Farmatsevt*, vol. 14, nos 47–8 (1906), p. 1365.
176. *The Lancet*, 16 January 1909, pp. 194–5.
177. 'The German Congress of Internal Medicine: alteration of the arteries produced by injections of adrenalin', *The Lancet*, 6 May 1906, p. 1222.
178. L. N. Lavrova, 'O deistvii ioda na patologicheskie izmeneniia v sosudakh, obuslovlivaemye vvedeniem zhivotnym adrenalina', *Arkhiv biologicheskikh nauk*, vol. 8, no. 3 (1908), pp. 205–36.
179. Ibid.
180. 'The prevention of arterio-sclerosis following the use of adrenalin', *The Lancet*, 28 November 1908, p. 1641.
181. L. A. Kovalevaia (In the journal her name is spelled thus; since Sidorkov spelled her name Kovaleva I have referred to her this way in the text), 'Vliianie preparatov fosfora na protsessy okisleniia v zhivotnom organizme', *Arkhiv biologicheskikh nauk* (St Petersburg), vol. 17, no. 3 (1912), pp. 293–320.
182. Toropov, 'Dvizhenie i rost', pp. 1298–1304.
183. *Rossiiskii meditsinskii spisok na 1916 god*, pp. 80–1.
184. Toropov, 'Dvizhenie i rost', p. 1305.
185. Lesnevskaia, 'Zhenshchiny-farmatsevty', p. 689.
186. K. Khrzhanovskii, *Polozhenie aptechnogo dela v Rossii v osveshchenii tsifr i faktov* (St Petersburg, 1913), p. 16.
187. *Tomsk gor. komissiia. Vo vrachebno-sanitarnyi sovet. Doklad komissii po revizii 1-i gorodskoi vol'noi apteki* (Tomsk, 1915), pp. 1–4.
188. Quoted in Borisovskaia, 'Iz istorii nauchnoi farmatsevticheskoi deiatel'nosti zhenshchin', pp. 31–2.
189. 'Vpechatleniia i zametki', *FV*, vol. 7, no. 5 (1904), p. 73.
190. While there still were cases of long hours and low pay, by 1910 less pay was remitted in room and board, 86 per cent received their *provizor* degree before twelve years of pharmacy practice, there was some upward mobility, etc. *Farmatsevty Rossii* (comp.) I. I. Korol'kov (Moscow, 1911), pp. 25, 17, 20–1 and *passim*. Pharmacies in large cities had 7-hour work days by 1910. Khrzhanovskii, *Polozhenie aptechnogo dela v Rossii*, p. 10.
191. *Tomsk gor. komissiia*. pp. 1–2.
192. This study will be expanded in my forthcoming book on pharmacies, pharmacists and the pharmaceutical industry in late tsarist, early Soviet Russia.

4 Women's rights, civil rights and the debate over citizenship in the 1905 Revolution

Linda Edmondson

One of the most startling features of the 1905 Revolution in Russia was the sudden entrance into the political arena of groups in society which had previously remained well outside it. Whereas the adoption of politics by some groups was seen as a fairly logical, even obligatory, development in a time of national crisis (the 'reluctant' Academic Union is a case in point) the politicization of other groups was unexpected and disconcerting.[1] Two prime examples of the latter are peasants and women, both of which categories were commonly regarded as either pre-political or apolitical. The entry of these groups into politics was not universally welcomed, even in opposition circles, and their claims for political rights met very similar objections concerning their supposed 'immaturity'. The fact that the demand for women's rights (though articulated in the main by educated middle-class women) was made on behalf of working-class and peasant women as well, served only to strengthen the opposition to it. As peasant women were the least literate of all social groups except nomadic tribes, it was easy to point to their assumed ignorance and their notoriously oppressed status within peasant society as reasons for not enfranchising them.

In radical circles the principle of women's suffrage caused few problems. It was written into the programmes of both the social democrats and the socialist revolutionaries and each party prided itself on its commitment to complete equality of all citizens, including unconditional universal suffrage. It was, in fact, over the formulation of suffrage demands that many a dispute was fought between radicals and liberals during 1905. While liberals were arguing among themselves about the very principle of universal suffrage, radicals were campaigning for a fully specified formula: not only 'universal, direct, equal and secret' (the so-called 'four-tailed' formula) but also 'without distinction of sex, religion or nationality' ('seven-tails').[2] Their campaign naturally attracted many of the most actively political feminists in 1905, who quickly realized that if 'universal' were not specifically extended to both sexes,

77

women's suffrage would be buried under the rubble of political faction fighting.

During most of 1905, many, though by no means all, liberals needed convincing that women's suffrage was a viable and necessary demand. It was adopted by the Union of Liberation in March only with a non-binding amendment – to a programme that was already non-binding because of other disagreements between factions. In May, the appearance of two delegates from the newly formed Union of Equal Rights for Women at the founding congress of one of the principal political organizations of 1905, the Union of Unions, apparently caused some consternation, and even five months later, in the heat of the October strikes, women's suffrage slipped into the programme of the Constitutional Democratic Party virtually by default.[3]

But while the liberals' unimpressive record on women's equality provides a clear demonstration of the difficulties the feminists faced, even in this most radical year of the liberation movement, consternation in the face of feminist demands was not such an illegitimate response if one considers how late in the day, and then how rapidly, women's suffrage entered the political debate. Only in the latter part of 1904 did the women's movement begin to tackle an issue that had been central to the movement in America and Britain for the previous half-century (with little to show for it so far, admittedly). And only in the uproar that followed the massacre of Bloody Sunday in January 1905, did women active in the Russian movement take decisive steps to launch a suffrage campaign.

The reasons for the late entry of the suffrage issue into the Russian women's movement seem clear enough. Feminism had first erupted in the early, reforming years of Alexander II's reign. Its ultimate aspiration in the 1860s was to establish a woman's right to independence and freedom and ensure her equal status as a citizen; its immediate practical objectives were to open the universities to women, greatly extend the range of employment opportunities and set up charities to aid women in need and to save them from prostitution. The movement's success over the next half-century was remarkable but limited: women did win the right to higher education, but were denied access to universities, state degrees and service status and pensions; they were able to find jobs in an expanding range of occupations hitherto closed (from medicine to telegraphy and clerical work) but always in subordinate positions, with lower pay and sometimes with a prohibition on marriage; they did build up effective charities, but these were hedged around with restrictions and prohibitions.

Politics was not an issue, in the sense of winning the right to vote and participate in government. There was no national legislature and, for much of the period, no freedom to campaign for one. But even at local level there was little pressure from women to gain access to the newly created zemstvos and municipal councils. However, politics quickly became an issue in a different sense. The schism between reformers and radicals – a central feature of the political landscape of the 1860s and 1870s – deeply affected the women's movement too. Radicals soon distanced themselves from reformists and within a decade most had left the women's movement altogether, to serve 'the people' and in some cases to immerse themselves in the terrorist organization of People's Will.[4]

This political schism had a profound impact on the future course of the women's movement. At the very point when feminists might have begun to build on their achievements and widen the scope of the movement, the assassination of Alexander II threatened to destroy everything that had been won in the previous twenty years. The only institutions that might have provided the focus for a suffrage campaign – the local government network of zemstvos and town dumas – were under attack, and in any case the chief preoccupation of feminists in the 1880s was to defend the gains they had already made, not to strike out into new and forbidden territory. The focus of their defensive action was higher education. This had become the greatest achievement of the women's movement to date, but an enterprise that aroused the most intense anxieties in conservatives, partly because many female radicals had started their adult lives as students of the women's courses, but more insidiously because the prospect of women acquiring abstract knowledge and the ability to reason conjured up fears (in Russia, as elsewhere) that they would lose their femininity, their supposed natural modesty and even their capacity to bear children.[5] As conservatives were in the ascendant in the period following the Tsar's assassination, the cause of women's higher education suffered grievously.

It slowly recovered in the mid-1890s, by which time women had come to be seen by the authorities as useful in certain professions, especially teaching, but increasingly also in medicine. They were also quite acceptable in philanthropy. But any attempt to link these activities to 'emancipation' or 'liberation' was highly suspect; proposals by women to organize in defence of their interests were consistently hampered by the sort of restrictions on associations that beset every social enterprise in this period. One organization that did brave the bureaucratic hurdles was the Russian Women's Mutual-Philanthropic Society (Russkoe zhenskoe vzaimno-blagotvoritel'noe obshchestvo) founded in 1895 in St Petersburg. Despite strict regulation of its activities and the departure of those less willing to compromise, it attracted a membership of 1,600 by 1899. But this proved to be the peak of its influence and from 1900 membership fell sharply.[6] By 1905, with only 716 members left, the society had lost its claim to be representative of feminist opinion, either in St Petersburg or in Russia overall.

In assessing the state of the women's movement on the eve of the 1905 Revolution, one can point to two factors which conspired to depress women's political initiative. The first is the more tangible: official discouragement and prohibition. The second is harder to pin down, largely because it is marked by an absence and a silence.

Since the 1860s, the Russian intelligentsia had boasted 'progressive' opinions on all matters concerning relations between the sexes. To be considered progressive meant to accept the canon of sexual egalitarianism established by the male publicists of the sixties. Reactionary outbursts, such as the influential ultra-conservative publicist Prince Meshcherskii was wont to indulge in, aroused either satirical mockery or righteous indignation as, for example, in 1901 when students in Moscow and St Petersburg protested against a particularly offensive squib from Meshcherskii, who had attacked demands for coeducation as merely the pretext for sexual licence in the lecture hall.[7] The campaign for women's higher education had attracted, and continued to attract, the sympathy and active support of many eminent professors, scientists in particular, without whom the higher courses could not have existed. In the same period, women had begun to publish under their own names, although it remained an uphill struggle to gain recognition, and no 'great names' emerged until the turn of the century.

But in journalism, where public opinion was moulded, women's contribution was confined almost entirely to the literary and review sections of the 'thick journals'; even in these their names featured mainly as authors of short reviews, poems and short stories and, above all, as translators of foreign authors.[8] They were almost nowhere to be seen in the political and current affairs sections, nor even very often in the specialist education journals – pedagogues were always male, while teaching was becoming a female profession, especially in elementary schools.[9]

To some degree, women's absence from the journals was a natural consequence of their exclusion from the elective offices of zemstvo and town duma and from university posts, where the liberation movement gathered recruits. But women did form part of the 'third element' (teachers, doctors, statisticians, etc. employed by local government) which was also a focus of the opposition; nevertheless they seem to have been expected (and maybe themselves expected) to assume mainly a supportive or organizational role in the realm of opinion making and in public affairs. Looking at the political, intellectual and cultural environment of educated Russia around 1900, it is hard to avoid the conclusion that women still existed on the margins – physically present perhaps, but treated as special cases, or else taken for granted as part of the furnishings, or serving an inspirational or an administrative function.[10] If this was so, their sudden appearance on the political stage in 1905 must have come as quite a shock.

Their marginal existence in the legitimate culture may have provided an additional incentive for the several thousand educated and politically conscious women who turned to the revolutionary parties between the 1870s and 1917. Although they tended to be very scornful of 'aristocratic' or (later) 'bourgeois' feminist activities and uninterested on the whole in discussing the 'woman question', the parties that they joined were both more respectful of women and formally committed to complete sexual equality. It has been estimated that from the 1870s to 1905, women constituted between 12 and 15 per cent of the membership of revolutionary parties, populist and Marxist. Beate Fieseler has calculated that about 2,100 women were active social democrats up to 1905. The proportion (though not the absolute number) of women fell after the 1905 Revolution, when the party became 'proletarianized'; nonetheless women achieved a prominence in the party and in the socialist revolutionary party that was denied them in liberal organizations.[11]

On the whole, their valued role was as organizers rather than theorists, but it is impossible to be sure whether their intellectual reticence resulted from a genuinely reduced interest in theory or from unconscious assumptions held by both sexes that men were the intellectual leaders. The vital difference between the revolutionary parties and the liberation movement up to 1905 lies in the nature of their organizations: in the former, women were generally welcome and accorded an active role; in the latter, women were often excluded or expected to assume only supportive functions.

By the end of 1904, a significant number of women had become impatient with their male liberationist colleagues and were anxious to establish their own credentials as politically conscious citizens. In September, Mariia Pokrovskaia, a doctor and long-time campaigner against state-registered prostitution, had set up a new journal, *Zhenskii vestnik*, which she maintained through thick and thin right up to the autumn of 1917. It was intransigently separatist and also moralistic in tone, neither of which characteristic recommended it to women in the liberation movement. But it made a dent in the standard rhetoric which proclaimed that in Russia men and women were equal in their lack of rights. Even before men acquired the vote in state elections, women had begun to see the necessity of arguing in their own words for rights of citizenship.[12]

The prospects were not encouraging. The government had no interest in widening the very limited proxy franchise that property-owning women could already exercise in elections to the zemstvo and town duma assemblies, and at no time during 1905 did it consider women's suffrage when projects for a state duma were discussed.[13] This came as no surprise. But in the autumn of 1904, even the liberal opposition was seemingly unaware of the issue, although a number of zemstvos had been advocating a limited female franchise in local government over the previous few years. As in the sphere of journalism, so in the political banquet campaign that the liberals launched in November and December 1904: women were present but apparently silent. There is only one recorded statement by a woman in defence of female suffrage at any of the major banquets. This foolhardy individual, one Zinov'eva, had risen to speak at the most prestigious of these banquets in St Petersburg on 20 November, and had reminded her fellow guests that the proposed suffrage resolution spoke of citizens (*grazhdane*) without indicating that this included women.[14] When she called for it to be amended to specify female citizens (*grazhdanki*) too, the esteemed writer Vladimir Korolenko is reported to have rebuffed her with a reply that was to become dismally familiar during the succeeding twelve months: 'Before us stands a common enemy, autocracy, to be overthrown. After we do that, we will discuss the differences and contradictions in a free state.' There was no reported response from the audience either to Zinov'eva's intervention or to Korolenko's rebuff.[15]

However, the accumulating dissatisfactions among feminists in the liberation movement were beginning to find an outlet. Zinov'eva herself had spoken in praise of students, whose political resolutions generally did specify male and female citizens. The revolutionary parties and often the left wing of the liberation movement itself were adopting the full suffrage formula. Perhaps most surprising and inspiring, Father Gapon's Assembly of Russian Factory Workers – the focus of labour organization in the capital in late 1904 – now boasted several women's sections, totalling about a thousand members, thanks to the enterprise and persuasion of Vera Karelina, a worker with years of experience in the labour movement. She had convinced Gapon that women's participation was vital both for their own interests and for the success of the assembly's work. Although the assembly did not address the question of a democratic constitution and universal suffrage, either officially or in its 'secret programme', the existence of the women's sections provided feminists in St Petersburg for the first time with a model of a mass organization of women.[16]

There was an immense and, as it turned out, unbridgeable gulf between the factory women whom Karelina attracted to the assembly and the teachers, doctors, medical assistants, writers and 'helpers of all sorts' who were tentatively discussing the formation of a women's rights organization.[17] Karelina was directing her efforts to the encouragement of a sense of self-worth and dignity in women who were accustomed to being desperately overworked, underpaid, pushed around and abused by employers, foremen, fathers and husbands. They were not at all used to thinking in terms of 'rights'; even the assembly's charter prohibited women from holding office. But within the lifetime of Karelina's organization (from October 1904 to Bloody Sunday) its members began to think of themselves as active participants, not as 'ballast', in Gapon's assembly. 'We were even discussing at our women's meetings how we could win rights of citizenship within the assembly.'[18]

Though the evidence is too sparse to make a conclusive assessment, it seems that Karelina's work may unwittingly have given a boost to the women's rights movement in St Petersburg. The links between left-wing liberationists and Gapon's assembly are well known. Liubov' Gurevich was one of a handful of women in the liberation movement who became involved in the assembly's work as Karelina's collaborators. After Bloody Sunday, Gurevich put together a pamphlet recording the history of the assembly, including the women's sections, and the events that led to the massacre.[19] During 1905 she became one of the most committed members of the Union of Equal Rights for Women, Russia's first feminist political organization. Although it has been more customary for historians to consider the possible influence of feminist *intelligentki* on working-class women, it is quite plausible that female participation in a mass organization like the assembly encouraged liberationist women to think of a separate political organization for themselves. True, there already existed the Mutual Philanthropic Society, and in the provinces a number of small women's groups had been formed in the previous few years. But feminists were still inhibited not only by official restrictions, which continued to be effective, but also by the tendency to subsume their own political interests under those of the liberation movement.[20] The success of Karelina's organization coincided with the growing awareness among feminists that women's suffrage was not on the liberationist agenda, and it may have had a greater influence on the women's movement than even feminists themselves realized.

Much of the history of political feminism in Russia is necessarily extremely speculative. The women's movement shared a fate common to all political movements in tsarist Russia, of being forced into a mould of historical interpretation after 1917 which distorted and obliterated much of its experience. Inevitably, the story that has been recreated by western historians in the past twenty years has borne the mark of that mutilation. Within the Soviet Union after the mid-1920s it became virtually impossible to document the pre-revolutionary activities of 'bourgeois' campaigners for women's rights, and to the best of my knowledge only one Soviet historian since then has reconstructed the history of their organizations.[21] What was left for legitimate research in the Soviet Union were the history of women's higher education, memoirs of the populists, and sketchy accounts of the 'proletarian' women's movement, all of which were distorted by the same ideological requirements.[22]

In emigration the record of the women's movement fared no better, and possibly worse. It suffered first of all from an inevitable and virtually exclusive preoccupation with the political history that had a direct bearing on the *émigrés'* current predicament. In that light, the struggle for women's suffrage seemed of incidental interest, especially so considering that it had been achieved and was no longer at issue. Then too, the *émigrés* took with them their pre-revolutionary habit of leaving politics and political memoirs to the men, with a few notable exceptions. But for those exceptions as well, a factual account of the women's suffrage movement was not a priority – on the contrary, one gets the impression that they almost wished to forget it, perhaps because it was an episode in their lives that contradicted their awareness of themselves as full and equal members of the liberation movement.[23]

The above is intended to draw attention to the difficulty of writing a full account of feminism in the 1905 Revolution. The problem lies less in describing the organizations and meetings, which were fairly well reported at the time, than in examining the reflections of their participants, especially their feelings about their status as women in a liberation movement that was led and dominated by men. In their published accounts of the women's movement, they stressed that it was integral to the wider political movement and that women in Russia had always been conscious of themselves as 'equal in their lack of rights' (*ravnye v bespravii*).[24] Indeed, they referred to themselves as 'equal-righters' (*ravnopravki*), spurning the word 'feminist' or 'suffragist' as too narrow to express their true commitment and situation.[25] But considering how readily many of their male colleagues disregarded their claim to equality, and considering how antagonistic towards those colleagues they were prepared to become during 1905, there is room to doubt whether 'equality in lack of rights' completely encapsulates their perceptions.

Confirmation that women were stepping out into independent political action came immediately after Bloody Sunday. For the first time, women organized their own political meetings in a number of Russian towns and cities to protest against the massacre, to register their growing opposition to the year-long war with Japan, to press their case for voting rights in the zemstvos and municipal councils, and to call for 'a fundamental legal order' guaranteeing the rights of every citizen. The first of these meetings was held in Voronezh on 11 January: 150 women signed a declaration to the provincial zemstvo calling for female suffrage 'without distinction of class, nationality or religion'.[26] Others were reported in Saratov, Moscow, Kharkov, Kiev. The texts of petitions and declarations varied considerably: the first Moscow declaration, signed by 468 women, was more a lament for the lives lost on distant battlefields and on the streets of St Petersburg. Other declarations, such as one signed by 955 Muscovites at the end of March, were a response to the Tsar's ukaz and rescript of 18 February, the first permitting private petitions and the second instructing the Minister of Internal Affairs to set up a commission to consider schemes for a national assembly.[27]

This second Moscow declaration, addressed to the mayor, was a self-confident statement requesting universal suffrage 'for all citizens of the Russian state without distinction of sex' and the eligibility of women for elected office in the city duma. It also called on the duma to defend 'the political rights of Russian women' when stating its views on a national legislature. The signatories justified their request on the grounds that women were already equal in 'many aspects of existing legislation' (for instance, in property rights), that women played an equal or significant role in many branches of the economy, that they paid taxes, contributed to the national culture, and served the nation as teachers, medical assistants, zemstvo and duma doctors. They trusted that the Moscow city duma 'which has stood in the foremost ranks of the contemporary social movement, will recognize the justice of our claims for an equal role with men in the country's political life'.[28]

As far as is known, many of these declarations were an uncoordinated expression of women's increasing confidence in staking a claim for political and civil rights. They continued unabated through the spring; one observer spoke of 'an extraordinary abundance of women's meetings and all sorts of "conferences" not only in Moscow and Petersburg, but also in Minsk and even sometimes in very out of the way corners of Russia'. The same writer noted that 'it was a rare town where women did not respond in one way or another . . . to the vast movement that had burst out everywhere'.[29]

However, some of these declarations had been coordinated, and they included the petition to the Moscow duma.[30] This was one of the first acts of the new organization that for the rest of the year was to steal the feminist limelight: the Union of Equal Rights for Women (Soiuz ravnopravnosti zhenshchin). The union was set up by a group of about thirty Moscow women at the end of February 'to struggle for women's civil and political rights'. It quickly established links with women in other towns (Saratov was apparently the first to respond) and by the time its founding congress took place on 6–9 May it could boast about twenty sections, the largest being in Moscow and Petersburg.[31] It was an intelligentsia union *par excellence*. Most of its founder members were graduates of the women's higher courses. They were writers, historians, publishers, editors, teachers, doctors, 'social activists'. Men were permitted to join; the only one to gain prominence was an educational-ist, Nikolai Chekhov, whose wife, Mariia Chekhova was the organiza-tional mainstay of the union throughout its three-year existence.

Before embarking on a recruiting campaign and before tackling the opponents and half-hearted supporters of women's suffrage in the liberation movement, the union had to settle an issue of potential dis-cord within its own ranks. Its leaders intended the union to affiliate to the political Union of Unions, which was in the process of coming together. But a minority of members objected to this proposal, for two reasons. The first was their belief that the women's union must pursue purely 'feminist objectives' and not involve itself with the liberation movement; the second, more specific, was their suspicion of a 'male' organization in which two constituent unions (academics and zemstvo activists) were openly opposed to women's suffrage.[32] Although the issue was quickly decided in favour of the 'broad path', it surfaced again late in 1905 and rumbled on into the following year.

It was also a factor at the founding congress, in the debates on the union's platform. The leadership had set out to appeal to women of all ethnic and religious groups in the empire and was therefore quite willing to accept the condition laid down by Polish, Jewish and Belorussian delegates that the platform should support the right of national and cultural self-determination. This demand provoked strong objections from those who feared its divisive potential and argued that it had no part in a women's rights programme. The 'feminists' were overruled, however, and delegates voted by 39 to 3 (with four abstentions) for the right to 'political autonomy and national cultural self-determination'.[33]

A second, and ultimately more serious, conflict over aims and tactics arose as a result of radicals' membership of the union. Although most of the leadership (and presumably the membership in general) belonged politically to the left and centre of the non-revolutionary liberation movement, a number of social democrats and socialist revolutionaries also joined, largely because it was the only women's rights organization in existence (barring the even more moderate Mutual Philanthropic Society). In April, a public meeting in St Petersburg – in effect, the foundation of the union's section in the capital – had been disrupted by a group of social democrats led by Aleksandra Kollontai.[34] It was not clear whether they wished to kill the union outright or whether they were attempting to radicalize it, but whatever was intended, the Petersburg section started out with a significant radical component. Kollontai herself refused to have anything to do with the union, but other social democrats were more flexible and the first elected council of the section contained at least one Bolshevik, M. M. Ianchevskaia, as well as an SR, Ol'ga Vol'kenshtein, who sat alongside the liberal Anna Miliukova and Ekaterina Shchepkina, future Kadets.[35]

Partly as a consequence of the radicals' membership, the union adopted a platform which not only advocated unconditional universal suffrage and civil rights, but also contained social and economic demands. Paragraph three of the platform reads like an amalgam of liberal feminist and socialist proposals, which is exactly what it was: equal rights for peasant women in any future agrarian reform; protection of women's work and compulsory insurance equal to men's; 'the admission of women to all spheres of social and public activity'; coeducation at all levels; and 'abolition of all exceptional laws relating to the question of prostitution and demeaning women's human dignity', i.e. abolition of the system of state regulation and compulsory police medical inspection. However, socialists failed to get their demand of an eight-hour working day written into the platform.[36]

The presence of a radical element in the union did not prevent the leadership from pursuing its primary objective, which was to persuade the liberation movement to adopt the full 'seven-tail' suffrage formula. This meant lobbying individual unions and their umbrella organization, the Union of Unions; petitioning zemstvo assemblies and municipal councils, and putting its case before the national congresses of zemstvo and duma representatives; holding public meetings and using the press wherever possible.[37] The union failed to set up its own journal until the middle of 1907, by which time the organization itself was moribund and the women's movement hemmed in and demoralized by the wave of reaction in the country's political life. During 1905, the press in the two capital cities showed a disappointingly diminished interest in the issue and reporting of events was perfunctory.

Censorship may have been partly responsible. The editor of a moderate pedagogical journal used the glasnost of the 'days of freedom' that followed the October Manifesto, to list the subjects banned in earlier days; these included the 'woman question' and feminism. Another journal, the left-wing *Pravda*, bore visible signs of censorship in its June survey of the women's movement. In addition, some meetings of the Union of Equal Rights were held in secret – the press was unable to report the union's foundation congress, except for a public meeting on the second day.[38] Censorship, especially of anything that might suggest working-class or peasant support for women's rights, or the involvement of revolutionaries, may have been far more pervasive than was ever reported at the time or subsequently.[39]

Whether or not this was a problem, it did not prevent the feminist journal *Zhenskii vestnik* from following the suffrage campaign carefully. But relations between the women's union and Pokrovskaia, who edited the journal virtually single-handed, were not close and the union could not depend on it to promote its activities during 1905. The following year, Pokrovskaia set up her own feminist organization, the Women's Progressive Party, and relations grew more distant still.[40]

To the supporters of the Union of Equal Rights, or the readers of *Zhenskii vestnik*, or members of the Russian Women's Mutual Philanthropic Society the case for women's suffrage was very simple. If they could not convince others of the wisdom of their cause by an appeal to the fundamental human rights of all citizens, they could cite the many ways in which women contributed to the welfare of the nation, to its economy, even to its continued existence. But to those who were not already convinced supporters of female emancipation and to those who were not persuaded by the arguments being put forward, the issue seemed 'complex', 'inopportune' or 'impractical'. What is remarkable, however, about the opposition to women's suffrage among liberals and even among some who counted themselves as radicals, is the shortage of clear arguments and reasoned (or even unreasoned) discussion to refute the feminists' case. On many occasions throughout 1905, feminists' opponents thought it sufficient to list their objections rather briefly, apparently trusting to the weight of prejudice or the known hostility of the government to settle the issue.

Unwillingness to engage in a debate can be explained at one level by the multitude of other pressing concerns in a year that was characterized

by crisis and uncertainty, outbreaks of violence, and situations demanding decisions, negotiations and polemics. In the political crisis of 1905
the question of women's suffrage genuinely was not very pressing.
However, the urgent demands of the year did not prevent editors of the
literary–political journals from continuing to publish immensely long
articles on a range of subjects that had no more (and often less) to do
with the crisis of the moment than did female emancipation. Yet the
space given over to a judicious consideration of female suffrage was
small indeed. Unless the censor was responsible for this silence, the
question arises: why should these articulate and opinionated men have
been so reluctant to grapple with the subject?

Reconsidering the history of Russian feminism in the 1905 Revolution, I have begun to see the absence of debate less as an indication of
indifference or as a preoccupation with other concerns – though these
were undoubtedly factors – and more as an inhibition created by the
emancipatory and egalitarian philosophies that the intelligentsia had
inherited from the hallowed sixties. As I suggested above, 'progressive'
opinion necessarily connoted a positive attitude towards the intellectual
and cultural aspirations of women and a set of egalitarian values concerning relations between the sexes. But as the question of women
sharing political power was almost completely irrelevant to the circumstances of Russian life in the second half of the nineteenth century,
liberals could maintain egalitarian principles towards women without
being asked to relate them to the problematic question of power and
authority.[41]

In 1905 they were asked to do so for the first time. Moreover, they
had themselves created a political discourse in which concepts of
equality, freedom, citizenship and rights predominated. The civil rights
rhetoric of 1905 spoke of 'equality before the law of all citizens', 'inviol-
ability of the person', 'freedom of conscience, speech, movement,
assembly and association'. Liberals of all persuasions, from Shipov to
the socialist-tinged left wing of the Union of Liberation adhered to this
rhetoric.[42] Suffrage was a far more complex and contentious issue, but
at least within the Union of Liberation and most political unions, some
formula containing the word 'universal' or 'general' quickly became the
norm. This very discourse gave energy to the movement for women's
rights. But as soon as feminists began to use the discourse for their own
interests, they encountered gentle mockery, outright hostility, uncomfortable silences and shifty glances from individuals many of whom they
had believed to be their allies.

Even men who favoured women's suffrage would not necessarily insist on it when faced with sustained opposition. Thus the programme adopted at the March congress of the Union of Liberation stated grandiosely:

no rights of the person and the citizen can be guaranteed until the law becomes an expression of the will of the people and until executive power is subjected to the control of a national representative assembly. For this it is essential that legislative power belong to the national assembly, organized on the principles of universal, direct, equal and secret voting, without distinction of sex.

Because a substantial minority withheld support for female suffrage 'for practical considerations', a rider was added permitting the minority to regard women's suffrage as 'inessential', thus depriving the clause of its entire force.[43] No wonder that *ravnopravki* in the liberation movement were so anxious to set up their own union. The drafters of the Union of Liberation's programme had sidestepped an issue that was to be the subject of heated disputes during 1905 – the question of enfranchising the male 'peasant masses' – yet they had found it wise to add a rider invalidating women's suffrage.

A similar response was forthcoming from a commission set up by the Moscow city duma to consider proposals for a national assembly. Its report was, *inter alia*, an indirect and brief reply to the petition sent by 955 Moscow women to the duma in March. The commission argued, a shade patronizingly, that universal suffrage was 'a powerful weapon for the development of the popular masses and for the inculcation in them of a feeling for legality and respect for law'. This it considered, reasonably enough, to be essential in a country that suffered 'from the prevailing lack of rights and arbitrary rule'. It concluded that there were no grounds for preserving distinctions based on estate (*soslovie*), property or education and no grounds for making the elections indirect. The only categories to be excluded were the 'usual' ones: women, children, lunatics and criminals. A minority had expressed no objections to female suffrage, but had not insisted on the issue being debated.[44]

Opinion certainly changed during the spring and summer and the Union of Equal Rights could claim much of the credit for the change. Yet despite victories for female suffrage in the Union of Unions, at a conference of municipal duma representatives and finally, after a sustained barrage of lobbying, in the November congress of zemstvo and duma representatives, ambivalence towards women's rights remained. Even after seven months of campaigning, suffragists were still forced to witness a scene almost identical to that enacted at the Union of Liberation congress in March, when the Constitutional Democratic Party came into existence in October. The proposal that women be specifically included in the suffrage formula was approved by a majority of only two – and that by accident, when two of the leading figures at the congress, I. V. Gessen and V. D. Nabokov left the hall to see what was going on in the street. The party's leader, Miliukov, who had been resolutely opposed to women's suffrage all year, successfully moved an amendment to make it non-binding on the party, and the amendment was not removed until the second party congress in January 1906. The bitter confrontation between Anna Miliukova and her husband on this issue was apparently one of the entertaining highlights of the Kadets' founding congress.[45]

The difficulty that women's suffrage presented to liberals who considered themselves open-minded in other respects was two-fold. Firstly, they had fettered themselves with a highly principled political rhetoric based on rights of citizenship. Secondly, they were constrained by an ideological heritage of sexual equality. To begin to argue at length against female enfranchisement would lay them open to the danger that in the process they would demolish their own egalitarian pretensions.

Without question, the most effective arguments against women's suffrage were those incorporating misogynist assumptions about female stupidity, irrationality, childishness, vanity, biological unfitness and even moral depravity. In general, assumptions about innate and acquired differences of personality between the sexes underpinned many of the arguments about women's suffrage – and not only the arguments of its opponents. If opinion was not swayed by natural rights theory or the utilitarian calculation that women would double the resources available to a democratic system, then reference could be made to the particular qualities that women would bring to politics. But it was riskier for a liberal to invoke them negatively: as overt misogyny was the happy hunting ground of the extreme right, it was impossible to resort to it without appearing to be politically reactionary. Thus it was simpler on the whole to be evasive.[46]

Of the two inhibiting factors, the second – the long shadow cast by the ideology of sexual egalitarianism – may, indeed, have been the more effective. For despite the rhetoric of citizenship, liberals did show themselves to be adept at expediency during 1905, a fact which disturbed feminists still further. It became apparent, for example, that arguments in favour of the enfranchisement of peasant men were based less on the principle of inalienable rights than on the fear of a peasant uprising. One of the clearest exponents of this view was Fedor Kokoshkin, who also opposed women's suffrage using a number of highly expedient arguments: the higher illiteracy rate of peasant women, the fear of an imbalance if working-class women used their vote more than women in the villages, or if Christian women voted more than Muslim.[47] The level of female illiteracy was certainly very high (about 86 per cent) but two-thirds of all men in Russia were illiterate too and would have been disenfranchised if literacy had been taken as a criterion of citizenship.[48]

Miliukov and others justified their opposition to female suffrage on the grounds that peasant men would desert those parties which gave their wives and daughters the vote. This was a legitimate apprehension, but peasant hostility to women's emancipation was not by any means the decisive factor in this context. The peasants whose votes were likely to go to parties on the left of the political spectrum (this included the Kadets) were susceptible to the argument that the enfranchisement of women would give the peasants a 'second army'. Such an argument helped to persuade delegates to the two congresses of the Peasants Union to vote for the full suffrage formula.[49] Peasants who were violently opposed to women's equality were likely to vote for right-wing nationalist parties and therefore were of no use at all to the Kadets. As it turned out, the peasant deputies elected to the First State Duma, who then formed themselves into the Trudovik group and allied with the Kadets, became the most steadfast supporters of women's rights throughout the short life of that assembly.[50]

The strength of the opposition to women's suffrage and the half-heartedness of some of its supporters, disguises the fact that there were also keen advocates of female equality among liberals. Lev Petrazhitskii, professor of jurisprudence, enabled the Kadets to dispose of the non-binding amendment at their second congress, and he announced himself willing to 'sacrifice' his 'reputation as a serious politician' in the First Duma to argue the desirability of women's entering politics.[51] Once female suffrage ceased to appear an eccentric diversion from 'serious' politics, once a few respected individuals had given it their blessing, others followed suit. A year after his influential rejection of the case for women's rights, Kokoshkin was to be heard in the Duma vigorously championing them. By 1908, even Miliukov had given in.[52]

Because the liberation movement provided such unreliable allies for much of 1905, the Union of Equal Rights for Women was forced to spend far more of its strength on persuading liberals to support its demands than it had either wished or foreseen. Consequently, the more interesting enterprise of creating a mass movement of women took second place. Though there are numerous, if scattered, pieces of evidence to suggest that working-class and peasant women were receptive to ideas about civil and political rights (as Karelina had found in the Gapon assembly) the organizations did not exist that could have mobilized them.[53]

Radicals in the Union of Equal Rights wanted it to shed its liberal connections and middle-class image, but their influence was not strong enough to force such a shift, and most of them departed early in 1906. As the social democratic party organizations refused to sanction separate work among women, the female populations of the towns and cities went unrepresented for the rest of the year.[54] A number of members of the Union of Equal Rights canvassed female opinion in several villages and sponsored declarations of peasant women from Iaroslavl and Voronezh provinces. But the union did not have the resources to do much more and once the revolutionary wave ebbed, it became risky for members to proselytize in the villages. Isolated reports suggested that peasant women were interested in the elections to the First Duma and keen to receive news about the Duma sessions, but after its dissolution little work was possible.[55]

The radicals in the union criticized it for being insufficiently political. Others criticized it for getting diverted from its primary goal by the October strike and the hectic political life that followed the October Manifesto. In the two capitals and in the sixty-seven other towns where sections had been set up, union members became totally engrossed in the meetings, marches and demonstrations that filled the 'days of freedom'. Protests against the pogroms unleashed by the right-wing Black Hundreds or against the government's resort to capital punishment were as important a part of their activities as meetings on women's rights. Their commitment to the Union of Unions involved them in fund-raising for famine relief or the political Red Cross, canteens for strikers and the unemployed and, in Moscow, first aid posts during the uprising that tore the city apart in December. All of this work, however essential, was a drain on their reserves and did not directly contribute to the progress of women's emancipation.[56]

Indirectly and in the long run, however, it may have helped women. Certainly it gave the union a political visibility that the older and more moderate women's organization, the Mutual Philanthropic Society, never achieved despite its persistent lobbying of officials and public institutions throughout the year.[57] The union gave the women who worked in it valuable experience of politics which they were less likely to acquire in other branches of the liberation movement, because for once they were in control of their own organization.

Moreover, the very feature of the union's activity that provoked criticism from 'pure' feminists like Pokrovskaia – that is, its close involvement in political life – may have broken down some influential liberal assumptions about women's political 'immaturity'. Previously, feminists had demonstrated women's commitment to the cause of Russia's social and political liberation by citing the examples of the Decembrist wives and the populist 'martyrs' of the 1870s and 1880s. But these were heroines who had assumed an unreal and almost mythical reputation. Their example seemed to confirm rather than deny the commonplace assertion that women could be only heroines or tyrants in public life.[58] There was no lack of legendary heroines in Russia's history; what the feminists in 1905 showed was the possibility of women taking an active and everyday role in politics.

Viewed from the perspective of December 1905, the achievements of the women's movement during the year seemed meagre. After the dissolution of the First Duma even those small gains appeared fragile. But looking back from the perspective of March 1917, when women were finally promised equal rights, one can perceive a slow and uneven progression from sceptical dismissal to resigned acceptance of feminist claims. The First World War and the February Revolution possibly hastened the change, but the suffrage campaigns of 1905–7 and the reawakened women's movement of 1912–14 undoubtedly loosened the foundations of resistance. The edifice finally collapsed after one major demonstration and a few rousing speeches only weeks after Nicholas II's abdication.[59]

In 1905 and 1906, the Union of Equal Rights came under fire from radicals for narrowing its demands to the issue of civil and political rights, instead of attacking the social and economic inequalities in Russian life. No less reprehensible was its lobbying of educated, middle-class liberal men, rather than the organization of women workers and peasants. Retrospectively, too, 'single-issue' suffrage campaigns (whether in Britain, America or Russia) have been criticized for tying the women's movement to an issue that barely touched the underlying causes of women's oppression.[60]

Whatever the justice of these criticisms, they overlook both the real and the symbolic significance of political rights. Feminists responded to socialist critics by claiming that no further change in women's social and economic status was possible without their participation in the political process. Whether or not they shared the radical vision of a social and economic transformation of Russian society, they argued that political change was the first essential step. Moreover, they could reasonably point out that if the opposition to female suffrage had not been so entrenched, the issue would have been settled very quickly, leaving them free to pursue their other aims. Even now, one cannot be sure if they were genuinely as surprised by the strength of the resistance to women's rights as they professed themselves to be, but in any case the campaign for the vote did consume much of their time during 1905.

The situation would have been different if the radical parties had regarded working-class and peasant women as a potential revolutionary force. But the social democratic and socialist revolutionary leaders were very slow to see the value of organizing women. They did not even calculate, as Gapon did, that women could do less harm if they were organized. For the whole of 1905 and well into 1906 and beyond, proposals for separate women's sections and for special appeals to women were dismissed as 'bourgeois feminism', even when individuals within the Union of Equal Rights and individuals outside it (like Kollontai in 1907) were successful in drawing groups of factory women, domestic servants or peasant women together.[61]

Because women were not considered to be a threat to the stability of the state, as peasants were in 1905, the movement to enfranchise them did not seem to be of major political significance at the time. But a historian who wishes to make sense of the confusion of ideas about citizenship, personal rights and responsibilities and the distribution of power and authority in the desired Russian state of the future, needs to pay attention to the discourse on women's rights and to the priorities that were set by political factions for the attainment of their various objectives. On the left, female suffrage was incorporated into a 'minimum programme' of immediate demands, and appeared not to be negotiable. Among the liberals who formed the Union of Liberation and later the Kadets, maybe half were convinced of the justice of the case for women's rights, but rather fewer prepared to fight for them.[62] Further to the right, support dwindled very noticeably.

Feminists had reason to feel most betrayed by the Liberationists and Kadets who withheld their support. These individuals had established their credentials on a radical programme for political change, which would replace the existing autocratic hierarchy with a fully democratic system guaranteeing equal rights to all citizens. They did not argue, as moderate liberals did, that change should be gradual or partial. Instead they swallowed their scruples about the immaturity, ignorance and volatility of the peasant masses or workers, when those masses were male. However, they were quite content to use the very same objections as arguments against the enfranchisement of women. This inconsistency exasperated feminists. Fortunately for them, the left wing of the liberation movement was prepared to use the issue in its fight with the centre. As a result, the more moderate elements in the movement were pushed into accepting female suffrage in their programme. Thus the first step was taken towards the full enfranchisement of women in Russia, although it still took twelve years more to reach that final destination.

Notes

I would like to thank Rochelle Ruthchild for reading an earlier version of this essay and for offering very helpful information and suggestions.

1. For the 'reluctant' Academic Union, see Samuel D. Kassow, *Students, Professors, and the State in Tsarist Russia* (Berkeley, 1989).
2. The three additional 'tails' were not always in that order.
3. The reported response of some members of the Union of Unions' executive committee to the arrival of two women delegates was: 'How did women get here? This must be some misunderstanding.' [E. Shchepkina] *Zhenskoe dvizhenie v otzyvakh sovremennykh deiatelei* (St Petersburg, 1905), p. 2.
4. For a full discussion of female radicalism in the 1860s and 1870s, see Richard Stites, *The Women's Liberation Movement in Russia. Feminism, Nihilism, and Bolshevism, 1860–1930* (Princeton, 1978), chs. 4 and 5; and Barbara Alpern Engel, *Mothers and Daughters. Women of the Intelligentsia in Nineteenth-Century Russia* (Cambridge, 1983). Rochelle Ruthchild points out that this schism has been exaggerated. Despite fierce disagreements, there were 'instances of overt and covert cooperation between female reformers and radicals' in this period. (Personal communication with the author.) However, the schism did destroy the possibility of extensive cooperation.
5. For a fuller discussion of this phenomenon, see my unpublished paper, 'Women's emancipation and concepts of sexual difference', given at the conference 'Women in the History of the Russian Empire', University of Akron/Kent State University, USA, 1988.
6. In Moscow, permission to form an equivalent society was repeatedly withheld. N. Mirovich, 'O pervom s″ezde russkikh deiatel′nits', *Russkaia mysl'*, no. 5 (1905), pt. 2, p. 134.
7. Kassow, *Students, Professors, and the State*, pp. 144–6; *Grazhdanin*, no. 78, 11 Oct. 1901, pp. 1–2. Meshcherskii was the editor and publisher of *Grazhdanin* and notorious for his reactionary provocations.
8. This was the case even on *Severnyi vestnik*, variously edited and published in the 1890s by Anna Evreinova and Liubov' Gurevich, both articulate and highly educated individuals who encouraged women's writing. They were later active in the movement for women's political rights. For Gurevich, see also Charlotte Rosenthal's chapter in this volume.
9. Women did not become more visible when political journals crossed the border. Even disguised under pseudonyms, only four were published regularly in Petr Struve's left liberal *Osvobozhdenie*: Ekaterina Kuskova, Ariadna Tyrkova, Liubov' Gurevich, Iuliia Toporkova. See K. F. Shatsillo, 'Novye svedeniya o psevdonimakh v zhurnale "Osvobozhdenie" ', *Arkheograficheskii ezhegodnik za 1977 god* (Moscow, 1978) pp. 111–14.
10. But see Charlotte Rosenthal's and Marina Ledkovsky's chapters for a more positive assessment of women's impact on literary life by the turn of the century; see also M. N. Yablonskaya, *Women Artists of Russia's New Age, 1900–1935* (London, 1990).

11. Beate Fieseler, 'The making of Russian female Social Democrats, 1890–1917', *International Review of Social History*, vol. 34, no. 2 (1989), esp. pp. 195–6.
12. On Pokrovskaia and *Zhenskii vestnik*, see Linda Edmondson, *Feminism in Russia, 1900–1917* (London, 1984) pp. 29–31; and Rochelle Lois Goldberg (Ruthchild), 'The Russian Women's Movement, 1859–1917' (PhD, University of Rochester, 1976), pp. 123–9.
13. Before 1890, a property-owning woman could nominate any male eligible to vote. After the government's restrictions on the zemstvos, she was limited to close male relatives. Edmondson, *Feminism in Russia*, p. 20.
14. The most common ways to indicate this were the formulae: 'citizens of both sexes' and 'without distinction of sex'.
15. Quoted by Jonathan Sanders, 'The Union of Unions: economic, political, and human rights organizations in the 1905 Russian Revolution' (PhD, Columbia University, 1985) p. 662. He quotes a police report (TsGAOR f. 102, ed. khr. 1250) which gives different wording from that of the published report in *Listok osvobozhdeniia*, no. 19 (1904), p. 4; no. 21 (1904) p. 4. However, the import is the same.
16. The assembly began as a police-sponsored organization to divert working-class discontent into safe channels, but itself became radicalized during 1904. The assembly raised the ill-fated workers' petition to the Tsar that was taken to the Winter Palace on Bloody Sunday, 9 January 1905. L. Gurevich, *9-e ianvaria. Po dannym anketnoi komissii* (St Petersburg, 1905), p. 6; Walter Sablinsky, *The Road to Bloody Sunday: Father Gapon and the St Petersburg Massacre of 1905* (Princeton, 1976); Gerald D. Surh, *1905 in St Petersburg. Labor, Society, and Revolution* (Stanford, 1989), pp. 116–25. For Karelina, see Rose L. Glickman, *Russian Factory Women: Workplace and Society, 1880–1914* (Berkeley, 1984) pp. 173–88.
17. Mariia Chekhova, quoted by Sanders, 'The Union of Unions', p. 655.
18. V. Karelina, 'Rabotnitsy v Gaponovskikh obshchestvakh', in P. F. Kudelli (ed.), *Rabotnitsa v 1905 g. v S.-Peterburge* (Leningrad, 1926), p. 21.
19. Gurevich, *9-e ianvaria*.
20. Restrictions continued well into 1905. A women's congress that had been planned since 1902 by the Mutual Philanthropic Society, had to be abandoned because the Ministry of Internal Affairs would not agree to the programme being widened beyond education and philanthropy. At the last minute, the St Petersburg governor-general, Trepov, demanded that all papers be submitted for prior inspection. The organizers cancelled the congress. See Edmondson, *Feminism in Russia*, p. 85.
21. Z. V. Grishina, *Zhenskie organizatsii v Rossii (1905 g. – fevral'/mart 1917 g.*, Avtoreferat dissertatsii (Moscow, 1978).
22. For example, S. N. Valk (ed.), *Sankt-Peterburgskie vysshie zhenskie (Bestuzhevskie) kursy, 1878–1918*, 2nd edn (Leningrad, 1973); L. D. Filippova, 'Iz istorii zhenskogo obrazovaniia v Rossii', *Voprosy istorii* (Feb. 1963) pp. 209–18; S. N. Serditova, *Bol'sheviki v bor'be za zhenskie proletarskie massy 1903 g. – fevral' 1917 g.* (Moscow, 1959). There are signs that Russian historians are breaking new ground. See G. A. Tishkin, *Zhenskii vopros v Rossii v 50–60 gg. XIX v.* (Leningrad, 1984); E. A.

Pavliuchenko, *Zhenshchiny v osvoboditel'nom dvizhenii. Ot Marii Volkonskoi do Very Figner* (Moscow, 1988); N. L. Pushkareva, *Zhensh- chiny drevnei Rusi* (Moscow, 1989). However, none of these works departs radically from previous interpretations and approaches. The long overdue re-emergence of feminism in Russia has recently led to a revived interest in gender issues and a desire to retrieve the submerged history of feminism before 1917. If this spirit of enquiry is allowed to breathe, women's history may at last find its deserved place in the new Russia, though as yet it is being expressed in newspapers and magazines, rather than in the publications of the historical profession.

23. E. D. Kuskova, 'Davno minuvshee', *Novyi zhurnal*, nos 43–5, 47–51, 54 (1955–8); A. V. Tyrkova-Vil'iams, *Na putiakh k svobode* (New York, 1952) and *To, chego bol'she ne budet* (Paris, 1954).

24. N. Mirovich, *Iz istorii zhenskogo dvizheniia v Rossii* (Moscow, 1908), p. 3.

25. The word 'feminist' acquired a pejorative sense early in the women's move- ment in Russia, and has retained it almost to this day. It seems to have been one foreign word that was *not* eagerly adopted by the intelligentsia.

26. Edmondson, *Feminism in Russia,* p. 35.

27. *Russkie vedomosti*, 4 Feb. 1905, p. 3; *Zhenskii vestnik*, no. 4 (1905), pp. 115, 121–2; no. 12 (1905), p. 366; *Pravda*, no. 6 (1905), pp. 276–9.

28. *Pravda*, no. 6 (1905), p. 277. In fact, women's property rights were not equal to men's – far from it – but women did have the right to retain their own property when they married, and in this respect had more rights than in many other countries. See W. G. Wagner, 'The Trojan Mare. Women's rights and civil rights in late imperial Russia', in Olga Crisp and Linda Edmondson (eds), *Civil Rights in Imperial Russia* (Oxford, 1989), pp. 65–84.

29. *Pravda*, no. 6 (1905), pp. 280–1.

30. Mirovich, *Iz istorii*, p. 5.

31. Ibid. pp. 4–5. Mirovich gives 26. The unpublished minutes of the congress give 19, including Moscow. Mirovich also misdates the congress 7–10 May. See *Protokoly zasedanii delegatov vserossiiskogo soiuza ravnopravnosti zhenshchin* (typewritten document in the London Library, Folio 1905). I have translated them in *Sbornik. Newsletter of the Study Group on the Russian Revolution* (Leeds, 1983), pp. 119–26.

32. Mirovich, *Iz istorii*, p. 5; *Protokoly zasedanii*.

33. *Protokoly zasedanii*.

34. *Pravo*, no. 16 (1905), cols. 1325–9; Aleksandra Kollontai, 'Avtobiogra- ficheskii ocherk', *Proletarskaia revoliutsiia*, no. 3 (1921), p. 268.

35. *Syn otechestva*, no. 98 (10 June 1905) p. 3.

36. Mirovich, *Iz istorii*, pp. 9–10.

37. Edmondson, *Feminism in Russia*, pp. 40–3.

38. *Vestnik vospitaniia*, no. 7/8 (1905) p. vii; *Pravda*, no. 6 (1905), pp. 281, 285; *Russkie vedomosti*, 8 May 1905, p. 3.

39. Caspar Ferenczi lists 'the emancipation of women' as one of a group of 'risky' topics to which the censors paid attention between 1905 and 1914. C. Ferenczi, 'Freedom of the press under the Old Regime, 1905–14', in Crisp and Edmondson, *Civil Rights in Imperial Russia*, p. 200. Censorship prob-

lems were not one of the hazards that members of the Union of Equal Rights complained about, though they did report many restrictions on meetings. After 1905, however, all their activities were impeded and many branches were closed.

40. Edmondson, *Feminism in Russia*, pp. 52–3.
41. For example, William Wagner has shown how Russian jurists supported the extensive reform of women's inheritance rights, as part of their wider attempt to establish Russian law on principles of civil equality and individual security. Wagner, 'The Trojan Mare'.
42. See my essay, 'Was there a movement for civil rights in 1905?' in Crisp and Edmondson, *Civil Rights in Imperial Russia*, pp. 263–85.
43. *Osvobozhdenie*, no. 69/70 (7 May 1905), p. 1.
44. *Novosti*, 3 June 1905, p. 4.
45. Tyrkova-Vil'iams, *Na putiakh k svobode*, p. 239; I. V. Gessen, 'V dvukh vekakh; zhiznennyi otchet', in *Arkhiv russkoi revoliutsii* (Berlin, 1937), vol. 22, p. 205.
46. See [E.Shch.] *Zhenskoe dvizhenie*, for the replies of zemstvists to a questionnaire on women's suffrage, prepared by the Union of Equal Rights. Many of the replies (for and against) contained assumptions about innate psychological differences between the sexes.
47. F. Kokoshkin, *Ob osnovaniiakh zhelatel'noi organizatsii narodnogo predstavitel'stva v Rossii* (Moscow, 1906).
48. In this period, 13.7 per cent of women were literate, and 32.6 per cent of men. The ratio of boys to girls attending school was about 3:1. Stites, *Women's Liberation Movement*, pp. 166–7.
49. V. Groman (ed.), *Materialy k krest'ianskomu voprosu* (St Petersburg, 1905), pp. 37–8; *Soiuz zhenshchin*, no. 1 (1907) p. 9.
50. L. Gurevich, *Zhenskii vopros v Gosudarstvennoi Dume* (St Petersburg, 1906).
51. L. I. Petrazhitskii, *O pol'ze politicheskikh prav zhenshchin* (St Petersburg, 1907); Edmondson, *Feminism in Russia*, pp. 69–70.
52. Ibid., pp. 68, 152.
53. In the spring of 1905, a Union of Working Women was set up in St Petersburg, but seems to have sunk without trace. [L. Gurevich] *Zhenskoe dvizhenie poslednikh dnei* (Odessa, 1905), pp. 10, 14–16; *Pravda*, no. 6 (1905), pp. 273, 282. During 1906, radicals from the Union of Equal Rights had a short-lived success with a Women's Political Club, and the following year Kollontai organized a 'working women's mutual aid society'. Edmondson, *Feminism in Russia*, pp. 64–5, 77–8.
54. Kollontai, 'Avtobiograficheskii ocherk', pp. 270–5.
55. *Sbornik 'Izvestii krest'ianskikh deputatov' i 'Trudovoi Rossii'* (Moscow, 1906), pp. 151–60.
56. *Ravnopravie zhenshchin. Tretii s''ezd soiuza ravnopravnosti zhenshchin. Otchety i protokoly* (St Petersburg, 1906).
57. P. N. Ariian (ed.), *Pervyi zhenskii kalendar' na 1906 g.* (St Petersburg, 1906), pp. 326–8.
58. See, for example, an Octobrist pamphlet during the First Duma election campaign, opposing women's suffrage on these grounds. Edmondson, *Fem-*

inism in Russia, p. 60. The feminists' own use of revolutionary martyrs raises a number of problems that have not been addressed by historians up to now. There was a tendency even among feminists who abhorred violence to pay hommage to female terrorists because they were fighting for freedom. Historians have been rather respectful of Russian terrorists and have not questioned the motives of the women who worked in People's Will, or the value of their activity. However, Richard Stites has pointed out the 'inappropriateness' of non-revolutionary feminists using the iconography of female terrorism. Stites, *Women's Liberation Movement*, p. 201, fn. 5.

59. Stites, *Women's Liberation Movement*, pp. 291–5; Edmondson, *Feminism in Russia*, pp. 164–9. But see Barbara Norton's essay in this volume, for evidence that even after women's suffrage had been promised, more campaigning was necessary to get the promise implemented.

60. Ellen DuBois has answered the criticism of Carroll Smith-Rosenberg and others, that 'woman suffrage has proved of little importance, either to American politics or to American women' (Smith-Rosenberg, 'The New Woman and the New History', *Feminist Studies*, no. 3 (1975) p. 186.) DuBois points out that suffragism in America was 'the first independent movement of women for their own liberation' and that the suffrage issue proved to be successful in creating a social movement 'of increasing strength and vitality'. Ellen DuBois, *Feminism and Suffrage. The Emergence of an Independent Women's Movement in America, 1848–1869* (Ithaca–London, 1978) pp. 17–18. In their far more circumscribed way, the Russian women's suffrage campaigns of 1905–17 performed a similar function. Failure came not because of their focus on political rights, but because the political and social environment was hostile to independent, non-revolutionary, political activity before 1917 (and way beyond).

61. See an unpublished paper by Rochelle Ruthchild, 'Feminism re-examined: gender, class and the Women's Equal Rights Union in 1905'. Ruthchild is the first historian to make an effective critique of the categorization of the feminists as 'bourgeois', an epithet that was hurled at them by their Marxist opponents and was subsequently preserved by Soviet (and some Western) historians.

62. This is a rough guess, based on the votes on women's suffrage at the respective congresses of the Union of Liberation and the Constitutional-Democratic Party in 1905.

5 Laying the foundations of democracy in Russia: E. D. Kuskova's contribution, February–October 1917

Barbara T. Norton

Like all of Russia's female revolutionaries, Ekaterina Dmitrievna Kuskova (1869–1958) forged her political career in a male-dominated oppositional movement that relegated women to a secondary, supporting role. Her forceful personality, however, along with an ability to articulate the demands of the moderate socialist and left liberal intelligentsia enabled her to overcome this marginalization and assume a place at the very centre of Russian revolutionary politics.[1] By 1917, Kuskova had achieved considerable prominence as a non-party social democrat, well known even beyond intelligentsia circles for her work as a journalist and an activist in the cooperative movement. By this time, too, she had entered the ranks of Russian feminists as an outspoken advocate of women's rights.[2] But it was socialism rather than feminism that informed Kuskova's politics in the period between the February and October revolutions, and she subordinated all other interests to the establishment of democracy in Russia. Moreover, throughout 1917 she continued, as she had in the past, to ignore her identity as a woman, remaining unconcerned with, if not actually unaware of, the extent to which her gender shaped her politics.

Any account of Kuskova's politics during this crucial year must remain incomplete until additional archival sources become accessible.[3] Nevertheless, available sources are adequate to construct a fairly detailed, if still preliminary, description of her efforts to lay the foundations of democracy in the period between February and October. While such a study may not substantially alter our general understanding of the two revolutions, it nonetheless broadens our angle of vision and adds depth and nuance to our picture of what is perhaps the central episode of modern Russian history. Most importantly, it reveals the extent to which this female radical managed to overcome the marginalization to which her gender consigned her. An examination of Kuskova's politics also provides a useful counterweight to the party-oriented analysis that characterizes the traditional historiography on 1917, and it sheds valuable light on the political significance of the little studied Russian cooperative movement. Finally, such a study serves to expand the important process of restoring women to their place in the history of 1917.[4]

For E. D. Kuskova, then in her late forties, the February Revolution was the culmination of a quarter of a century of determined struggle for Russia's liberation from autocratic oppression. Like so many other veterans of the oppositional movement, she greeted the news of the Petrograd uprising with a mixture of astonishment and exaltation, seeing in the revolution the promise of 'the triumph of personality and freedom', 'the slow but unswerving transformation of the whole social order, the freeing of enslaved humanity from the yoke of economic inequality'.[5] Kuskova had spent the years since the 1905 Revolution working on behalf of Russia's highly secret political Masonic organization to unite the country's oppositional intelligentsia.[6] Now, as information about the Petrograd uprising of 23–7 February reached her in Moscow, she joined with political Masons and other democratically minded public figures to establish a Committee of Public Organizations (Komitet obshchestvennykh organizatsii) to assume local control and maintain public order in Russia's second capital. Kuskova's extensive experience as an editor and publisher, as well as a journalist, made her an ideal choice to head the Committee's Commissariat for the Protection of the Freedom of the Press (Kommissariat po obespecheniiu svobody pechaty).[7] Her selection for this post – for which there was no dearth of qualified men available – was testimony to the high regard in which she was held by her male colleagues, radicals and liberals alike.

Kuskova was fully aware that the preservation of a free press, like all else in newly liberated Russia, depended finally upon defending and expanding the freedoms won by the revolution. Hence, her primary concern in the immediate aftermath of February, and throughout 1917, was laying the foundations for the further evolution of democracy. The formation of the Provisional Government on 1 March, with a cabinet that included six of her political Masonic associates, had signalled the beginning of what she hoped would be Russia's fundamental transformation to a society both politically and socially democratic. Although Kuskova had long ago broken with organized Marxism, she remained a 'critical socialist', adhering to the revisionist Marxist conviction that social democracy would be achieved only after political democracy had prepared the way, gradually, within the capitalist system. Consequently, she was quite content with the purely political agenda announced by Russia's new government on 3 March.[8]

The major feature of the Provisional Government's programme was its commitment to the principle of representative government and to the convocation of a Constituent Assembly that would create a new constitutional order for Russia. It was this commitment that set Kuskova's own political agenda.[9] In her view, the country's most pressing problem was the need to ensure that the Constituent Assembly would be democratically elected by an informed and responsible citizenry. The first task, therefore, was to obtain a truly democratic franchise for the assembly; the second, to prepare the population for participation in elections.

A genuinely democratic franchise would, of course, include women. Yet, it was by no means certain that the Provisional Government was committed to female suffrage. A campaign by the feminist League of Women's Equality (Liga ravnopraviia zhenshchin) during the second and third weeks of March succeeded in wresting a promise from Prime Minister G. E. L'vov to include women in the new electoral law.[10] But Kuskova was not willing to take anything for granted. She realized, moreover, that political rights, while important in themselves as a major step towards women's equality, would amount to little if women and other elements of the population remained insufficiently conscious of their duties and responsibilities as citizens. The quest for women's suffrage thus had to go hand in hand with the civic education of the still politically unsophisticated elements of Russian society.

On the evening of 23 March, Kuskova took this message to a meeting of Moscow women arranged jointly by the League of Women's Equality and an organization of women students. Addressing herself to the students, she urged them to join forces with their older sisters in the struggle for emancipation and to safeguard the freedoms of the February Revolution. It was crucial that the young women prepare themselves and the Russian people for the forthcoming elections by working with political parties and organizations like the League to develop the political consciousness and responsibility of the masses.[11] However, it was not the parties or the League but the cooperative movement that was to play the pivotal role in her own political strategy.

On 25 March, Kuskova joined more than 700 other cooperators from across the country for a four-day, All-Russian Congress of Cooperatives in Moscow, convened for the purpose of defining cooperation's role in strengthening Russia's new order.[12] She was one of only a handful of women in attendance, a reflection of the fact that in cooperative as in other politics women rarely achieved positions of leadership. But she quickly made her presence felt. Addressing the gathering on the first evening, Kuskova outlined in detail her vision of cooperation's unique opportunity to guide Russia through the transition to socialism. In her view, the cooperatives, because of their extensive network and broad base of support among all segments of the population, were better situated than any other organizations, including the political parties, to serve as a conduit for democratic ideas and a mechanism for preparing the country for self-government. While this would require abandoning cooperation's traditionally apolitical stance, to do otherwise in the present circumstances would be nothing short of criminal. Cooperation must become the coordinating centre for the formation of a democratic bloc to secure and extend the revolution.[13] 'Cooperators must try in every possible way', she insisted, 'to unify the political and social activities of the democracy' in order to rally the various tendencies within it and aid its struggle 'for the full democratization of the entire political and social order of Russia'.[14]

Turning her attention to the Constituent Assembly, Kuskova told her audience that they should apply all their energies to preparing the masses, and particularly the peasantry, for the forthcoming elections and for responsible participation in the new national legislature. She then proposed a number of measures with which to accomplish this, including the establishment of cultural centres in the countryside, villages and towns that would organize meetings, provide speakers and distribute agitational literature. She suggested, too, that cooperators establish local short-term courses around socio-political issues to raise the civic consciousness of the masses. Not surprisingly, she further urged the creation of publishing houses and a special press to promote the discussion of political and social issues.[15]

No doubt Kuskova expected objections to her programme for politicizing the cooperative movement. And some delegates did express opposition to diverting the movement from purely economic concerns. But the sentiment of the majority of the delegates was clearly on her side, with the eminent economist, M. I. Tugan-Baranovskii, among others, championing the cause of political involvement along with her. When the debates ended, the congress unanimously approved the new orientation, a decision that was to change the thrust of much cooperative activity for the remainder of 1917.[16]

That same evening, Kuskova also presented to the congress a resolution regarding the cooperatives' relationship to the Provisional Government. It emphasized the importance of a strong, authoritative government that could take responsibility for both domestic reconstruction and conducting the war against Germany, thereby guaranteeing the convocation of the Constituent Assembly. The resolution expressed full support for the individual cooperators who had entered the new cabinet and for the Provisional Government itself, 'in so far as it will unswervingly carry out the democratic programme it has announced'.[17] According to the Moscow daily *Russkie vedomosti* (*Russian Bulletin*), she received an enthusiastic ovation for this resolution, which was quickly adopted by the congress.[18]

In her statements to the cooperators, Kuskova had mapped out a political strategy for the months ahead; what remained now was to implement it. As she began to prepare for the elections to the Constituent Assembly, her anxieties about the franchise surfaced once again. These were revealed at the All-Russian Congress of Women that opened in Moscow on 7 April. Attended by such luminaries of the revolutionary movement as the old-time Populist V. N. Figner, Socialist Revolutionaries E. K. Breshko-Breshkovskaia and M. A. Spiridonova, and the Marxist V. I. Zasulich, the congress served as a forum for the discussion of women's rights issues.[19] For Kuskova, the suffrage issue was paramount. On the second day of the gathering, she warned the participants that, Premier L'vov's assurances of early March notwithstanding, their right to vote in the forthcoming elections was far from secure. Explaining that she had been informed by the Minister of Justice, A. F. Kerenskii, that the government did not intend to include women in the electoral law, she called upon the delegates to demand a special decree assuring women's right to vote. This they immediately resolved to do.[20]

Later in the congress, it was suggested that no basis existed for including women on the newly constituted electoral commission, composed as it was of prominent jurists. Kuskova objected strenuously to this view and insisted that, as members of Russia's public organizations, women had every right to demand inclusion among the latter's representatives on the commission. Once again the delegates responded and adopted a resolution demanding a place on the electoral commission. Kuskova's prodding had clearly strengthened their resolve to claim their rights as citizens of the new, democratic Russia.[21]

It would be several months before the electoral commission would complete its work, but Kuskova seemed confident that the franchise was at last secure. In any case, there were other matters demanding her attention. Foremost among them was the political course she had charted for the cooperatives. In the aftermath of the March Congress, she and other members of the Moscow Union of Consumers' Societies had established the Cooperative Printing Society (Kooperativnoe tovarishchestvo izdatel'skogo dela) for the publication of a daily paper along with books, pamphlets and other materials to disseminate the ideas of cooperation and democracy.[22] The newspaper, appropriately named *Vlast' naroda* (*Power of the People*), was of special significance to Kuskova, and its programme clearly reflected her political strategy. The programme called for 'the strengthening of the democratic republic, the building of the idea of democracy (*narodovlastiia*) in the consciousness of the broad masses', as well as for 'the protection of the interests of the working classes and the unification of the labouring masses in the creative work of transforming the whole economic order on the basis of socialism'.[23] Designed to be the mouthpiece for the broad democratic coalition on which Kuskova pinned her hopes for Russia's future, *Vlast' naroda* attracted liberal contributors like I. P. Belokonskii and V. V. Vodovozov, as well as such prominent socialists as the Popular Socialist Party leader, S. P. Mel'gunov, the Socialist Revolutionaries V. I. Burtsev and M. V. Vishniak, the Mensheviks P. P. Maslov and A. N. Potresov, and the non-party social democrat and well-known writer, A. M. Gor'kii. The paper soon became the principal forum for Kuskova's observations and analysis of Russian political developments. It was also to be one of the strongest supporters of the Provisional Government.

The appearance of *Vlast' naroda* at the end of April coincided with the first serious internal crisis of the Provisional Government. The ensuing resignation of the Octobrist Minister of War, A. I. Guchkov, and the Kadet Foreign Minister, P. N. Miliukov, greatly distressed Kuskova who feared for the fate of liberal-radical solidarity.[24] The announcement of a new, coalition government on 5 May, however, did much to allay her fears, not the least because the cabinet now included seven political Masons. The following day, her column in *Vlast' naroda* contained a plea to 'close tightly socialist and democratic ranks . . . and create the conditions for successful practical work jointly with the government'.[25] The practical work she had in mind involved measures designed to counter Bolshevik influence among an increasingly discontented working class. Despite signs of improvement in industrial productivity, rising food prices at the end of April coupled with Lenin's return to Russia earlier that month had provided new opportunities for the Bolsheviks. As May wore on, Kuskova grew alarmed at the rising tide of restlessness among the workers, and she urged the government to formulate some basic principles to regulate the country's economic life until the convocation of the Constituent Assembly. What was needed, she suggested, were temporary controls on wages, lockouts and profits in order to demonstrate good will and emphasize the fact that there would be no return to the old order.[26]

Although Kuskova was deeply sympathetic to the suffering of the working classes, now in their third year of wartime deprivation, she believed that fundamental economic reform was the exclusive prerogative of the Constituent Assembly. The limited economic measures she sought were thus intended primarily to take the pressure off the Provisional Government so that it might continue the struggle against Russia's external enemies. Only the successful conclusion of the international conflict could provide the security and stability she considered necessary to address the country's profound socio-economic problems. Here her views corresponded fully with those of her Masonic colleague Kerenskii, newly appointed Minister of War. Like him, she sought a peace without annexations or indemnities on the basis of national self-determination, the formula endorsed by the Petrograd Soviet of Workers' and Soldiers' Deputies. Until such a plan could be fully elaborated, however, the successful conduct of the war remained a priority.[27] 'The conclusion of the dreadful war and the creation in the Russian state of a purely democratic, purely republican constitution', she wrote in early June, had to be the country's first concern. Moreover, this process could only take place through the united action of all democratic organizations 'in support of the coalition ministry and the line of the Congress of Soviets of Workers' and Soldiers' Deputies'.[28]

In Kuskova's estimation, it had always been a mistake to perceive the interests of the Provisional Government and those of the workers' and soldiers' soviets as divergent. She was secure in her conviction that, under the guidance of political Masonry,[29] both government and soviets had as their primary goal the defence of the revolution from internal as well as external threats. It was not the so-called 'dual power' that Russia had to fear but the division that existed between the revolutionary intelligentsia and the politically unsophisticated masses. As unrest in the cities and countryside intensified throughout June, Kuskova revealed her concern about 'the country's general lack of culture (*nekul'turnosti*)' and 'the general unpreparedness to decide fundamental questions of law and economy'. At the same time, she praised the Congress of Soviets for recognizing the need for an 'all-socialist bloc' in the Constituent Assembly elections. 'Only the firm rallying of all resolute forces of the democracy can avert the coming danger', she reiterated. 'All influential elements of the [socialist] parties and the soviets must immediately set about the organization of this united bloc of all democratic forces.'[30]

Although Kuskova focused her attention on the tasks before the socialists, she never wavered in her insistence that the fate of the revolution and the country's further democratic evolution depended also upon democratically minded liberals. Her reaction to the Kadets' departure from the Provisional Government on 2 July was a measure of the firmness of this conviction. Writing in *Vlast' naroda* about the new cabinet crisis, she angrily chastised the Constitutional Democratic Party for its recent shift to the right. This represented an even greater danger for Russia than did the anarchistic politics of the extreme left, she lamented; for it revealed that broad layers of the bourgeoisie completely failed to grasp the significance of the revolution or understand that changed political circumstances required new and more flexible political tactics.[31] Yet, even as Kuskova criticized the Kadets, she urged them 'immediately to reverse their decision and send into the Provisional Government people who are not afraid of the Soviet of Workers' Deputies, people who believe in the principle of the state (*gosudarstvenno-mysliashchikh*) and who act decisively'.[32]

Kuskova must have feared the worst for the fate of the revolution when, in the midst of this second cabinet crisis, Bolshevik and anarchist insurgents attempted to seize power in Petrograd. She produced several articles for *Vlast' naroda* in the wake of these July Days reproaching the Bolsheviks, in particular, for their 'pernicious tactics' of 'defeatism and civil war'.[33] In her view, Lenin's politics amounted to nothing less than a 'policy of treason', 'a knife in the back not only of the army but also of the revolution'.[34] This said, however, she hastened to emphasize that her criticisms ought not be construed as hatred of Bolshevism. Ever the advocate of democratic solidarity, Kuskova appealed for 'the unification of all tendencies of revolutionary democracy, including Bolshevism'. She was convinced that freedom would 'cleanse the most sympathetic layers of Bolshevism of demagoguery and blend them together with the rest of the democracy in one common, creative line of socialism'.[35]

The outcome of the July crises must have been reassuring. Not only had the Petrograd Soviet rejected demands by the insurgents that it take power, but it had even initiated arrangements to bring troops to the government's defence. Further, when a new government was announced at the end of the month, the alliance with the liberals remained intact, and the cabinet's political Masonic contingent had increased to ten. Kuskova's satisfaction with this turn of events was undoubtedly enhanced by Kerenskii's assumption of the premiership and the fact that her husband, S. N. Prokopovich, now joined the government as Minister of Trade and Industry.[36]

With Prokopovich's entry into the government, Kuskova began to divide her time between Moscow and Petrograd. Already on 22 and 23 July, she provided *Vlast' naroda* with the first of what would be a continuing series of 'Petrograd letters' describing the political atmosphere and events in the capital.[37] Her new vantage point would enable her to keep her readers informed about the government's efforts to secure and extend the achievements of the revolution.

As July drew to a close, Kuskova expressed her concern over mounting pressure on the government to enact radical reforms. 'Socialism planted in sterile soil', she reminded Kerenskii's predominantly socialist cabinet, 'not only will not take root, but it will destroy that capitalism through which we must inevitably pass.'[38] It was important that the liberal members of the government continue to help hold in check all socializing tendencies. This required that the Kadets, in particular, maintain their commitment to coalition government. But the party's July congress raised doubts in her mind about their inclination to do so. Warning that coalition for the sake of appearances was of no use to Russia, Kuskova emphasized that the fate of the revolution depended not merely on the solidarity of the left but on 'a true union of all the available forces of the country'.[39] It was her hope that the forthcoming Moscow State Conference, slated to begin on 12 August, would serve to bring the Kadets and other progressive forces closer to such a union.

This hope was soon disappointed. The Moscow Conference, organized by the Provisional Government in its quest for national support, quickly became mired in partisan politics. Composed of some 2,500 representatives of the country's various social, professional, political and national groups, the three-day gathering proved a dismal failure. For Kuskova, who attended as a representative of the cooperatives, it merely highlighted the sharpening class conflict and political polarization that had come to characterize Russian life since June. As she noted shortly afterwards, the initial 'class truce' established at the conference quickly gave way to the usual collision of parties, groups, moods and convictions.[40]

On the heels of the ineffectual Moscow State Conference came the attempted military coup by General L. G. Kornilov and the consequent dissolution of Kerenskii's coalition cabinet. For the first time since February, Kuskova's optimism about Russia's future began to flag. In her 'Petrograd letter' of 30 August commemorating the six-month anniversary of the revolution, she wrote with profound sadness:

It is already impossible now to talk about the victory of a united revolution . . . The revolution itself, in the person of labouring democracy (*trudovoi demokratii*), is split into two opposite camps: in one – forces rally who defend class dictatorship . . . in the other – elements of labouring democracy who decisively protest against dictatorship, who defend the idea of compromise . . . Above these two tendencies within the revolution rises and grows stronger a third tendency, the varied elements of the wealthy classes who aspire to a dictatorship of the bourgeoisie, to the suppression of the political and social forces of labouring democracy . . . The elements of national compromise are in a most difficult, almost hopeless position.[41]

In these circumstances, she conceded soon afterwards, a victory for counter-revolutionary bourgeois forces was very possible:

The *Kornilovshchina* – this is the Russian June Days. This is Versailles and Paris, 1871. This is the clash of the Commune with the bourgeois world . . . This is not a simple uprising against the present composition of the Provisional Government. This is the collision of two . . . principles, of two strata and two foundations of a future Russia.[42]

Nevertheless, Kuskova would not give in to despair. The revolution might still succeed if it could strengthen its will 'to crush . . . the forces of anarchism in its midst and promote the creative forces, the able forces of "state organization" (*gosudarstvennosti*)'.[43] But this was Russia's only hope; bourgeois counter-revolution would triumph if the democracy did not 'deploy its creative forces in the spirit of the national (and not its class) interests', if it acted in isolation 'without an attempt to carry out the programme of coalition administration of the country'.[44]

Amid growing social polarization and intensifying political fractiousness, Kuskova remained a determined voice for 'national compromise'. It may well have been her desire to encourage compromise on the part of moderate social democrats that had led her, sometime earlier, to join the Moscow Menshevik organization.[45] She did not participate in party work, however, and involved herself in Menshevik affairs only to the extent of urging all party factions to endorse coalition government. Thus, during the first week of September, she and a number of other Menshevik defencists publicly protested against a resolution by the party Central Committee opposing further Kadet participation in the government. In a statement that appeared in several radical newspapers on 7 September, the group warned their party that a non-coalition cabinet would only provoke counter-revolution and civil war.[46] To Kuskova, the collaboration of the Kadets remained *sine qua non* for Russia's further democratic evolution.

The main cause for concern was no longer the Kornilov offensive, which had been halted by a joint liberal–socialist effort, but the forthcoming Democratic Conference, scheduled to open soon in Petrograd in order to reconstruct the government (temporarily in the hands of a five-member Directory). Summoned at the initiative of the soviets' Central

Executive Committee, this was to be a gathering of representatives of all democratic organizations and organs of local self-government. In her 'Petrograd letter' of 8 September, Kuskova contemplated with alarm the prospect that the conference might endorse a government absent of any representation for Russia's propertied groups. Such an eventuality, she felt, would amount to nothing less than 'the seizure of power by revolutionary democracy' and could only result in 'the isolation of it and the government from all other, non-democratic elements' of society. This would represent 'a brilliant victory by the idea of Bolshevism', the outcome of which would be not merely another crisis of authority but 'the temporary rule of demagogues of all types and ranks'.[47]

This did not mean that Kuskova shared the view of those who sought to broaden the constituency of the conference. On the contrary, she directly rejected a proposal by the Council of All-Russian Cooperative Congresses to include representatives of all segments of society. 'A repetition of the Moscow Conference', she countered, 'would not give the country anything new. It would be the same arrangement of forces, the same irreconcilable crossing (*skreshchivanie*) of opinions and desires.' What was needed was for cooperators to assume a leading role in the Democratic Conference to represent the sober voice of reason among those intoxicated by 'the idea of the unlimited rule of democracy'.[48] She would reiterate this position at the Extraordinary All-Russian Cooperative Congress in Moscow.

On 11 September, approximately 150 cooperative leaders assembled in Moscow for a special three-day congress to consider participation in the Democratic Conference. Speaking on the second day, again, to a predominantly male audience, Kuskova told her listeners that it lay within the power of the cooperative movement to determine whether the country would have 'a commune or a coalition'. Her remarks met with an enthusiastic response.[49] And it must have pleased her very much indeed when the congress not only resolved to participate in the Democratic Conference but instructed its delegates 'to form a temporary bloc . . . in union with the tendencies in the socialist parties that adhere to a state perspective (*gosudarstvennoi tochki zreniia*), and with those non-socialist groups and parties . . . that have striven and are striving to consolidate the achievements of the revolution and social reforms'.[50]

When the Democratic Conference convened on 14 September Kuskova was present as a member of the cooperative delegation, one of the few women to attend this gathering of nearly 2,000 people.[51] Two days later, she telephoned the editorial offices of *Vlast' naroda* with a report on the proceedings. In it she described the atmosphere of the

conference as chaotic, observing that, with the exception of the cooperators and the Bolsheviks, none of the groups or factions could agree
among themselves on a desirable government for Russia.[52] This situation continued until 20 September when the conference, deadlocked on
the question of coalition, decided to transfer responsibility for constitut-
ing a new government to a smaller Democratic Council established for
that purpose.[53] Kuskova's frustration at the failure to endorse coalition
was evident when she told the readers of *Vlast' naroda*: 'There is no
united front of the revolution. There is no united front of the
democracy. This is the final, this is the main, fundamental result and
conclusion of the conference.'[54] Still, she refused to abandon all hope.
Perhaps the newly constituted Democratic Council, of which she was a
member, might yet steer the country through 'the raging waves of
anarchy'. If it could not, Russia was 'doomed to full destruction and
indubitable ruin'.[55]

By the final week of September, following negotiations with representatives of the Democratic Council, Kerenskii was at last able to
announce the formation of a new coalition cabinet, one which again
contained a significant number of political Masons.[56] Kuskova now
reminded the ministers – including her husband, this time in the post of
Minister of Food Supplies – that they 'must do everything possible to
defend fully the interests of the democracy *within the limits of a
bourgeois order*'. Moreover, only the organized support of the masses
could ensure that the government would move 'in the direction of the
democracy and not in the direction of the propertied [*tsenzovykh*] elements'.[57] That such support had not been forthcoming earlier Kuskova
attributed not to the pace of reform but to the ineffective work of the
democracy, and the socialist parties in particular. On 29 September, she
offered a detailed critique of the socialist parties in another article for
Vlast' naroda. Her analysis led her to conclude that, with the exception
perhaps of the Bolsheviks, these parties could not be successful in
organizing the masses for the elections to the Constituent Assembly
(fixed in July for 17 September but subsequently postponed until 12
November). Consequently, a supplement to the parties was necessary,
one which only the cooperatives could provide. It was not a question of
forming 'a special "cooperative party" ', she asserted, but 'a question
of the salvation of the country'.[58]

Already, at the beginning of August, Kuskova had proposed to the
First All-Russian Congress of Workers' Cooperatives in Moscow that
cooperation expand its role in the preparations for the Constituent
Assembly elections. But her proposal, which included the suggestion
that the cooperatives offer their own lists of candidates, had been poorly

received by the worker cooperators, many of whom supported the socialist parties.[59] Now, as the Provisional Government, the revolution and Russia itself struggled for survival, she hoped that the value of an independent cooperative presence in the elections would be obvious to all.

On 5 October, Kuskova put her case before the 200 or so cooperative leaders gathered in Moscow for the second Extraordinary All-Russian Congress of Cooperatives. In an impassioned speech to an attentive audience, she dispatched one by one the objections to a direct electoral role for the cooperatives. She also repeated her criticism of the socialist parties, stressing the impracticality of their programmes and pointing, additionally, to the defeatist stance that many socialists had adopted towards the war. Kuskova recalled with particular distaste the recent demand of the newly radicalized Moscow Menshevik organization for an immediate armistice. Emphasizing her point about the harmful nature of such a position, she declared dramatically: 'If I, here, with this hand, cast my ballot for the list of that party to which I belong . . . I would cut off this hand because . . . I would have cast my ballot for defeatists.'[60] There was absolutely no question in her mind: capitulation to foreign enemies would not serve the interests of the masses. As she had warned earlier, cooperators could not vote for 'parties or tendencies advocating unity . . . with anti-state and defeatist elements'.[61] Consequently, while they might still work with moderate socialists, cooperators could no longer rely on the socialist parties in the forthcoming elections.

This time, while not without opponents – including most worker cooperators – Kuskova's call for direct, independent electoral activity found a generally receptive audience. Indeed, many of the cooperative leaders had already reached similar conclusions. For people like the Menshevik, V. A. Anisimov, and the Socialist Revolutionary, A. V. Chaianov, her arguments served as an important catalyst. As *Russkie vedomosti* noted: 'If there was a moment at the congress when it seemed that a single, common decision began to triumph, it was at the time of this passionate, gifted (*talantlivoi*) speech.'[62] After a lengthy debate, the congress approved the position that Kuskova had so eloquently championed. Cooperators were instructed to assist 'the formation of blocs with the socialist parties and factions adhering to a state perspective' or to align with individual parties and fractions in order to exert influence on the composition of their electoral lists. In the event that blocs or individual alliances were not possible, local cooperative organizations were to put up separate lists of candidates.[63]

In recognition of Kuskova's role in formulating cooperative policy, the men on the Council of All-Russian Cooperative Congresses selected her for inclusion in the cooperative electoral lists.[64] This was a singular mark of respect, especially when bestowed upon a woman. Kuskova lost no time initiating her campaign, apparently travelling soon after the Moscow congress to a provincial congress in Tver to garner support for the cooperative lists. Here she warned once more of the bankruptcy of the socialist parties and their inability to relate to the masses.[65]

Kuskova's criticism of the socialist parties and her blatant disregard for Menshevik party discipline had not gone unnoticed by the Moscow Menshevik organization. Already on 6 October, the party bureau had decided to call her to account for her public comments, demanding that she appear at their next meeting to explain having 'so compromised' the party. By the time the bureau's communiqué reached her, however, she was once again in Petrograd, occupied with the work of the recently convened Provisional Council of the Republic, as the newly expanded Democratic Council was called. Unable, but also unwilling, to return to Moscow at the bureau's beckoning, Kuskova replied by letter, her annoyance obvious: 'I would be . . . very grateful if the party bureau did not simply fling at me the accusations of "compromising" the party, but precisely and definitely indicated exactly what part of my public-political (*obshchestvenno-politicheskoi*) work compromises the party.' This was not mere disingenuousness on her part; she firmly believed that the welfare of any party rested on its members' willingness to challenge erroneous and dangerous decisions by party leaders. Thus, she proceeded to chastise the Menshevik leadership anew for their descent into defeatism and for a political stance that had only contributed to Bolshevik successes in recent local elections. She closed her reply defiantly, rejecting the idea that her public activity should be judged by 'people, who although calling themselves Mensheviks, in reality have nothing in common with the principles of this social democratic tendency'.[66]

Kuskova's failure to appear before the Moscow bureau as requested was sufficient pretext for the Menshevik leaders to expel her from the party. Such independence was not to be tolerated, especially from a woman. No doubt the arrival of her unrepentant letter shortly thereafter confirmed the bureau in the correctness of their action.[67] It is unlikely that Kuskova was seriously troubled by her expulsion from the Menshevik organization. Party membership had meant little to her and, as things stood, it was probably only a matter of time before she left of her own accord.[68] In any event, her attention was now on more important matters, with the Council of the Republic sitting in regular session and the campaign for the Constituent Assembly in full swing.

The Council of the Republic, composed of representatives of all

major parties and public organizations, had officially opened in
Petrograd on 7 October.[69] Intended to function as a temporary
legislature until the Constituent Assembly convened on 20 November,
this Preparliament, as it was popularly known, began its work with a
consideration of Russia's deteriorating military situation. But the first
session had done little more than reveal again the serious differences
that divided the various segments of society. Kuskova, for one, was
appalled at the endless wrangling that continued even as the German
army approached the outskirts of the capital. At the Council's second
session on 12 October, she addressed the assembly with words both of
reproach and entreaty. Was it possible, she asked, that after seven
months of wrangling, people had come to the Preparliament simply to
continue quarrelling? It was time to move beyond talk and arguments:

At the moment, when it is a question of defending the city where we are
accustomed to carry on our disputes, in the name of the cooperatives I would
like to appeal to you not only with a request but with a plea to put aside
declarations, or at least transfer them to other tribunes, and . . . I would call
upon you to make this revolutionary Preparliament a businesslike institution.

Divergent interests would remain, of course, 'but at the moment', she
reminded her audience, 'not one question can be solved without first
establishing order in the country'. Long opposed to the use of force
against the population, Kuskova felt that the situation had now become
so serious 'that all means should be exhausted immediately, down to
coercion, in order to channel the masses into an arm of organized
defence of their motherland'. The task before the Council, she concluded, was to support the Provisional Government, to 'enable the
authority to orient itself as to the forces it deals with and [to see] what
agreements are possible between the varied interests that tear the
country apart'. Her address ended with a final appeal to the Preparliament 'to find those points of unity that would really ensure the defence
of the country and the state from devastation'.[70]

Kuskova's words made a strong impression on her listeners. Most
sympathetic were the moderate, conciliatory elements in the Council.
So impressed with the speech was Popular Socialist A. S. Zarudnyi that,
at its conclusion, he rushed to kiss Kuskova's hand,[71] a gesture that
underlined her anomalous female presence in this predominantly male
forum. But even as harsh a critic as the independent social democrat
N. N. Sukhanov, who dismissed her remarks as 'absolutely without a
core and without a firm idea', acknowledged the 'outward success' of
her speech. On the right, the Kadet I. V. Gessen felt that 'This speech
. . . opened a window vent (fortochku) and made it possible to breathe',
while for Miliukov her remarks 'produced that impression that a truth-

ful and courageous word always produces in a milieu accustomed to conventional hypocrisy'.[72] It remained now for Kuskova to translate this oratorical success into practical results.

She and her cooperator colleagues quickly set to work drafting a so-called 'formula of transition' around which they hoped to unite a majority of the Preparliament. Despite support among a wide range of parties and groups across the political spectrum, the formula was narrowly rejected by the full assembly when it came to a vote on 18 October.[73] This would prove to be Kuskova's last attempt to organize a political prop for Kerenskii's beleaguered government. Her profound disappointment and anger at the outcome of her efforts were clearly evident in *Vlast' naroda* on 19 October. Reflecting on the Preparliament's failure to provide the government with either the public support or the moral sanction it so desperately needed, she lamented: 'instead of [creating] a genuinely revolutionary fusion of all state-minded people, without exception, for the support of its authority and the conferring of firmness and decisiveness to its activity, we argue about . . . [sic] land committees'. A special wrath was reserved for those of her socialist colleagues who 'still twiddle old programmes and old proclamations, not seeing that someone evil and more resolute wants to snatch from them the fate of Russia . . . [sic]'.[74] She could only hope that the Constituent Assembly would convene in time to assume the mantle of authority from the Provisional Government.

As the date for the opening of the Constituent Assembly drew near, Kuskova's chances for election to the long awaited national legislature appeared to be quite good. By the third week of October, her name had been entered among the top two or three on numerous electoral lists, ranging from those of independent cooperators and cooperator–socialist alliances to the feminist list compiled by the League of Women's Equality. In Moscow, Petrograd and several points between, this energetic champion of democracy was considered by many to be a prime candidate for Russia's new democratic parliament.[75] But the events of 24–26 October were soon to change everything.

Since mid-month, Petrograd newspapers had daily been reporting rumours of an imminent Bolshevik-led uprising. Yet, like so many other radical intelligentsia preoccupied with the problems of Russia's external defence, Kuskova had little time to attend to talk of insurrection.[76] By 24 October, however, rumour had become reality. Shortly after noon that day, Kerenskii appeared before the Preparliament to announce that the uprising was at hand.[77]

The following morning, as Kuskova accompanied her husband on his way to a cabinet meeting, the couple were detained near the Winter

Palace by a group of insurrectionaries. Prokopovich was arrested, but she was allowed to proceed to the Preparliament for what would prove to be its final session.[78] Early in the afternoon of 25 October, the Council of the Republic was dispersed by a contingent of soldiers and sailors. Kuskova spent the remainder of the day in frequent telephone contact with those cabinet members sequestered in the Winter Palace, keeping them informed of the general situation in the capital and of efforts being made for their rescue. Shortly before midnight, as the situation grew desperate, she reported to the Minister of Posts and Telegraphs, A. M. Nikitin, that a large deputation of supporters was on its way. But neither from this quarter nor any other did the hoped for rescue materialize. In the early morning hours of 26 October, the ministers in the Winter Palace were placed under arrest by the Bolshevik-led Military Revolutionary Committee.[79] The October Revolution had brought an end to the eight-month rule of the Provisional Government and, with it, an end to Kuskova's efforts to lay the foundations of democracy on the ground prepared by the February Revolution.[80]

During the course of 1917, E. D. Kuskova's intellectual acuity, determination and rhetorical abilities placed her at the very centre of Russian political life. Throughout the critical months from February to October, she took part in most of the significant events of the day, working side by side with the male leaders of the liberal and radical intelligentsia. But the respect and influence she enjoyed were achieved at a price, the price of submerging her identity as a woman.

Kuskova's political thought revealed a genuine and deeply held concern for women's rights that placed her firmly in the ranks of Russian feminists. With the exception of the suffrage battle, however, her politics during 1917 were not the politics of feminism. This was due in part to her conviction that genuine equality for women would come only with Russia's fundamental socio-economic transformation. But it had another source as well. The achievement of her 'honorary male' status in revolutionary circles had required her, consciously or unconsciously, to ignore the part that her sex played in shaping her politics.

Yet, gender played a critical role in determining the nature and limits of Kuskova's political opportunities and ambitions. There remained important bastions of male power, such as the Council of Cooperative Congresses and the Provisional Government cabinet,[81] that no female, regardless of her prominence, could realistically hope to penetrate. Moreover, in a political culture that mirrored patriarchal society in assigning women a nurturing and supportive role, Kuskova had only so much room to manoeuvre without violating the conditions of female political participation. Thus, the role she defined for herself as the moral voice of democracy and conscience of the February Revolution remained within the limits of acceptable behaviour for a woman. Gender was a factor, too, in influencing her political strategy and tactics. Whether she realized it or not, her strategy of compromise as opposed to competition, and her tactics of persuasion rather than manipulation, were essential elements in her political success.

Given the constraints of Russian political culture, it is not surprising that Kuskova's politics were not conventional, partisan politics. While she remained a convinced social democrat, Marxist ideology was of little immediate importance to her. Indeed, with her emphasis on 'state-mindedness' and the need for responsible and lawful behaviour, she often sounded more like a liberal than a socialist. In contrast to the majority of social democrats, moreover, she clearly understood the importance of including progressive propertied elements in all discussions about Russia's future. What mattered was the establishment of a firm foundation on which further peaceful democratic development could occur. All else was secondary.

In assessing the effectiveness of Kuskova's politics during 1917, it is easy to point to her failure to cement a broad democratic coalition. But if her efforts at reconciling the diverse elements of the country's revolutionary leadership were ultimately unsuccessful, the attempt nevertheless represented a significant contribution to the politics of the period. Her unwavering commitment to above-party, above-class cooperation may appear naive in the circumstances of intense class conflict and sharp political polarization that characterized Russian life throughout most of the year. However, it can be argued that this path alone offered an acceptable way out of the country's political impasse. For democracy to succeed, it was necessary before all else to reduce ideological combat through compromise and understanding. Only then could political leaders begin to formulate a resolution to the enormous social and economic difficulties confronting them. But regardless of how Kuskova's contribution is evaluated, it is impossible to deny this female radical a prominent place in the history of 1917.

Notes

I am indebted to Adele Lindenmeyr and Christine Ruane for their very helpful comments on an earlier version of this essay.
  1. Kuskova's involvement in the revolutionary movement had begun in the

mid-1880s. Although a confirmed Marxist by the early 1890s, she maintained no connection with organized social democracy after the end of the decade. She was one of the founders of the Union of Liberation (Soiuz osvobozhdeniia), helping to establish the Constitutional Democratic (Kadet) Party during the 1905 revolution. After 1905, she remained without party affiliation, channelling much of her energy into Russia's political Masonic organization (known after 1912 as the Grand Orient of the Peoples of Russia (Velikii vostok narodov Rossii)), where she played a leading role in the campaign to unite the oppositional intelligentsia.

2. Kuskova's emerging feminism was evident already in 1908, at the first All-Russian Congress of Women, when she suggested that Russia's radical socio-economic transformation held the key to women's liberation. See Linda H. Edmondson, *Feminism in Russia, 1900–1917* (Stanford, 1984), pp. 93–103 passim. Kuskova's growing interest in women's issues was further evidenced by her participation in a 1912 congress on women's education and by her entry on 'the woman question' in the Granat encyclopedia ('Zhenskii vopros', *Entsiklopedicheskii slovar'*, 7th edn, vol. 20 (Moscow, n.d.), cols. 162–77).

3. Most important are Kuskova's own papers. Those from 1917 itself, if they have been preserved, are most likely in the Soviet Communist Party archive. Materials from her years in emigration after 1922 are in the Soviet-held Prague Archive, only now becoming available to Western scholars, and in the Bibliothèque Nationale in Paris where they remain under a recently renewed embargo until the year 2008.

4. Kuskova's case is illustrative of the neglect that intelligentsia women have suffered at the hands of Soviet and Western historians alike. The historiography on 1917 includes only passing references to her; and even G. Ia. Aronson's 'E. D. Kuskova. Portret obshchestvennogo deiatelia', *Novyi zhurnal*, vol. 37 (1954), pp. 236–56, treats her politics in this period superficially.

5. E. D. Kuskova, 'Dnevnik', *Vlast' naroda* (hereafter *VN*), 11 June 1917, p. 2. Her recollections of the 'February Days' are found in 'Mgnovenie (27 fevralia 1917 g.)', *Dni*, 15 March 1923, and letter to S. P. Mel'gunov, 21 December 1950, British Library of Political and Economic Science (hereafter BLPES), Mel'gunov Archive, group 45, box c.

6. On Kuskova's Masonic affiliation, see Barbara T. Norton, 'Russian political Masonry and the February Revolution of 1917', *International Review of Social History*, vol. 27, pt. 2 (1983), pp. 240–58.

7. Organized during 28 February–1 March, the Moscow Committee quickly set up a variety of commissariats, commissions and committees to deal with all aspects of civil administration. *Sbornik materialov komiteta moskovskikh obshchestvennykh organizatsii*, pt. 1 (Moscow, 1917). Kuskova's appointment as press commissar is reported in *Russkie vedomosti* (hereafter *RV*), 18 March 1917, p. 3.

8. As Kuskova would put it later: 'The country is for political revolution. But it is not for socialism', Kuskova, 'Dnevnik', *VN*, 2 June 1917, p. 1. Her Marxist revisionism is discussed in Barbara T. Norton, '*Eshche raz ekonomizm*: E. D. Kuskova, S. N. Prokopovich and the challenge to Rus-

sian social democracy', *The Russian Review*, vol. 45, no. 2 (1986), pp. 179–202.

9. According to A. F. Kerenskii (*Russia and History's Turning Point* (New York, 1965), p. 89), the Provisional Government's programme was worked out by Russian political Masonry prior to the February Revolution. Thus, Kuskova may well have had a hand in formulating that programme. Regarding Masonry's role in the creation of the Provisional Government, see Barbara T. Norton, 'The establishment of democracy in Russia: the origins of the Provisional Government reconsidered', *History of European Ideas*, vol. 11 (1989), pp. 181–8.

10. Edmondson, *Feminism in Russia*, pp. 165–6.

11. *RV*, 24 March 1917, p. 5.

12. The delegates to this congress, which met at Shaniavskii University, represented some 35,000 cooperatives with a total membership of approximately 10,000,000. 'The All-Russian Cooperative Congress in Moscow', *The Russian Cooperator* (hereafter *RC*), May 1917, p. 93. Kuskova had been active in cooperation for more than a decade and was a prominent member of the important Moscow Union of Consumers' Societies (Moskovskii soiuz potrebitel'skikh obshchestv).

13. 'Po dokladu E. D. Kuskovoi: "Uchastie kooperativov v podgotovke k Uchreditel'nomu sobraniiu" ', in *Rezoliutsii, priniatye na pervom Vseros-siiskom s"ezde predstavitelei kooperativnikh soiuzov, ob"edinenii i komitetov v Moskve 25–28 marta 1917 g.* (Moscow, 1917), p. 11; and *RV*, 28 March 1917, p. 6.

14. 'Po dokladu', p. 11. See also *RV*, 28 March 1917, p. 6; and *RC*, May 1917, p. 93. In Kuskova's usage, 'the democracy' (*demokratiia*), referred to all politically conscious elements of the left whose primary concern was the welfare of the Russian masses.

15. 'Po dokladu', p. 11.

16. *RV*, 28 March 1917, p. 6; 'All-Russian Cooperative Congress', p. 93; and V. F. Totomiants, 'The All-Russian Congress of Cooperative Unions', *RC*, June 1917, p. 112.

17. 'Po dokladu', p. 12.

18. *RV*, 28 March 1917, p. 6.

19. *RV*, 7 April 1917, p. 6. About seventy delegates attended.

20. *RV*, 9 April 1917, p. 6.

21. Ibid. When the electoral commission began its deliberations at the end of May, it would include two members of the League of Women's Equality, and the electoral law formulated and ratified in July would finally enfranchise women. O. N. Znamenskii, *Vserossiiskoe uchreditel'noe sobranie* (Leningrad, 1976), pp. 125–7; and Richard Stites, *The Women's Liberation Movement in Russia* (Princeton, 1978), p. 294.

22. *RC*, July 1917, p. 135.

23. *VN*, 28 April 1917, p. 1. Initially one of four co-editors, Kuskova gradually assumed much of the editorial responsibility for the paper. Letters to A. F. Damanskaia, 9 June 1949, Archive of Russian and East European History and Culture, Columbia University, Damanskaia Collection, box 41; to L. O. Dan, 15 August 1951, International Institute of Social History (here-

after IISH), Dan Archive, XII, packet 7; and to N. V. Vol'skii, 4 May 1956, Hoover Institution on War, Revolution and Peace (hereafter HIWRP), Vol'skii Collection, box 5.

24. The resignation of Guchkov, a long-time Mason, was a particularly severe blow to Kuskova, and she sharply rebuked him for his impatience, and for misunderstanding the needs of the revolution. Kuskova, 'K ukhodu A. I. Guchkova', *VN*, 3 May 1917, pp. 2–3.

25. Kuskova, 'Dnevnik', *VN*, 6 May 1917, p. 2.

26. Ibid., 7 May 1917, p. 3, and Kuskova, 'Proletaite i soediniaites'! *VN*, 19 May 1917, p. 2.

27. Kuskova, 'Dnevnik', *VN*, 28 May 1917, p. 2, and 31 May 1917, p. 1.

28. *VN*, 11 June 1917, p. 2.

29. On the Masonic–soviet connection, see Norton, 'Establishment of democracy'.

30. Kuskova, 'Dnevnik', *VN*, 18 June 1917, p. 3.

31. Kuskova, 'Tri linii', *VN*, 4 July 1917, p. 1.

32. Kuskova, 'Ubezhavshie', *VN*, 11 July 1917, p. 1.

33. Kuskova, 'Dnevnik', *VN*, 6 July 1917, p. 1.

34. Kuskova, 'Slovo skazano', *VN*, 7 July 1917, p. 1.

35. Kuskova, 'Prosim ob"iasnit', *VN*, 9 July 1917, p. 2.

36. Prokopovich, an eminent economist, was also a political Mason.

37. Kuskova, 'Petrogradskie pis'ma', *VN*, 22 July 1917, p. 1, and 23 July 1917, p. 2.

38. Kuskova, 'Na lozhnom puti', *VN*, 25 July 1917, p. 1.

39. Kuskova, 'Kadetskii s"ezd', *VN*, 29 July 1917, p.1.

40. Kuskova, 'Russkie koshmary', *VN*, 22 August 1917, p. 1, and 'Petrogradskie pis'ma', *VN*, 30 August 1917, p. 1. For the proceedings of the conference, which met in the Bolshoi Theatre, see *Gosudarstvennye soveshchaniia* (Moscow, 1930).

41. Kuskova, 'Petrogradskie pis'ma', *VN*, 30 August 1917, p. 1.

42. Ibid., 31 August 1917, p. 2.

43. Ibid.

44. Ibid., 1 September 1917, p. 1.

45. The date and circumstances of Kuskova's return to organized social democracy are obscure and perplexing. Contemporary evidence on the matter is scanty, while her own recollections are singularly unhelpful. Thus, she writes to Menshevik friend Vol'skii (2 July 1955, HIWRP, Vol'skii Collection, box 5): 'we [she and Prokopovich] joined again before some elections in 1917 (I do not remember what ones)'. That it was the Moscow Menshevik organization Kuskova joined (the second largest after Petrograd) is evident from E. Gurevich, 'Pobedim my', *VN*, 17 October 1917, p. 3.

46. *VN*, 7 September 1917, p. 2; and *Den'*, 7 September 1917, p. 3. For the Menshevik political configuration in this period, see Ziva Galili, *The Menshevik Leaders in the Russian Revolution* (Princeton, 1989), pp. 353–4.

47. Kuskova, 'Petrogradskie pis'ma', *VN*, 8 September 1917, p. 3.

48. Ibid., 10 September 1917, p. 3.

49. *VN*, 13 September 1917, p. 2.

50. P. N. Miliukov, *Istoriia vtoroi revoliutsii*, vol. 1, pt. 3 (Sofia, 1921), p. 37.
51. Held in the Aleksandrinskii Theatre, the Democratic Conference included 1775 representatives, about 165 of whom were cooperators, ibid., pp. 34, 37, 49; and V. V. Kabanov, *Oktiabr'skaia revoliutsiia i kooperatsiia (1917 g. – Mart 1919 g.)* (Moscow, 1973), p. 115. Kuskova's effort to promote liberal–radical solidarity at the conference is noted in A. V. Tyrkova-Williams, *From Liberty to Brest-Litovsk* (London, 1919), pp. 226–7.
52. Kuskova, 'Vtoroi den'', *VN*, 17 September 1917, p. 3. In point of fact, even the cooperators were divided, with a sizeable workers' group having seceded from the delegation over the issue of coalition. A. Sonev, 'At the crossroads of politics', *RC*, January 1918, p. 20.
53. On the creation of the Democratic Council, see *VN*, 22 September 1917, p. 2.
54. Kuskova, 'Na demokraticheskom soveshchanii', *VN*, 21 September 1917, p. 1.
55. Kuskova, 'Konets–nachalo', *VN*, 24 September 1917, p. 3. Kuskova's election to the Democratic Council (the only woman among twenty-four cooperative representatives), is reported in *VN*, 23 September 1917, p. 2.
56. That Kerenskii's new cabinet included only six Masons suggests that even Masonic solidarity was weakening.
57. Kuskova, 'Legkaia i trudnaia rabota', *VN*, 28 September 1917, p. 2.
58. Kuskova, 'Kooperatsiia i politika', *VN*, 29 September 1917, p. 1.
59. P. A. Garvi, 'Rabochaia kooperatsiia v pervye gody russkoi revoliutsii, 1917–1921', p. 13, undated manuscript in HIWRP, B. I. Nikolaevskii Collection, no. 19, box 2. A Menshevik labour organizer who opposed the kind of political activity Kuskova was advocating, Garvi was among those who erroneously interpreted her position as an attempt to create a separate cooperative party. His view is shared by at least two historians who make the point, explicitly or implicitly, in another context. See Elsie Terry Blanc, *Co-operative Movement in Russia* (New York, 1924), p. 151; and Catherine L. Salzman, 'Consumer societies and the consumer cooperative movement in Russia, 1897–1917' (PhD dissertation, University of Michigan, 1977), p. 457.
60. *RV*, 6 October 1917, p. 5.
61. Kuskova, 'Kooperativnomu s''ezdu', *VN*, 4 October 1917, p. 2.
62. *RV*, 6 October 1917, p. 5. A subsequent report identified Kuskova as a leader of the majority tendency. *RV*, 7 October 1917, p. 6.
63. *RV*, 7 October 1917, p. 6; and *VN*, 7 October 1917, p. 2. Salzman is obviously mistaken in maintaining that the idea of offering separate cooperative lists (which she attributes to the Kadet A. V. Merkulov) 'were firmly rejected by socialist cooperators'. 'Consumer societies', p. 457.
64. *VN*, 8 October 1917, p. 4.
65. *Soiuz potrebitelei*, 30 November 1917, p. 63, cited in Salzman, 'Consumer societies', p. 458. Also, Kabanov, *Oktiabr'skaia revoliutsiia*, p. 119.
66. Gurevich, 'Pobedim my', p. 3, See also *RV*, 18 October 1917, p. 4.
67. The decision on Kuskova's expulsion was taken on 11 October. Her letter did not reach the Moscow bureau until four days later. Gurevich, 'Pobedim my', p. 3.

68. This episode made so little impression on Kuskova that, when recalling it years later, she completely misremembered the date and the circumstances. Letter to Vishniak, 8 May 1957, HIWRP, Vishniak Collection, box 5, folder b.

69. The Council met in the Mariinskii Palace with an eventual membership of 555 people. I. F. Slavin, 'Krizis vlasti v sentiabre 1917 g. i obrazovanie Vremennogo soveta respubliki (Predparlament)', *Istoricheskie zapiski*, no. 61 (1957), pp. 55.

70. *RV*, 13 October 1917, p. 4. Kuskova had been reluctant to use force on principle; but she had also worried about the reaction of the army and the 'bolshevized and already unbridled' masses, 'V chem zhe vykhod?', *VN*, 12 August 1917, p. 2.

71. *RV*, 13 October 1917, p. 4.

72. N. N. Sukhanov, *Zapiski o revoliutsii*, vol. 6 (Berlin, 1923), p. 266; I. V. Gessen, 'V dvukh vekakh', *Arkhiv russkoi revoliutsii*, vol. 22 (1937), p. 376; and Miliukov, *Istoriia*, p. 144. Gessen and Miliukov's sentiments were echoed by Kadet colleagues P. A. Buryshkin (*Moskva kupecheskaia* (New York, 1954), p. 346), and Tyrkova-Williams (*Liberty to Brest-Litovsk*, p. 233).

73. *RV*, 14 October 1917, p. 4, 17 October 1917, p. 3, and 19 October 1917, p. 3. See also Miliukov, *Istoriia*, pp. 144–8. Support for the proposal ranged from the Social Democratic Unity (*Edinstvo*) group and the Peasants' Union on the left to the trade-industrial group and the Cossacks on the right.

74. Kuskova, 'V kom zhe opora?', *VN*, 19 October 1917, p. 2.

75. For some of the lists, see *VN*, 15 October 1917, p. 4, 19 October 1917, p. 4, and 25 October 1917, p. 3.

76. Serving as a member (the only female) of the Preparliament's Defence Committee, Kuskova was actively involved in assessing the country's fighting capacity. 'Nakanune oktiabr'skogo perevorota. Vopros o voine i mire. Otchety sekretnykh zasedanii Vremennogo soveta respubliki', *Byloe*, no. 12 (6) (1918), pp. 37–8.

77. *RV*, 25 October 1917, p. 4.

78. *Izvestiia Petrogradskogo soveta rabochikh i sol'datskikh deputatov*, 26 October 1917, pp. 3–4.

79. Kuskova recounts her activities of 25–26 October in 'Noch'', *VN*, 28 October 1917, p. 2, the first published eyewitness account of the Bolshevik seizure of power, and letter to Mel'gunov, 22 August 1938, BLPES, Mel'gunov Archive, New Material, box JJ, packet 29. Her final hours in the Preparliament are described in V. D. Nabokov, 'Vremennoe pravitel'stvo', *Arkhiv russkoi revoliutsii*, vol. 1 (1921), p. 85.

80. While she remained in Russia, and also after her expulsion from the country in 1922, Kuskova would oppose the Bolsheviks' seizure of power, optimistic until the very end of her life (in 1958) that the process of democratization begun in February 1917 would one day be resumed.

81. Although S. V. Panina served in the government as Assistant Minister of Education and as Assistant Minister of Welfare, no woman was ever appointed to a full ministerial post.

6 Mariia L. Bochkareva and the Russian amazons of 1917

Richard Abraham

We are all familiar with those entertainments which bring on a troupe of dancing women when the action begins to drag. All too often they are silent. And so it is in many of the accounts, on celluloid (and now magnetic tape) as well as in print, of the story of the Russian Provisional Government of 1917. We must all have seen those pictures of its female defenders giggling like oversized girl scouts on Palace Square on the morning of the Bolshevik triumph. For those of us with a Communist Party formation, the only permitted eye-witness account until the death of the 'Great Helmsman' was that of John Reed. Reed was, of course, a socialist. More to the point, he was accompanied on his travels through Russia by Louise Bryant, who may not be recognizable as a sister to all varieties of contemporary Anglo-Saxon feminism, but who had a strong sense of fellow-feeling for Russian women of widely differing political views.

Reed caught up with the women soldiers of the Provisional Government just as the Bolsheviks were about to storm the Winter Palace. A young officer described the disposition of forces to him:

'The Women's Battalion decided to remain loyal to the Government.'
'Are the women soldiers in the Palace?'
'Yes, they are in the back rooms, where they won't be hurt if any trouble comes.' He sighed. 'It is a great responsibility.'

At the conclusion of the siege, when Read and his companions had allegedly narrowly escaped being shot as provocateurs, they asked about the fate of the women soldiers:

'Oh – the women!' He laughed. 'They were all huddled up in a back room. We had a terrible time deciding what to do with them – many were in hysterics, and so on. So finally we marched them up to the Finland Station and put them on a train for Levashovo, where they have a camp . . .'

And in a dry appendix, Reed disposed of the scandal created by anti-Bolshevik allegations that the women had been raped.[1]

124

In a fine analysis of the Bolshevik Revolution published on its fiftieth anniversary, Robert Daniels anticipated some of the findings elaborated by Alexander Rabinowitch nine years later. Yet Daniels' *Red October* contains the following deplorable section on the women soldiers:

Cadets replaced the regular guard at the railroad stations, and the garrison of the Winter Palace was strengthened by a bicycle battalion and, of all things, the 'Women's Battalion of Death'.

This curious unit of bourgeois girls was recruited by Kerensky after the Russian rout in July with the idea of shaming the Russian men into fighting better. They had done nothing but sit in a Petrograd suburb, however, until they were called in to help defend the government on the morning of October 24. 'I saw these unfortunates when they passed under the windows of the French Embassy', wrote Ambassador Noulens, 'on the way to take up their position. They marched in step, affecting a martial spirit which was obviously contradicted by their plump figures and their feminine waddle.'[2]

Quite apart from its uncritical recycling of Noulens' manifest anti-feminist animus, and Daniels' redundant give-away phrase, 'of all things', this passage is riddled with factual inaccuracies.

In August 1970, I found Boris Solonevich's *Zhenshchina s vintovkoi* in Nicholas Martyanov's shop in New York. I was attracted by its lurid cover, straightforward Russian and modest price. Written in girl-scout magazine style, it moves from heavy politics to the hilarious story of how the women coped with male uniforms and back to individual personal stories, often tragic but sometimes heroic. The story it told contradicted the version given by Daniels at almost every point. The 'Women's Death Battalion' (actually only a *kommanda*) had already been disbanded before the siege of the Winter Palace and while some of its members did take part in that event they did so as members of another women's unit. The 'Women's Death Battalion' included women of every social class, being commanded by a peasant, Mariia Leont'evna Bochkareva (née Frolkova), who had already served with distinction in male units at the front. Bochkareva emerges from the narrative as an authentic Russian *podvizhnitsa* (self-sacrificing heroine). Her unit was formed in May and, after confronting Bolshevized soldiers in Petrograd, had received the blessings of Mrs Pankhurst before setting out for the Western Front. There, it had fought competently and bravely, suffering casualties and taking German prisoners. It was disbanded in September when it became clear that it had failed to transform the psychology of the male soldiers and in the face of growing Bolshevik threats to the lives of the women. The women's sexuality was also treated as a source of strength on some occasions and not exclusively as a debilitating weakness. The book claims to be not a novel but the slightly fictionalized reminiscences of one of the soldiers, who signs herself proudly, '*poruchik* (lieutenant) of the Russian Army, Nina Krylova, Cavalier of the Order of St George the Martyr Triumphant'.

What really made me sit up, however, was Nina Krylova's outspoken feminism. While the world's press was then (1970) saluting or reviling Kate Millett and Germaine Greer for their moral courage in developing feminist theses, Nina Krylova and her comrades had allegedly asserted most of the same things in Russia in 1917, and she had insisted on recording them (over the vociferous objections of her own menfolk) in Brussels under German occupation in the early 1940s! If she was to be believed, the Russian amazons had not been benighted instruments of reaction, but conscious protagonists of a progressive social force representing half or more of humanity. Here is an example:

But the [February] Revolution had already happened. Woman had won for herself rights of which she had been deprived during the course of millenia – THE RIGHTS OF AN EQUAL MEMBER OF SOCIETY. Woman would never again permit her rights to education, to her own life, to her own heart, to the opportunity of giving birth when SHE wanted to, to construct a life according to her own plans, and not according to the plans of a man. And the world would soon see who was morally superior: man with his simplistic crude mind and callous soul, or woman, with her understanding, sensitivity and humanity.

The passage ends ironically, conceding that women might after all want their menfolk to be able to carry them over the threshold (the only remaining reason for women to prize male physical strength). It is followed by a poignant footnote:

All my menfolk, Zhora [her husband], Goria [her son] and even my friend, the writer Boris Solonevich, wanted me to throw this passage out of the book, since it supposedly slowed down the dynamic of the story and so on. We know these male tricks: the slightest pinprick to male vanity and 'chuck it out'! I insisted that it went into the book.[3]

It was not just male and Marxist prejudice that made me wary of using Krylova's memoir as a source. To begin with, it contains a number of extremely obvious factual errors. Thus, at a meeting held to recruit women volunteers allegedly at the Cinizelli Circus on 21 May 1917, we find Kerenskii (already Prime Minister!) delivering the 'rebellious slaves' speech he had actually given a month earlier.[4] Solonevich (and Krylova?) seemed to be trying a little too hard to extort the reader's sympathy. Krylova's introduction suggests that the book was written so that her fifteen-year-old son could explain to his Belgian classmates how he came to be the son of 'two Russian officers', while Solonevich's footnotes suggest that she was then deported by the Nazis and killed by

Allied bombing, while he himself completed the book in a Belgian prison awaiting deportation to the USSR as an alleged collaborator. I feared that Solonevich the writer might have over-dramatized his subject. For example, the narrative begins with Krylova listening to Lenin at the Finland Station on 3 April 1917. During the ensuing sidewalk debate, she meets a wounded volunteer soldier, who turns out to be her future husband, *and* Mariia Bochkareva, her future commanding officer. I already disliked Solonevich's novel *Zagovor Krasnogo Bonaparta*, perhaps for giving Stalin a rational motive for his purge of the Soviet officer corps.[5]

When I began to prepare my book on A. F. Kerenskii for the press in 1982, I quickly located Bochkareva's own book (as told to Isaac Don Levine), *Yashka, My Life as Peasant, Exile and Soldier*, the reports of Emmeline Pankhurst's visit to Russia, Mariia Bocharnikova's article, 'Boi v Zimncm dvortse', and reread the memoirs of a number of the best women observers of the events of 1917. Ironically, it was probably George Katkov who did most to provoke my interest in the women soldiers. In 1980, Katkov, whose work on the February Revolution had earned him great respect, published a sequel entitled polemically, *Russia 1917. The Kornilov Affair. Kerensky and the break-up of the Russian Army*. This was a work that anyone writing on Kerenskii was bound to confront. The formation of the 'Women's Death Battalion' and of some of the national units were amongst the responses of Kerenskii and his military advisers to the break-up of the army.[6]

When I mentioned to Dr Katkov that Bochkareva has published an account which not only describes the rise and fall of the 'Women's Death Battalion' but also comments directly on relations between Kerenskii and Kornilov, he warned me against believing Isaac Don Levine since he had been a friend of Kerenskii. The trouble with this was that Bochkareva's account is extremely critical of Kerenskii, prompting Levine himself to confess in the introduction that, 'The reader gets a picture of Kerensky in action that completely effaces all that has hitherto been said of this tragic but typical product of the Russian *intelligentsia*.'[7] What Levinc means is that this picture 'completely effaces all that has hitherto been said' *by Levine* about Kerenskii. None of Kerenskii's enemies can have been the least bit surprised at it, especially as Bochkareva was a prominent 'Kornilovite' who accompanied the Supreme Commander-in-Chief on his crucial visit to the Prime Minister on 10 August 1917.[8] In other respects, the book confirmed and amplified for me Nina Krylova's description of the creation, achievements and failures of the 'Women's Death Battalion', and its commander's relations with leading Russian personalities and with

Mrs Emmeline Pankhurst. This is not surprising as Solonevich acknowledges that he consulted *Yashka* before the publication of *Zhenshchina s vintovkoi*.[9]

Bochkareva's book is fascinating for quite other reasons as well. It is a biography, which describes the life of a Russian peasant as she escapes from a beating father to a beating husband to a beating lover. Neither before nor since have I encountered an almost first-hand account of the existence of a pre-revolutionary Russian peasant woman which presents such an unvarnished picture of her existence. It describes, for example, two attempts (one successful) by men in authority to extort sexual favours from her.[10]

Part 2 of Bochkareva's book describes her discovery of her military vocation, her ultimately successful attempts to enlist as a soldier 'by the grace of the Tsar' and her distinguished military service. The final section of the book relates her adventures following the October Revolution when she eluded Bolshevist soldiers, paid a visit to Kornilov and the Volunteer Army and finally left Russia to seek foreign military intervention.[11]

Ever since 1917, feminist radicals have been hostile towards Bochkareva. A good example is Sylvia Pankhurst, who, in describing her own mother's visit to Russia, gives short shrift to the Russian amazons: 'She saw the ill-starred companies of women, fitly named the "Battalions of Death", paraded for the Front under their peasant leader.'[12]

The reports of Mrs Pankhurst's visit to Russia and related material, which appeared in *Britannia* in the summer and autumn of 1917, are unambiguous in supporting military values and in asserting that women can demonstrate them as well as men. The first Russian soldier whose photograph appears is not Bochkareva but a Mlle Kudatgora, dressed in cossack uniform, who 'has received the Russian Military Order of Valour'. In a subsequent issue, it is reported that, 'Mrs Pankhurst regards Mme Botchkareva as one of the most remarkable characters she has ever met both for her single-minded determination and innate courage.' In a laconic telegram, Mrs Pankhurst confirmed that the 'Women's Death Battalion' did indeed fight bravely and successfully at the front: 'First Women's Battalion number two hundred and fifty took place of retreating troops. In counter attack made one hundred prisoners including two officers. Only five weeks training. Their leader wounded. Have earned undying fame, moral effect great. More women soldiers training, also marines.' This assessment was, of course, designed to raise morale among British women assisting the war effort, but a memorandum by Bernard Pares intended for the more sceptical

readers of British Military Intelligence substantially confirms the factual
aspect of this telegram.[13]

The 'as told to' memoirs of Krylova and Bochkareva substantially
confirm and enlarge this brief account of the battle at Smorgon, close to
the present Minsk–Vilnius highway, on 7–11 July 1917. Krylova enjoys
relating the story of the German officer ashamed at the discovery that he
has been captured by women, and swearing, 'Teufel! Donnerwetter!
Gefangen durch Frauen! Unmöglich! Teufel!' Eventually they have to
tie his hands to prevent him from making away with himself. Bochkareva supplies an important qualification, however. While she confirms that the women endured bombardment and returned fire
effectively from their trenches, she claims that their attack was reinforced by some 75 officers and 300 men from neighbouring units after
the majority of men in those units had refused to support their attack.
Their triumph was therefore that of a mixed gender formation.[14]

The Stavka (Army GHQ) communiqués describing this action convey
the barest minimum information about the women's role in the action.
The first one does not mention them at all. Mrs Pankhurst's enthusiasm
for this first military engagement of a women's unit in modern history
was evidently not at first shared by General Brusilov. The second communiqué published on 12 July indicates the preoccupations of Stavka:

To the South-West of Dvinsk our units, after a heavy artillery bombardment,
occupied German positions on both sides of the Dvinsk–Vilno railway. After
that, whole divisions, without any pressure from the enemy, spontaneously
retreated to their original trenches. Several units refused to carry out military
orders during the battle. Units of the 24th. Division, The Tul'skii, Lokhvitskii
and Surazhskii regiments and the Death Battalion acted heroically. As on other
fronts, the gallantry and heavy losses of the officers are noticeable.

Only an acute reader would have known that women had taken part at
all.

A supplementary report makes it clear that this was still a success for
the Western front at a time when the South–West front, the scene of
Kerenskii's main offensive on 18 June, was reeling under a German
counter-attack. Reporting the capture of 2,000 German prisoners during the attack at Smorgon, a military communiqué adds a piquant detail:
'The prisoners have a depressed look, displaying shocking hostility
(porazhaias' ozloblennost'iu). Among the prisoners is a whole battalion
with its commander, band and medical personnel.' The final reports on
those involved in this action add further intriguing details:

The party of wounded in the battles in the direction of Vilno report the extreme ferocity of the Germans, who preferred death to capture. This is the explanation for the relatively small number of healthy prisoners. The field of battle was littered with German corpses.

The Women's Battalion, which received its baptism of fire, also suffered. The wounded women soldiers have been conveyed to Minsk.[15]

One cannot help wondering whether the Germans did not fight harder, and resent capture more fiercely, because they knew that they were being tested against women.

An account by the Belorussian Kamenshchykau illustrates the cynical tactics used by Bolshevik agitators to discredit the battalion, ensuring that its military success would remain a political failure. Kamenshchykau misdates the battle, and does not read like an eye-witness:

From the morning of 6 June, a preparatory artillery bombardment was made on the German positions in the direction of Vilno in the area of the 10th. Army on the Western Front. To encourage the soldiers, who were reluctant to go on the offensive, Kerenskii sent the 'famed' women's battalion of Bocharova [sic]. When the artillery preparation was finished on the morning of 10 June, the order was given to storm the German trenches, but the soldiers demanded that Bocharova's battalion should go over the top first. How great was the pleasure of the soldiers, when, after the first artillery rounds from the Germans, the 'famed' battalion broke off their attack. With cries and screams, the 'gallant' women soldiers scattered among the bushes, and the soldiers had to search them out in the woods. Only after darkness was Bocharova's battalion reassembled in one place.

After that the soldiers declared that they would not go on the offensive, for if the screams of Bocharova's 'gallant' battalion could not break the German defences, then it was obviously beyond the strength of simple soldiers like themselves.[16]

Similarly, John Reed alleges that the soldiers of the First Petrograd Women's Battalion hid in back rooms throughout the siege of the Winter Palace by Bolshevik forces on the evening of 25 October 1917. One has to ask why, if they were such cowards, they did not all go straight home? (The normally scrupulous Leninist historian, V. I. Startsev suggests that this is exactly what they did, but this is contradicted by too much direct testimony.) No one seriously denies that these women were among the last loyal defenders of the Provisional Government of 1917 and few now deny that that government was a good deal more likely to hand over power to a democratically elected parliament than those who opposed it in October 1917. Yet we are asked by stereotype-ridden films and secondary literature to believe that the women who defended the Winter Palace were misguided, stupid and cowardly, and perhaps lucky to avoid the sexual violation they had thoughtlessly provoked (or which they groundlessly feared), once the siege was over.

We do at least know that they did not huddle in back rooms all the time, for on 24 October, David Soskice, a member of Kerenskii's staff saw them patrolling the area outside the Winter Palace. 'We saw the Women's Battalion regulating the movements of the crowds and arresting anyone who showed resistance.'

Both Krylova and Bocharnikova give vivid and virtually identical accounts of the siege, describing the defence of one of the main entrances of the Winter Palace on to Palace Square, until their unit of some thirty women, several of them veterans from Bochkareva's Battalion, was finally ordered to retire into the Palace. Bocharnikova claims that the women were the last to resist: 'when on the barricade, the cadets had already laid down their arms, the women volunteers still held on'. General Knox, who concerned himself with the women's safety, was slightly sceptical of Bolshevik charges that 'they had resisted to the last at the Palace, fighting desperately with bombs and revolvers', but he was convinced that they had fought as long as possible.[17]

Before I return to the evidence relating to the treatment of women soldiers in captivity in the Winter Palace, Levashovo and elsewhere, and the way in which this has overshadowed subsequent discussion of the successes and failures of the Russian amazons of 1917, I would like to indicate the scope of the movement headed by Bochkareva, the way in which relations between women of different social classes were reflected in it, and the way they interacted with an increasingly Bolshevist mood amongst the male units that surrounded them.

On the 8–9 August 1917, Bochkareva travelled to Moscow, where, as she says, 'I had been invited to review the local Women's Battalion, organized in imitation of mine. There were many such battalions formed all over Russia.' In his report to the British War Office, Bernard Pares described the recruitment of women as part of a more general effort to recruit volunteers to replace demoralized conscript units. By early August, there were apparently some 50,000 men and 4,000 women volunteers known to the semi-official All-Russian Central Volunteer Committee which he consulted. Bochkareva suggests that there were about 1,500 women in the Moscow Battalion, but the atmosphere was not conducive to careful counting. The Moscow women's immodest dress, make-up and casual attitude provoked her to a dressing-down. The meeting degenerated and threatened to become violent. According to Bochkareva herself, only the personal intervention of General Verkhovskii, Commander-in-Chief Moscow, prevented violence.[18]

At some point in the summer or early autumn, the First Petrograd Women's Battalion was formed. This was the unit some of whose members took part in the defence of the Winter Palace on the night of the

Bolshevik coup. According to its sole member to publish an account, who bore the confusingly familiar name, Mariia *Bocharnikova*, the battalion suffered only inconsequential losses during that engagement (one killed, one injured), though a few of the volunteers escaped and disappeared afterwards. The head-count taken when they were finally disarmed by Red Guards at Levashovo came up with 600 volunteers in four companics of 150 each. Louise Bryant interviewed some of them after the October Revolution and discovered that one had been recruited in Mogilev. On 11 July, *Novoe vremia* had reported that the women's volunteer movement was making great strides. The Ekaterinburg depot had already sent 700 women to Moscow and Petrograd while the Tashkent depot had enrolled 200. A British press report reprinted in *Britannia* also mentioned six-foot tall women in the marines (*Morskoi Ekipazh*) and we have already encountered Mlle Kudatgora (the name sounds Georgian), while the British nurse, Florence Farmborough confirms that 'a woman soldier, or boy soldier, was no uncommon sight in the Russian army', having treated two for wounds herself.[19]

Oddly enough, there is greater uncertainty about the numbers of the most famous of all the women's units, the Mariia Bochkareva Death Command itself. To explain why this is so, we must bear in mind the novel and unprecedented institutional framework within the armed forces established as a result of the February Revolution, for conflict over this almost terminated the existence of the Battalion before it could leave for the front.

During the decisive phase of the February Revolution of 1917 (27 February–1 March), a critical situation arose in the Petrograd garrison. The vast majority of the rank and file soldiers joined the revolution while the vast majority of the officers remained loyal to their oaths to the Tsar. The impromptu Soldier Section of the Petrograd Soviet dictated 'Order No. 1' to the Menshevik lawyer, N. D. Sokolov. Designed to cover a temporary emergency in a geographically limited area remote from the front, it was published in *Izvestiia* and then broadcast to the whole army. Attempts by officers at the front to question its authenticity or relevance simply increased its authority (and that of the soviets) with the men. Essentially, 'Order No. 1' transformed the hierarchical and harshly disciplined army of the Tsar into an egalitarian and democratic citizen militia in which orders were replaced by peaceful persuasion. Moderate socialists in the Provisional Government and the soviets hoped that it would be consistent with military efficiency, but both Bolsheviks and conservatives saw it as undermining the cohesion of the Russian Army. The Provisional Government's conservative first War and Naval Minister, A. I. Guchkov, was no more successful at mitigat-

ing the destructive (or revolutionary) impact of 'Order No. 1' than its
socialist second Minister, A. F. Kerenskii, over whose signature a modi-
fied version of the order, renamed The Declaration of the Rights of the
Soldier, appeared on 11 May 1917.[20]

Bochkareva considered 'Order No. 1' to be prejudicial to army discipline, as serious a matter in her eyes as pacifism or cowardice. For her
the formation of a women's battalion capable of putting the male
soldiers to shame was incompatible with the committee system introduced by 'Order No. 1'. She had no intention of permitting the committee system in her unit. It is not surprising then, that her project soon
won the support of Duma President Rodzianko and the new Supreme
Commander-in-Chief, General Brusilov. She describes how Kerenskii,
the ink barely dry from signing The Declaration of the Rights of the
Soldier, granted her unit an entirely illegal exemption from it. She
suggests that a crucial consideration for the socialist war minister was
our old friend, the double standard!

He told me that he had heard about me and was interested in my idea. I then
outlined to him the purpose of the project, saying that there would be no
committees, but regular discipline in the battalion of women.

Kerensky listened impatiently. He had evidently made up his mind on the
subject. There was only one point of which he was not sure. Would I be able to
maintain a high standard of morality in the organization? He would allow me to
recruit it immediately if I made myself answerable for the conduct and reputation of the women. I pledged myself to do so. And it was all settled. I was
granted the authority there and then to form a unit under the name of The First
Russian Women's Battalion of Death.

As Bochkareva was soon to find, things were far from 'settled'.[21]

Still, on the basis of these assurances, Bochkareva began recruiting
volunteers between the ages of 18 and 35. To be on the safe side, she
insisted on statements of authorization from parents or guardians of
women under 21 and made them all sign a document renouncing their
rights under the Declaration of the Rights of the Soldier. Bochkareva
says that 1,500 volunteered after her first meeting; Krylova, writing two
decades later, gives a figure of 3,500. Perhaps there were several meetings since they agree that 2,000 were enrolled by their first parade in
barracks on 26 May at which Bochkareva was assisted by instructors
from the Volynskii Guards Regiment. They were divided into two battalions and further subdivided into companies and platoons.[22]

Bochkareva then began to weed out the weaker sisters, having all the
women's hair shaven and confiscating all personal property but bras-
sieres, giving no time off and not sparing the pronoun ty (the intimate
'thou' forbidden by the Declaration) nor traditional Russian mat (i.e.

cursing, which was also prohibited). Many of the women, encouraged no doubt by those Bochkareva saw as Bolsheviks, but who may as well have been SRs or Mensheviks, soon repented of their signatures on Bochkareva's illegal pledge. The result was a mutiny. It is hardly surprising that Bochkareva's and Krylova's accounts diverge sharply in their description of what must have been a traumatic event for both of them. Both, however, agree that she spoke to the mutineers in her usual sharp tone and commanded the battalion to split into supporters and opponents. According to Bochkareva, only some 300 remained loyal to her. Krylova suggests a more even split, with 900 remaining loyal to the commander. Bochkareva says that she then left the barracks and offered to resign, while Krylova has her cursing the rebels and throwing them out into the night at gunpoint! On the numbers involved, the British sources tend to support Bochkareva, reporting 200 parading at St Isaac's before their departure for the front, while Pankhurst's telegram mentions 250, a figure confirmed by Bryant. A further discrepancy arises from the fact that Bochkareva claims that when the battalion was joined by 375 men at the battle of Smorgon, the combined force numbered 1,000, while Krylova describes the unit as still functioning after losing 100 killed and 192 wounded in the battle. Until Soviet military archives are available for inspection we will never be certain. The outcome of the mutiny entirely satisfied Bochkareva, who shared Lenin's preference for quality over quantity. Kerenskii gave verbal support to the mutineers but, faced by Bochkareva's obduracy, let her get away to the front on 29 June with her by now clearly illegally constituted unit.[23]

The numbers of women soldiers recruited by the Provisional Government in a few short weeks during the summer of 1917 justify the description of this campaign as a 'movement', i.e. a socially significant phenomenon, testifying to the willingness of substantial numbers of young Russian women to subject themselves to the most rigorous and potentially fatal examination of their equality with men. Bolshevik success in mobilizing women is legendary, and it is true that the Bolsheviks mobilized far more women, 66,000 in 1920, which represented a much larger proportion of the 6 million strong Red Army, than Bochkareva's followers did of the 10–13 million strong Russian Army of 1917. However, we must remember that Bolshevik recruitment took place over a far longer period. The disparity wanes further when we bear in mind that only a small minority of the Bolshevik women soldiers (about 1,500) actually served in combat roles, earning, for example, only 100 decorations as compared with 15,000 for men.[24]

Louise Bryant, the closest of our informants to the Bolsheviks, simply writes off the experience of the Provisional Government's women soldiers (*with the possible exception of Bochkareva herself*) as irrelevant (or perhaps a negative example) to the Soviet government:

Women in Russia have always fought in the army. In my opinion the principal reason for the failure of the woman's regiment was segregation. There will always be fighting women in Russia, but they will fight side by side with men and not as a sex. Botchkarova herself fought several years before she organised the Death Battalion at the instigation of Kerensky and Rodzianko.

While I do not share Bryant's view that the regiment failed, it is true that some Russian women had always fought as *individuals*, as they would again in the Second World War. What Bryant fails to note is the way in which Bochkareva's unit placed the question of fighting women on the agenda for society, and for women in particular. Many male observers of the events of 1917 either ignore or mock the women soldiers. Almost all the women observers were fascinated by them. On the distant Romanian front, Florence Farmborough concluded her account of the impact of the news of the formation of the women's battalion with the words, 'We sisters were of course thrilled to the core.' When General Knox was begged by the women defenders of the Winter Palace to enroll them in the British Army, he gave a most curious reason for his refusal: 'I told them that Englishwomen were not allowed to fight, and that they would be jealous if their Russian sisters were permitted to go to the front.'

According to Bochkareva herself, Lenin and Trotskii in person asked her to assist them after the October Revolution, which suggests that they respected her ability to mobilize women even though they disliked her politics. Unlike Kerenskii and Rodzianko, they had no religious prejudices about chastity so segregation was irrelevant to them. I have little information about women in the White armies. It may be significant that one of the women who served in women's units subsequently joined the White armies as a nursing sister, but Krylova says that 'I know that many of our soldiers later bravely fought in the ranks of the Volunteer Army, but there were no more separate women's units'.[25]

To what extent were the Provisional Government's women soldiers 'bourgeois girls' as the popular view has it? Meriel Buchanan insists that 'in a spirit of high-hearted self-sacrifice the women of Russia joined hands', and goes on to stress the non-class or perhaps cross-class nature of their undertaking: '"When the soldiers see their wives and daughters fighting, surely they will be struck by shame and follow us," so the women argued, and peasant girls, women of the middle class and of the nobility cut their hair short, put on uniform and went through all the training of regular soldiers.'[26]

Krylova is particularly interesting on this aspect of Bochkareva's battalion:

It would be difficult to say immediately, whom these twenty centuries of young women comprised. As I have already written, there were not a few titled personages, very many women university students ... there were also many nurses. I don't know what percentage, but there were also many simple widows, whose husbands had perished at the front. It would have been difficult to find peasant girls in Petrograd, but there was certainly at least one century of soldiers, whose faces and figures so much resembled Bochkareva's, that it would have been difficult to doubt their peasant origins.

It was curious that several girls and ladies of wealthy or aristocratic (*znatnykh*) families, found themselves in the battalion together with their former cooks and chambermaids. Thus a truly democratic battalion emerged . . .[27]

General Knox, who was in a position to know, asserts that 'these women were volunteers recruited from all classes, but mostly from the *Intelligentsia*'. Perhaps the most incontrovertible testimony to the presence of working-class women amongst the volunteers comes from Bryant, who tracked down a number of working-class members of the First Petrograd Women's Battalion after the Bolshevik coup, including Kira Volakettnova, a poor dressmaker, and Anna Shub, a Jew from the Pale.[28]

Of course, the women volunteers were by no means an exact microcosm of Russian young women in 1917. Krylova reports that 90 per cent of the Women's Death Battalion were literate, a much higher figure than for the younger female population as a whole, even in Petrograd. In addition, 50 per cent had secondary education, virtually a monopoly of those who might reasonably be called 'bourgeois' or at least 'petit-bourgeois', while a full 25 per cent were (or had been) university students, generally indicative of upper bourgeois status. In addition, thirty women were already Cavaliers of the Order of St George before they enrolled as soldiers by virtue of their service at the front as nurses. Within the battalion, class differences may have been ignored, but caste soon emerged as a major factor in the hierarchy. As Krylova puts it: 'It is true that the chancelry was temporarily in the hands of elderly officers from the War Ministry, but we had to establish internal order ourselves. So it is not surprising that soldiers from military families, as for example I, were soon promoted to positions of command.' These women included Krylova, the daughter of a colonel, 'Tasia' Dubrovskaya, the daughter of a general, Princess Tatueva, daughter of a Georgian aristocratic family, and Magdalina Skrydlova, daughter of a famous naval hero of the Russo-Turkish War of 1878 and a less successful

Commander-in-Chief Pacific Fleet during the Russo-Japanese War, who used his influence to secure supplies for the women during periods away from the front.[29] These distinctions made themselves felt at moments of crisis. During the mutiny over the committee system, Krylova reports that almost all the promoted women remained loyal to Bochkareva. Bochkareva herself describes the loyal rank and file as follows: 'Most of the remaining women were peasants like myself, illiterate but very devoted to Mother Russia. All of them but one were under thirty-five years of age. The exception was Orlova, who was forty, but of an unusually powerful constitution.' Krylova's account of the mutiny suggests that it was set off by visitors to the barracks who were workers rather than by intellectuals; Bochkareva's description of the mutineers as *'Piterskaia svoloch''* (Petrograd scum) is unfortunately lacking in sociological precision.[30]

Bryant also describes a moment of incipient class conflict in the history of the First Petrograd Women's Battalion. According to Bocharnikova, only the NCOs (*unter-ofitsery*) were women in the battalion, which was joined by a woman officer (*zhenshchina-praporshchik*) in the Winter Palace. (If Nina Krylova was indeed a genuine historical personality, this can only have been her.) Bryant relates the words of Anna Shub, then in Bolshevik custody:

Tears welled in her eyes. 'I felt as if I myself could die of shame. I didn't know what to do. And then, just before the Winter Palace fell, one of the aristocrats of the Death Battalion came in and asked us to go down and join the Cossacks to fight the revolution.'

'I am a Jew,' said Anna, 'and I come from within the Pale. Liberty is dearer than life to me. And I . . . I was actually asked to do this thing!'

This should not be taken too literally, not least because the cossacks left, as we shall see, before the women were involved in serious fighting. To summarize on the basis of admittedly very fragmentary evidence, one might conclude that the noble objective of creating democratic women's military formations was little more successful than the subsequent 'democratic counter-revolution'. What did emerge were units commanded, in the main, by women members of hereditary military families, fully supported by only a small proportion of the most pious and patriotic lower-class women, many of them mourning widows. Bryant was therefore correct in concluding that 'class struggle permeated everything and it hurled the women's regiments into the maelstrom with everything else.'[31]

I have argued in this chapter that the Russian women soldiers of 1917 set themselves not one but *two* important objectives. Perhaps only a minority of them were conscious feminists when they enrolled, but visits from figures such as Mrs Pankhurst and consciousness-raising sessions from Nina Krylova and her schoolfriend Lelia Kolesova must have raised their awareness of feminism; Krylova offers a number of intriguing examples of this which foreshadow comments by famous Anglo-Saxon feminists. They set out to prove that women could be good soldiers, that is, that women could compete with men in an arena which men have regarded as their exclusive terrain since the onset of patriarchy. I suggest that the evidence supports the contention that these Russian women succeeded on behalf of women everywhere in this objective, but that they have been robbed of this success by contemporary and subsequent commentators for politically sectarian as well as macho motives. Undeniably, they failed in their second and principal objective. They had almost no effect at all on the mentality of men, irrespective of whether the men supported or opposed them, providing a cautionary tale for women who seriously believe that chivalry can significantly modify male behaviour.

To begin with the exceptions that prove the rule, we must consider the heroic conduct of the 350 (Bochkareva's figure) Russian men who joined her battalion at the battle of Smorgon. Apparently, they demonstrated both gallantry and chivalry. The question is, was this a significant *modification* of their behaviour? Weren't these men dying for a chance to behave like this, a chance denied them by the majority of the men in their own units? General Knox demonstrated great courage and chivalry by going in person to Smolny to demand the release of the women captives by the Military Revolutionary Committee, not least by pleading for their safety with someone he described as 'a repulsive individual of Semitic type'. Yet, he was only too glad of an opportunity to give some Russian officers a dressing-down, 'telling them that no nation except the Russian had ever allowed its women to fight, and certainly the British nation never would'.[32] Not much sign of modification here.

Their German enemies certainly gave the women no quarter, though Krylova claims that,

the deaths of our soldiers were experienced . . . much more sharply by men in the rear. Protopresbyter Shabashev later told me that he had to send many of our battalion on their way.

Our women died without groans or complaints, if anything more quietly than the men soldiers. But the impression they made was even more shattering . . .

Father Shabashev remembered the death of Elena Nedzvedskaia, who had received 28 wounds, with lively emotion. 'They killed a child, a little girl (*devochka*) clothed in army uniform and "legally" recognized as a soldier . . .'

Florence Farmborough claims that three wounded women from Bochkareva's battalion were treated by her unit. She found them 'sadly
shocked'. There are even more unpleasant possibilities. Krylova reports
that eight women were missing in action, presumed blown to pieces.[33].
In 1983, when I was considering a book on this subject, I came across an
anthology of First World War photographs assembled by a collective of
West German art students, including a photograph captioned 'Russian
woman soldier'. It was a virtually pornographic photograph of a woman
naked below the waist and with torn military uniform above it.

The men Bochkareva really hoped to influence were the pacifist or
'Bolshevized' rank and file of the Russian Army, as she made crystal
clear in her Manifesto: 'You, the valiant warriors, our soldiers of free
Russia, you who have retained the sense of honour, of shame, and of
courage in your hearts. We turn to you. When will you raise your
powerful voice and finally silence the cowardly lips of shameful Russian
jackals, dressed in soldiers uniform?' When she confronted rebellious
soldiers face to face, she usually began by talking to them as a fellow
veteran, but if they persisted, she lashed them with contempt. All the
sources agree that this method of dealing with the men was almost
totally unsuccessful. The women were mocked and threats were made to
their honour and their lives. The windows of their barracks were
smashed. Bolshevized soldiers did everything they could to dissuade
them from fighting the Germans as they did not want action to recom-
mence on a largely dormant front. When this failed they did their best to
demoralize the women, even, allegedly, firing at their backs (or perhaps
over their heads from the rear). Following Kornilov's mutiny, the situation became desperate and Bochkareva had to inform her soldiers that
the battalion must be disbanded. They were relieved:

They could not stand it much longer where they were. They were prepared to
fight the Germans, to be tortured by them, to die at their hands or in prison
camps. But they were not prepared for the torments and humiliation that they
were made to suffer by our own men. That had never entered into our calcula-
tions at the time that the Battalion was formed.[34]

The same pattern was repeated when the First Petrograd Women's
Battalion marched to the defence of the Provisional Government.
Knox, who, as a soldier knew more about these things than Noulens,
watched them too: 'They made the best show of any soldiers I have seen
since the (February) Revolution, but it gave me a lump in the throat to
see them, and the utter swine of "men" soldiers jeering at them.' The
behaviour of other 'loyal' troops was scarcely any better. Just before the
cossacks deserted the Winter Palace one of their junior lieutenants
justified himself to the cadet Sinegub,

When we came here, they told us all sorts of stories, that almost the whole town would be here with the icons, or at least the military schools and the artillery, but in fact it turned out to be just Yids and females (*zhidy da baby*), yes and the government, also half Yids. But the Russian people stayed out there with Lenin.

Sinegub cursed him for deserting 'women and children', but it made no difference.[35]

After the women were captured, lurid rumours swept Petrograd. The Right SR, Sorokin, reported that 'the fate of the women was even worse than our imaginations had been able to picture. Many had been killed, and those who escaped merciful death had been savagely ravished by the Bolsheviki. Some of these women soldiers were so vilely abused that they died in frightful agony.' Sorokin would have said anything to discredit the Bolsheviks, but it would be unwise to assume that anti-Bolsheviks started these rumours. Sinegub remembered hearing bursts of machine-gun fire *after* the capture of the Winter Palace, and the chilling words of a Bolshevik guard:

'They're shooting them', a soldier broke the silence.
'Whom?' I asked.
'The women volunteers!' . . . and, after a pause, he added:
'Look, they're wretched females. (*i baby bedovie*) One platoon held out. The lads are consoling themselves. The women are with us. And so if someone refuses, or if she's ill, put the *svoloch'* [filth] to the wall!'

It is quite possible that this was a 'wind-up'. Proletarian exultation took many forms that night.[36]

The allegations were investigated by General Knox and Louise Bryant, observers of diametically opposed political views. Both concluded that while the women had been abused and, in some case, assaulted, there had been no gang rape. Mariia Bocharnikova was not convinced that this was the end of the story, herself providing a detailed and circumstantial story of a serious case of humiliation and indecent assault, and offering a haunting picture of what may have happened to some of the women, (who were easy to track down because of their shaven or closely-cropped hair), out of the sight of foreign observers:

A group of 40 volunteers travelled home. In Petrograd, sailors captured them and took them to Kronstadt. A letter from the parents of one of those taken with this group was received. They dealt with the fate of their daughter. Their lot is unknown, they did not come home. A second group of 36 persons was captured by soldiers in Moscow and taken to a barracks. From one of the volunteers ours received a letter, in which she informed us about what had happened, and concluded, 'I am not in a position to tell what was done to us . . . It would have been better had they shot us, than let us go after what we had been through . . .'[37]

This is all what English judges call 'hearsay', but then, allegations of violence against women often are.

Public revulsion against those who had permitted boys as young as seventeen and girls as young as eighteen to face such ghastly possibilities was deep-seated and widespread. For once, the monarchist Countess Marie Kleinmichel spoke for most of society, 'While these lion-hearted girls were dying for him, Kerensky the Dictator had long since fled, without a thought for all those who had died for him in vain. In my opinion, as a woman, it is one of the most sinister pages of his history.'[38]

Kerenskii had gone to find troops to relieve the siege, but this is only slightly unfair on him and certainly explains his rather ungracious failure to publish a line of praise for the women. Their other patrons did little better. I have found nothing about the women from the pen of Rodzianko. Kornilov was killed before he could fully account for himself and his statement to the Shablovskii Commission was a defensive legal document. To have mentioned Bochkareva in that context would have been to put a noose round her neck. Krylova cites a short tribute from Brusilov, without indicating where it was first published:

The further conduct of my young maidens (*devits*) belongs to history. Their glorious conduct on the front, return to Petrograd, firm defence of the Provisional Government and the Winter Palace against the Bolsheviks, and martyred fate in the hands of the bestialized soldiers, all serves as a shining example of that high patriotism and correct understanding of the concept of duty, of which, unfortunately, few could boast at that time.

Krylova also cites the journalist, Boris Suvorin, who frankly confesses why so many men who owed them gratitude could not bring themselves to praise the Russian amazons of 1917: 'The battle at Smorgon will remain an eternal shame for our time, but will, again and again, adorn Russian Woman with an unexpected garland.'[39] In other words, the better the women fought, the less 'patriotic' men liked to talk about them!

Perhaps enough water has flowed down the Neva for people to take a more generous view. Perhaps there are now men and women everywhere, who can read with admiration Krylova's words, 'Each of us felt ourselves not just a Russian woman defending our country (as every wolf defends her lair), but also a representative of half the population of the whole globe, going into an examination, to prove that *even* in military matters, a woman can be a worthy soldier . . .'[40]

Notes

1. An example of relatively positive treatment of the women soldiers occurs in the 1967 Granada TV–Novosti coproduction, *Ten Days that Shook the World*. John Reed, *Ten Days that Shook the World* (New York, 1960), pp. 117, 144, 155. A 'positive' photograph of the women soldiers appeared in *Ogonek*, no. 41, October 1990.
2. Robert V. Daniels, *Red October: The Bolshevik Revolution of 1917* (London, 1967), pp. 136–7; cf. Joseph Noulens, *Mon Ambassade en Russie Soviétique 1917–1919* (Paris, 1933), vol. 1, p. 117; (Noulens only arrived in Petrograd in July 1917); Alexander Rabinowitch, *The Bolsheviks Come to Power* (New York, 1976), pp. 261–2.
3. Boris Solonevich, *Zhenshchina s vintovkoi* (Buenos Aires, 1955), pp. 62–3. (Henceforth: *Zhenshchina*).
4. Ibid., p. 34ff; cf. Richard Abraham, *Alexander Kerensky, The First Love of the Revolution* (New York–London, 1987), pp. 186–7.
5. *Zhenshchina*, pp. 3, 11, 12ff, 150. B. Solonevich, *Zagovor krasnogo Bonaparta* (Buenos Aires and Seattle, 1958).
6. Maria Botchkareva, *Yashka, My Life as Peasant, Exile and Soldier* (as set down by Isaac Don Levine) (New York and London, 1919); *Britannia* (formerly *The Suffragette*), 6 June, 13 June, 29 June, 13 July, 20 July, 27 July, 3 August, 10 August, 31 August, 16 November 1917; Ariadna Tyrkova-Williams, *From Liberty to Brest-Litovsk* (London, 1919); Meriel Buchanan, *Dissolution of an Empire* (London, 1932); Louise Bryant, *Six Red Months in Russia* (London, 1919); George Katkov, *Russia 1917, The Kornilov Affair, Kerensky and the Break-up of the Russian Army* (London, 1980).
7. Botchkareva, *Yashka*, p. xi. (The British Library copies have the American edition stamped on 1 April 1919 and the British edition stamped on 22 July 1919).
8. Ibid., pp. 222–3; Abraham, *Kerensky*, pp. 253–4.
9. *Zhenshchina*, p. 11.
10. Botchkareva, *Yashka*, pp. 29, 51–3.
11. Ibid., pp. 247–339.
12. E. Sylvia Pankhurst, *The Life of Emmeline Pankhurst. The Suffragette Struggle for Women's Citizenship* (London, 1935), pp. 160–1.
13. *Britannia*, 29 June, 13 July, 3 August 1917; Public Record Office, London (hereafter PRO) WO 106 (War Office: Directorate of Military Operations and Intelligence), p. 1140, Memorandum on the Russian Volunteer Army by Professor Pares.
14. *Zhenshchina*, pp. 124ff.; Botchkareva, *Yashka*, pp. 206ff.
15. *Moskovskie vedomosti, Novoe vremia, Rech'*, 11–13 July 1917.
16. B. Kamenshchykau, *Za úladu Savetaú (1917 god na Zakhodnim frontse) Uspaminy* (Minsk, 1959), p. 56.
17. B. Hollingsworth, 'David Soskice', Soskice Papers, House of Lords Records Office, London; cited in Abraham, *Kerensky*, p. 315; V. I. Start-

sev, 'Poslednii den'Vremennogo pravitel'stva', in V. A. Ovsiankin (ed.), *Iz istorii velikoi oktiabr'skoi sotsialisticheskoi revoliutsii i sotsialisticheskogo stroitel'stva v SSSR* (Leningrad, 1967), p. 111; *Zhenshchina*, pp. 157, 161–2; Mariia Bocharnikova, 'Boi v Zimnem dvortse', *Novy zhurnal*, no. 68, 1962, pp. 216–17; Maj.-Gen. Sir Alfred Knox, *With the Russian Army 1914–1917* (London, 1921), vol. 2, pp. 712–13.

18. Botchkareva, *Yashka*, pp. 220–1; PRO, WO 106, p. 1140.
19. Bocharnikova, 'Boi v Zimnem dvortse', p. 222; Bryant, *Six Red Months*, p. 214; *Novoe vremia*, 11 July, 1917; *Britannia*, 29 June, 13 July 1917; Florence Farmborough, *Nurse at the Russian Front* (London, 1974), p. 300.
20. George Katkov, *Russia 1917. The February Revolution* (London, 1967), pp. 367–74; I. I. Mints, *Istoriia velikogo oktiabria*, vol. 1: *Sverzhenie samoderzhaviia* (Moscow, 1967), pp. 585–91; Abraham, *Kerensky*, pp. 194–6.
21. Botchkareva, *Yashka*, pp. 151–7.
22. Ibid., pp. 158–62; *Zhenshchina*, pp. 34ff., 54.
23. Botchkareva, *Yashka*, pp. 167ff.; *Zhenshchina*, pp. 76–8; *Britannia*, 13 July, 3 August 1917; Bryant, *Six Red Months*, p. 212.
24. P. M. Chirkov, *Reshenie zhenskogo voprosa v SSSR (1917–1937 gg.)* (Moscow, 1977), pp. 153–60; For the sizes of the two armies, see L. M. Gavrilov and V. V. Kutuzov, 'Istoshchenie liudskikh rezervov russkoi armii v 1917 g.', in A. L. Sidorov (ed.), *Pervaia mirovaia voina* (Moscow, 1968), pp. 146–7; John Erickson (JE), 'The Red Army', in *The Blackwell Encyclopaedia of the Russian Revolution* (Oxford, 1988), pp. 185–7.
25. Bryant, *Six Red Months*, p. 212; Botchkareva, *Yashka*, pp. 261–3; Farmborough, *Nurse*, p. 300; Knox, *With the Russian Army*, vol. 2, p. 713; Bocharnikova, 'Boi v Zimnem dvortse', pp. 216–17; *Zhenshchina*, p. 166.
26. Buchanan, *Dissolution of an Empire*, pp. 216–17.
27. *Zhenshchina*, p. 54.
28. Knox, *With the Russian Army*, vol. 2, p. 711; Bryant, *Six Red Months*, pp. 213–16.
29. *Zhenshchina*, pp. 5–56, 64–6, 77–8; Botchkareva, *Yashka*, p. 199; AN SSSR, Institut istorii, *Boevaia letopis' russkogo flota* (Moscow, 1948), pp. 252–3, 278, 322; Marie, Countess Kleinmichel, *Memories of a Shipwrecked World* (London, 1923), p. 266.
30. Botchkareva, *Yashka*, p. 174; *Zhenshchina*, pp. 76–8.
31. Bocharnikova, 'Boi v Zimnem dvortse', pp. 216–21; *Zhenshchina*, pp. 156–7; Bryant, *Six Red Months*, pp. 210, 216.
32. Knox, *With the Russian Army*, vol. 2, pp. 712–13.
33. *Zhenshchina*, pp. 103, 137.
34. *Britannia*, 10 August 1917; Botchkareva, *Yashka*, p. 242 and passim; *Zhenshchina*, passim.
35. Knox, *With the Russian Army*, vol. 2, p. 705; A. Sinegub, 'Zashchita Zimnego dvortsa', *Arkhiv russkoi revoliutsii*, 22 vols. (Berlin, 1922–37), vol. 4, p. 165.
36. Pitirim Sorokin, *Leaves from a Russian Diary* (London, n.d.) (Cambridge University Library copy stamped 2 October 1925), p. 103; Sinegub, 'Zashchita', p. 192.

37. Knox, *With the Russian Army*, vol. 2, pp. 712–14; Bryant, *Six Red Months*, pp. 212–19; Bocharnikova, 'Boi v Zimnem dvortse', pp. 225–7.
38. Kleinmichel, *Memories*, p. 267.
39. *Zhenshchina*, 103, 157.
40. Ibid., p. 94.

7   Russian women writers: an overview. Post-revolutionary dispersion and adjustment

Marina Ledkovsky (Astman)

By the turn of the century and throughout the Silver Age, Russian women writers had moved into the ranks of the profession, becoming increasingly visible and recognized by their peers as well as their audience. Some women writers were very successful and earned considerable rewards, others not. But by and large, this movement pointed towards a progressive acceptance of women writers as meaningful participants in the creative process of Russian literature and their eventual full integration into the dominant canon. The events of the First World War, the Revolution and the Civil War brought about significant changes in this promising development. 'The revolution and the civil war split Russia in two, literally and figuratively: one lost the very name of Russia and became first the RSFSR and then the USSR; the other, defeated by Lenin's government, rejecting and escaping the newly created RSFSR, constituted itself into a Russia beyond the borders, Russia Abroad.'[1] An approximate periodization should provide some orientation in the further development of Russian women writing in the post-1917 period.

As is well known, in the early period of the division 'both Russias' continued to promote modernism in its various forms at least until well into the twenties.[2] The creative impact of the aesthetic ideas and the religious–philosophical concepts of the Silver Age never succumbed completely to the cataclysms of war, revolution and civil war;[3] it came forth in full force from 'under its rubble' and was shared by writers on both sides until Trotskii's ominous assault on the processes of literature in 1924.[4] After that attack the literary activities of 'both Russias' gradually moved in different directions as experimentation in art and literature began to wither in the Soviet Union; it dried up completely with the imposition of the doctrine of socialist realism at the first congress of the newly established writers' union in 1934.

At this point the gulf between *émigré* and Soviet writers had reached its lowest depth: while *émigrés* had won absolute freedom in exchange for their painful losses,[5] Soviet writers were forced under the total control of their government. Only with Stalin's death in 1953, and the gradual cultural liberalization, did literary developments in Russia Abroad and in the homeland start to converge once again. The various stages of post-Stalin literature included a vigorous renewal of interest in modernist trends begun in the Silver Age, and an ever-increasing fascination with the culture and literature of Russia Abroad.

In the diaspora, the refugees of the 1917 holocaust endeavoured to accomplish the task they had set themselves by rejecting the coarse regimentation of the Soviet government. Their primary objective was 'to preserve and carry on the culture of their homeland in the hope of its return to a Russia freed from Bolshevism'.[6] The focus of this endeavour was concentrated on language and literature as the most obvious manifestation of their cultural heritage. The concern with the creative word, its purity, versatility and efficacy, taken over from the Silver Age programme, remained constant through every phase of *émigré* literature and was fervently cultivated by women writers. The first, most brilliant period belongs to the twenties and thirties with its most important cultural centre in Paris. There is a hiatus during the Second World War, when *émigré* writing is stifled by occupation, hardship, renewed flight and resettlement to new centres (New York, San Francisco); some writers perish in the process, some survive by going underground and come back in the postwar period to continue their creative activity by joining forces with the new refugees of the second wave. The last stage, beginning in the seventies, is marked by the new influx of fresh talent forced out of official Soviet literature and moving voluntarily or involuntarily to the West to participate in the free literary enterprise of Russia Abroad.

There are two more factors which are important for the understanding of the Russian literary process of the past seven decades: one is the unbroken spiritual bond between the writers in the homeland and those in dispersion and their intense interest in each side's literary output – in contrast to the Western Slavists' almost total indifference to *émigré* literature; the other is the establishment of publishing houses in exile, most notably in Berlin in the early twenties,[7] but also in Prague, Belgrade, Riga, Kharbin, Paris, New York and San Francisco. In the beginning, Berlin was the publishing centre and through it contacts and exchanges were established for as long as Soviet Russia was not sealed off from the rest of the world. Many Soviet authors travelled abroad – a few stayed for good. But more importantly, Soviet authors were able to have their works published outside Russia. This was especially advantageous, as a shortage of paper, ink, printing presses and so on had plagued the homeland for years after the Revolution. Thanks to this lively exchange, modernism survived in Soviet Russia for a while. In the 1960s, the practice of *tamizdat* resumed, whereby Soviet writing was smuggled out of the country and published abroad.[8] In the present situation (1991) only a shortage of paper in the Soviet Union seems to stand in the way of a free exchange of new publications and reprints between the two Russias.

Within this framework women writers have continued to forge their way ahead in Soviet Russia and the diaspora. They appear to have enjoyed significant success in spite of extraordinary moral and physical hardships, which *émigré* women writers have shared with their Soviet sisters in peculiarly complementary ways. Their numbers and the recognition they have gained as major contributors to literature are impressive.[9] On the other hand, it is also true that throughout the period of Soviet dictatorship ideological censorship silenced and repressed women writers for political, male-oriented reasons: as, for example, Akhmatova, Kollontai, Parnok and Shkapskaia, Berggol'ts, Ginzburg, Zernova and many more became victims of purges; feminist-oriented writers, such as Baranskaia and Ganina and several other women authors, were reprimanded and called to order; those considered unacceptable radicals like Gorbanevskaia, Goricheva, Ratushinskaia, Voznesenskaia, Mamonova were jailed and expelled. The list could go on. Marina Tsvetaeva's ostracism by prejudiced, politicized *émigrés* in the diaspora, although it has been grossly exaggerated, is another distressing fact.

In the early post-1917 period, women writers who had their roots in the Silver Age, were attracted to the publishing opportunities beyond Soviet confines. They continued to create poetry in their idiosyncratic, modernist manner and published their works mainly in West European centres. Most of the poetry of Akhmatova, Parnok, Shkapskaia, Shaginian and many others was published in Berlin, Leipzig and Sofia. This practice came to a standstill after 1925; and at home, these poets were barely published, with the exception of the versatile conformist Marietta Shaginian. Akhmatova's case is well known. The silencing of Sofiia Parnok and Mariia Shkapskaia deserves comment.[10] The basic reason was that their work was 'discordant with their time (*ne sozvuchno s epokhoi*)'. Parnok was aesthetically not radical enough in form for the modernist critics, insufficiently revolutionary in her themes for the ideologues, and too dedicated to introspection and self-awareness as the ultimate goal of existence. Mariia Shkapskaia's unique poetry about motherhood likewise did not satisfy the expectations of Soviet officials. Shkapskaia chose a very private, yet at the same time universal theme of woman and her baby, but not that of happy motherhood glorified in the posters of the Revolution; instead the themes of sorrow, of anxiety, of prescience, of loss and failure became the texture of her art. Such a view of motherhood was not acceptable to the optimistic leaders of a future-oriented society. Shkapskaia never published her experimental poetry after the announcement of the 'Policy of the Party in the Field of Belles-Lettres' in July 1925; she turned to work in journalism until her death in 1952. Another case is that of Aleksandra Kollontai, who had to abandon her vision of a truly liberated 'new Soviet woman' and comply with the demands of the party.

In contrast, Marietta Shaginian can serve as a formula of adjustment to the prescribed norms for Soviet literature in those turbulent times. Several of her contemporary or somewhat younger fellow women writers followed suit to fit into the restrictive conditions of the Soviet venture. They unquestioningly pledged their support to the new centralized plan of Soviet art and gradually rescinded their former commitment to innovative experimentation. At first, they still participated in different modernist groupings of the twenties, but eventually accepted the ensuing prescriptions of socialist realism.

As the dominant themes of the new literature were the Revolution and the Civil War, Shaginian turned away from writing poetry and explored these new themes in stories about the intelligentsia and their adjustment to the new era. A series of Shaginian's 'Textile Stories' followed between 1922 and 1926. In order to comply with a request to attract readers' interest, she wrote the detective story 'Mess-Mend – A Yankee in Petrograd' which was serialized in international communist papers and raised their circulation. When all the forces of society were mobilized behind the first five-year plan (1928–32) and the writers were urged to concern themselves with such themes as industrial plants, collective farms etc., 'Shaginian came up with *Hydrocentral* (1931), a carefully researched novel about a huge construction project.'[11] At the first congress of the union of Soviet writers in 1934, its members had to accept the programme of the Communist Party and strive to participate in 'Socialist Construction'. Sure enough, Shaginian encouraged her fellow writers to exploit the poetic power of that theme, referring to Blok: 'The poet Blok called upon all of us "to hear the music of Revolution". The real music is only beginning now: listen to it, comrades! Because the real music of the Revolution is socialist construction!'[12] Of course, the quality of Shaginian's writings suffered significantly from her all too eager adjustment to the party line; and yet, undeniably, Shaginian deserves recognition as an unusually ingenious and talented, if conformist, writer who managed to function successfully within the limits drawn by the establishment. Her creative career still awaits a competent scholarly monograph that would analyse her work in dissociation from her political entanglement.

Several gifted women writers followed Shaginian's example of adjustment to the new terms of existence, thus narrowing their true artistic scope. Vera Inber, who like so many fellow writers made her start in literature with a Symbolist collection of poems in 1914, joined the Constructivists, who advocated the reduction of art to simple formulae making it intelligible to the masses. However, soon Inber would be criticized by the official press for being too concerned with domestic themes and for depicting Soviet reality too superficially and lacking in heroism. She suffered repression and met with difficulties in publishing her work until the war. Similarly, Elizaveta Polonskaia, the only woman associated with the Serapion Brothers, had started out with Symbolist poetry. Eventually she turned to journalism, to translations and to writing children's books, as so many Silver Age authors did looking for a loophole of survival.

But there were many who refused to bend their genius to the regime's regulations. Some would not be published for long periods (for example, Akhmatova and her friend Mariia Petrovykh), others, such as the recently discovered exceptional avant-garde poet and musicologist Elizaveta Mnatsakanova, never even ventured to reach the reading public through official channels. Mnatsakanova combines musical structures with transrational language to create a singular, evocative view of the world in her poetry. Her poems have only recently been published in the West.[13]

Still others like Ol'ga Forsh, who began writing at the height of the Silver Age modernist experimentation, continued to practise modest innovative methods. Forsh succeeded in producing expressionist, ornamental prose, especially remarkable in her *Crazy Ship*, an entertaining and witty account of the post-revolutionary intelligentsia and the carnavalesque years in the Petrograd House of Arts of the early twenties. When rebuked by censorship for her licentious book, she resorted to creating historical novels on safe topics, but also of considerble interest and literary value.[14] She never totally refrained from experimentation in narrative prose. Throughout her creative career she continued to toy with grotesque imagery and to imbue her text with innovative linguistic vitality.

Generally, most women writers of that period conform to the requests of the government and produce tendentious works in support of the wide-ranging industrial and collectivization plans. They are among the first to depict the coming of mechanization to the Soviet country. Thus,

Anna Karavaeva, a Bolshevik who belonged to the *Pereval* group and contributed regularly to *Krasnaia nov'*, published her novel *Lesozavod* [Sawmill] in 1928. The novel deals with the introduction of modern machinery into the lumber industry. Karavaeva was later the editor of the Komsomol organ *Molodaia gvardiia* (1931–8) and became a staunch supporter and heedless enforcer of socialist realism during Stalin's rule.

Another member of *Pereval*, Ekaterina Strogovaia, wrote about women workers in a small manufacturing town in Russia's backwoods. Her story 'Country Women' was ostensibly, if not convincingly, attacking 'antisocial activities' and the survival of a pre-revolutionary life style.

Lidiia Seifullina was successful in creating 'village literature' with portrayals of positive peasant types growing into dedicated Bolshevik activists. Aleksandr Voronskii, the editor of *Krasnaia nov'*, considered her work a continuation of the 'village' tradition of Populist writers, of Grigorovich, Turgenev, Bunin and others.[15] Seifullina dedicated her abilities to blatantly realistic depictions of Siberian peasantry. Vireneia, the heroine of Seifullina's eponymous novel of 1925, serves as an example of the period's iconography patterned on Gor'kii's *Mother*. The simple-minded peasant girl develops into a responsible revolutionary and eventual martyr to the cause. Ironically, L'vov-Rogachevskii, a contemporary critic, hailed Seifullina for her 'virile' prose and juxtaposed her style favourably to Boris Zaitsev's technique: 'V ee kisti chuvstvuetsia muzhskaia sila i smelost' . . . Esli Boris Zaitsev napisal po-zhenski svoiu Agrafenu, to Seifullina po-muzhski sdelala krepkii, novyi, obaiatel'nyi obraz.'[16]* Zaitsev's subtle image is rejected in favour of this male critic's taste for a rather crudely passionate and strikingly flawless heroine of the revolution. This conformist prose and poetry (in retreat at that period) is restrained, straightforward, lacking in inventiveness and elegance, seeking refuge in somewhat trite landscape descriptions and occasionally in quite vibrant dialogues.

Meanwhile, a rich, versatile experimental literary activity is taking place in the various centres of dispersion. Well established women writers of the Silver Age, Zinaida Gippius, Marina Tsvetaeva and others[17] participate as steady contributors in the publication of journals, almanacs and newspapers from the very outset of emigration in 1920–1. They continue to write prolifically in various genres, following existing trends and creating new ones for modern writing. Marina Tsvetaeva's Paris years, in spite of all their vicissitudes, witness her best work, in the

---

* 'The stroke of her brush conveys a man's strength and boldness . . . If Boris Zaitsev's Agrafena was written with a feminine touch, there was masculinity in Seifullina's robust, new, fascinating image.'

opinion of most critics.[18] She produces richly varied lyric poetry in her unique manner which defies categorization. In the 1930s, she also contributes brilliant essays on Russian literature and autobiographical prose pieces to the most prestigious *émigré* journals. Whether these exceptional creations would ever have reached the public eye in different environments and circumstances remains a futile conjecture.

The younger generation of *émigré* women writers begins to make its appearance by the 1930s. They are continuing the effort of the Silver Age artists to find innovative ways to express their experience; they are also more deeply involved in the intellectual trends of their host countries. Most are interested in European writers and thinkers: Nietzsche's impact can be traced in many works, as can the attraction of the methods of the great masters of contemporary Western prose – Joyce, Proust, Mann, Kafka, Malraux – and the current literary and artistic trends of Cubism, Dadaism, Surrealism and Existentialism. In complementing the materialist direction of literature in the homeland, women writers together with their male peers of Russia Abroad concentrate on the spiritual and philosophical aspects of life. An awareness of and a longing for a higher dimension, beyond reason and rationalization, informs most of their writings.[19]

The most capable younger women writers explore modernist techniques in various genres and produce numerous novels, short stories and poetry. A concern with the complexity of the human psyche, with theosophy and anthroposophy enriches their fiction and verses. In some of their writings Nietzschean cynicism seems to alternate with the gnostic views of Markion (for example, in various works by Bakunina, Velichkovskaia, Golovina and Kuznetsova). Spiritual desolation against an alienating environment, the desire to penetrate the existential void inclines many women writers to Orthodoxy, to the 'Christianization of life', advocated by eminent priests and theologians at the various ecclesiastical centres in the diaspora. As the result of an intense, awakened religious consciousness, several women authors are dedicating their talents to religious and theological writings, to the composition of new liturgical texts for complete religious services which are adopted by Church authorities. A rough count has yielded approximately thirty known religious women writers.

In all the great centres the younger poets gather in literary clubs around prominent masters; the best known emerge in Paris, but Prague, Riga, Belgrade and Kharbin should not be discounted. The poetry of the young Parisians has acquired the generic label of the 'Parisian note'. Georgii Adamovich, the major mentor of the 'Parisian School', advises his young followers to practise restraint, honesty and simplicity, 'two lines about the most essential things': evil and suffering, mortality and good.[20] Among the most representative women contributors to the 'Parisian note' is Lidiia Chervinskaia, while the more striking Anna Prismanova, Alla Golovina, Galina Kuznetsova and Raisa Blokh have no direct ties to any school. Yet, they are steeped in the formal traditions of Russian literature and trace their links with great women poets, past and present. Thus, Anna Prismanova gains strength for the search of her inner self from lines by Karolina Pavlova chosen as epigraph for her third collection of poems *Salt*:

> Kto tshchetno ishchet – ne bednee
> togo, byt' mozhet, kto nashel.

> Who searches in vain is not poorer
> than he who already has found.

These concluding lines intone Prismanova's sombre verses in the quest for the 'incarnation of existence'.[21] In other poems she pays tribute to the martyr poet Raisa Blokh and, interestingly, to the Brontë sisters. Ties to the female literary tradition seem to be of special value to Prismanova.

The younger *émigré* poets of the fertile thirties have contributed lasting verse to the treasury of Russian poetry, which prompted Georgii Adamovich to thank destiny for having made them exiles, implying that only in freedom could they have created those works of enduring importance.[22]

The Second World War had a smothering effect on Russian literature in both Russias. In exile it almost disappeared under the onslaught of the Third Reich; in the homeland it called forth some moving patriotic verse, especially about the 900-day siege of Leningrad (Akhmatova, Berggol'ts, Aliger and Inber endeavoured to write profusely about this grim experience), and repetitive, endless war novels. The war events have haunted Soviet women writers for three decades at least. Iuliia Drunova, Margarita Aliger and I. Grekova among others have returned to this theme regularly. New talents like Vera Panova emerged with the most famous war novel *Sputniki* (1945) for which she won the Stalin prize; nevertheless, she was rebuked for dealing too extensively with the private lives of individuals rather than the heroics of the collective effort. The reprimand was well taken and Panova remained a loyal, low-key, officially approved writer; together with several women novelists she turned to the discussion of topical problems of Soviet society in the postwar years. Family relations, the rearing of children, the dilemma of moral choice and civic duty, the portrayal of heroic women as 'auxiliaries to their men' – the 'Builder' heroes[23] – provided the focus of their attention. Other female authors elaborated those same themes, sometimes timidly questioning the validity of this patriarchal pattern.[24] Generally, in the last few years before Stalin's death Soviet 'conflictless' literature had reached an impasse.

The post-Stalin thaws gradually brought back vitality into that almost lifeless method of writing. Heretofore 'forbidden' themes came into the open. Galina Nikolaeva's *Running Battle* (1957) was the first novel to deal with the reactions to Stalin's death; it also included the new theme of Stalin's repressions. Subsequently, other women authors bore witness to the horrors of Stalin's purges in shattering poems and memoirs, which were complemented by the reminiscences of the second wave *émigré* women writers.[25]

A vigorous poetic revival started with the 1960s, bringing forth exciting experimentation, novel techniques and avant-garde themes. Remarkable women poets competed successfully with their noisy male peers. Bella Akhmadulina, Novella Matveeva, Iunna Morits and more recently Elena Shvarts and Olesia Nikolaeva, widely recognized as first-rate, are the best known of a score of excellent women poets.

In women's prose of more recent years, motifs of the 'double-shift-syndrome' (much earlier exposed by Margarita Aliger in several poems and in her 'Autobiography' of 1961),[26] of single motherhood, of solitary independent women, of ageing and retirement, alcoholism and sickness, inadequate health care, envy, adultery and betrayal have become an important constant. Frequently, this fiction focuses on women's struggle to survive the multiple duties and claims on their time and energy, while searching for some lasting meaning of existence. Most works still reveal the basic quest for liberation, be it from tedious, never ending domestic chores or oppressive social conditions.[27] The appearance of the brilliant Tatiana Tolstaia, one of the few writers who rises above her contemporary Soviet Russian environment and deals with universal human flaws, has promoted women writers into the first ranks of Russian literature. Tolstaia's unconventional, exuberant fiction offers a new vision of existence, a different perspective of universal culture from that of most contemporary Russian writers. One can only hope that the Tolstaia phenomenon will arouse due interest in women's overall contribution to modern Russian literature.

In post Second World War Russia Abroad women writers resumed their literary and publishing activities with full vigour, replenished by the talents of the second and the later third wave women authors. Most of the new *émigrés* proceeded to the United States and settled there. In Paris the first wave refugees licked their wounds and took up publishing. Shakhovskaia became the editor-in-chief of *Russkaia mysl'*, probably the best *émigré* Russian newspaper for twenty years; the poets Sofiia Pregel' and Irina Iassen headed a publishing enterprise *Rifma* that cultivated *émigré* literature, mainly poetry. Ever since, many female writer-editors have headed Russian publishing enterprises promoting Russian books, journals and dailies.[28] This seems to have become a firmly established practice in European centres. *Emigré* women, like their Soviet peers, have also continued to write in all genres. First-rate women poets, writers and literary critics of the second wave joined the ranks of the 'old' *émigrés* – Ol'ga Anstei, Lidiia Alekseeva, Irina Bushman, Iraida Lekhkaia, a cubo-futurist, Nonna Belavina, Valentina Sinkevich and many more produced idiosyncratic, subtle poetry still keeping a spiritual bond with their lost native country, but enjoying the freedom to create, be it in an alien land. Irina Bushman should be singled out especially as perhaps the most brilliant poet of postwar Russia Abroad. She has produced three volumes of unpublished remarkable poetry and has been working on a *Poema* on Giordano Bruno for the past fifteen years. Giordano's unusual fate has captivated her imagination and talents since childhood. Giordano's liberal humanism, his restless wanderings and trials evoked a sense of kinship with the Russian refugees' lot. Lidiia Alekseeva's poetry about the 'eternal [Russian] wanderer' directly inspired the creation of the *poema*.

The memoir genre forms a major contribution to the literature of Russia Abroad. It will require a special critical assessment. Many women writers have left memorable reminiscences that will find their way back home and prove to have exceptional value.

The third wave likewise has blessed the literature in exile with great talents: some outstanding, others less remarkable, but still deserving attention. Poetry, prose writers, critics, publicists are equally represented: Gorbanevskaia, Ratushinskaia, Rozanova, Vosnesenskaia and Goricheva are among the most noteworthy. Tat'iana Goricheva is one of several contemporary religious poets continuing the uninterrupted trend of religious and liturgical female writing since the first decades of emigration. Thus, contrary to the opinion of some observers, Russia Abroad is quite vital and active, in spite of the unpropitious conditions for creativity. It should be recalled that Russian refugees were lost in an alien environment, frequently faced with a hostile reception and poverty (especially painful after the luxury lost in the homeland); 'yet creative life went forward. The fact that the *émigrés* were totally free to create in whatever way they chose'[29] [except for the Nazi years] should not be underestimated. 'Neither government nor public opinion interfered with their creativity.'[30] These were exceptional conditions that 'had not been attained even in the heydays of the newly gained freedom in the late months in 1905, or the early weeks of 1917'.[31]

The common impulse of the members of Russia Abroad (and women writers form a significant and important part of it) to retain and reinforce the traditions of Russian literature, seems finally to bear fruit. As Raeff suggests, it will or may have striking consequences for the development of Russian culture and perhaps for Russian public life as well. Just like the return of the Orthodox traditions to the Church, this would be a major legacy of Russia Abroad to the future Russia at home. The intensity in *émigré* culture and the awe before it in the homeland point to a full integration of the culture of Russia Abroad into the history of all Russia.

In an overview, it seems that female authors in both Russias continue to favour the short form of novella, short story, poem or essay. Critics and women writers themselves have offered some valid if stereotyped explanations for this preference: the hardships and complexities of a modern woman's life might prevent her from engaging in long-term projects; poetry and the short narrative, as more flexible and focused media, correspond better to the emotional character of women's thought. But history shows that some women are indeed capable of producing memoirs of considerable size. This again is attributed to the female special capacity 'to preserve and transmit memory, to effect the link between generations'.[32] The argument, though, that safeguarding 'cultural continuity through memory is not a gender-specific prerogative'[33] seems justified in view of the availability of numerous volumes of memoir literature by both genders. Besides, a solid body of novels, especially valuable historical novels, long narrative poems (the *poema*) and quite remarkable plays written by Russian women have also appeared over the past seventy years. Women engage successfully in literary criticism and in philosophical-publicistic essays of wide range. The question arises whether it is possible to distinguish a special mode of female writing within the course of the literary process.

The formalists' ideas of the revolutionary nature of literature (Tynianov, Shklovskii) do not seem to apply to the evolution of women's writing. There is certainly a continuity of genres, methods and themes that gives women's literature a definite shape throughout its development. On the other hand, the formalists' stand on the examination of the entire literary process, including works of heretofore neglected literature is well taken in connection with women's writing. What remains incomprehensible is their disregard for a rich body of literature right next to them and open for investigation.

In order to arrive at a formulation or rather discovery of certain
semantic or semiotic patterns in Russian female writing, a series of
linguistic, structuralist and semiotic investigations of the narrative form,
poetic semantics and verse structure should be initiated.* Only such
painstaking research can yield significant results and eventually reveal
new ways of evaluating women's input into the Russian literary process.
Philological and literary scholarship of the Moscow–Tartu school should
be applied to this area of Russian literature. It might well uncover
Bakhtin's carnavalesque element in several interesting pieces written by
women. Ol'ga Forsh seems to introduce it in her *Crazy Ship*, as an
underlying layer which creates the basic comical tone of the work. It
seems to be used according to the 'classic semiotic analysis', as the
'archaic method of a ritual neutralization of underlying binary opposition'[34] to mitigate the rather gruesome reality presented, which
otherwise would repel the reader. This work has apparently not been
chosen for scrutiny by the Moscow–Tartu school. Forsh's works, Prismanova's short stories, Akhmatova's 'Poem Without a Hero', the prose
of Tolstaia and Petrushevskaia, and other female writings need more
serious analysis that would allot them their deserved place in literature.

As can be seen, scores of women writers of both Russias have firmly
established themselves as significant contributors to their native
literature in spite of adverse conditions for creative activity and the still
existing prejudice and covert resistance to official recognition. Yet, the
full integration of Russian women's writing into the total range of
cultural manifestations still awaits its realization. The 'traditional
canons of literature' have begun to accept a more enlightened and
modern view of literary creation. Such a positive attitude might help to
assess the true significance of Russian women writers' contribution to
literature and culture.

Notes

Research for this article – part of a larger project, *A Guide to Russian Women
Writers from the Period of Catherine the Great to Our Time* – was supported in
part by a grant from the International Research and Exchanges Board (IREX)

* Editor's note: This process has already begun, as was demonstrated in several
  panels of the 1990 World Congress for Soviet and East European studies in
  Harrogate.

and with funds provided by the Andrew W. Mellon Foundation. Neither of these organizations is responsible for the views expressed.

Preliminary research for the entire project was also supported by a National Endowment for the Humanities Travel to Collections award, a travel grant by the American Philosophical Society, as well as several associateships at the Summer Research Laboratory of the Russian and East European Center at the University of Illinois Champaign-Urbana. All this support is deeply appreciated.

1. Marc Raeff, *Russia Abroad – A Cultural History of the Russian Emigration, 1919–1939* (New York–Oxford, 1990), p. 3. I have adopted Raeff's felicitous label, 'Russia Abroad', as it designates succinctly the realistic geographical dispersion and at the same time the spiritual unity of the Russian diaspora.

2. The year 1925 is usually given as the cut-off date for experimentation in the Soviet Union; in reality it continued there into the late twenties.

3. Here I permit myself a different opinion from the one expressed by Raeff in his *Russia Abroad*, p. 101, as will be shown in my following discussion.

4. Lev Trot'skii viciously attacked the great Silver Age writers, mocking Anna Akhmatova and Marina Tsvetaeva especially, for their departure from realism and their half-hearted support of communism, and labelling them 'fellow-travellers' in his tract *Literature and Revolution*.

5. M. Aldanov, 'O polozhenii emigrantskoi literatury', *Sovremennye zapiski*, no. 61 (1936), p. 401. Aldanov writes: 'We have won freedom. Even the most enthusiastic admirers of Soviet literature cannot seriously insist that it is free. Whereas we write what we want, how we want, and about what we want.'

6. Raeff, *Russia Abroad*, p. 74. I am greatly indebted to Professor Raeff's clear analysis of the first wave *émigrés'* important ideology.

7. A list of 188 publishing enterprises, based on most recent research, in Berlin alone between the years 1918 and 1928 is adduced in *Russia Abroad*, p. 77. See also L. Fleishman, R. Hughes, O. Raevsky-Hughes, *Russkii Berlin 1921–1923* (Paris, 1983).

8. Edward J. Brown, *Russian Literature Since the Revolution* (London, 1969), pp. 307ff.

9. The present research, still incomplete, has resulted in lists of about 700 names of post-1917 women writers in 'both Russias'.

10. See Barbara Heldt's excellent analysis of 'Four modern women poets' in her seminal study *Terrible Perfection. Women and Russian Literature* (Bloomington, IN, 1987), pp. 116–43.

11. Victor Terras, 'Soviet literature 1925–1953', in Charles A. Moser (ed.), *The Cambridge History of Russian Literature* (Cambridge, 1988), p. 484.

12. Brown, *Russian Literature*, p. 31.

13. Gerald J. Janecek, 'Paronomastic and musical techniques in Mnacakanova's *Rekviem*', *Slavic and East European Journal*, vol. 31, no. 2 (Summer 1987), pp. 202–19.

14. For example, *Firstborn of Freedom* on the Decembrists; a Radishchev Trilogy and on the Pauline era, *The Mikhailovsky Castle*.

15. Robert A. Maguire, *Red Virgin Soil, Soviet Literature in the 1920s* (Princeton, 1968), pp. 294–5.
16. V. L'vov-Rogachevskii, 'L. Seifullina', in *Noveishaia russkaia literatura* (Moscow, 1927), pp. 411–12.
17. Notably N. Teffi, L. Stolitsa, E. Nagrodskaia, I. Odoevtseva, N. Berberova, L. Deisha (Georgii Peskov), Lappo-Danilevskaia.
18. Stepun, Weidlé, Struve, Mirsky.
19. *Cf.*, P. Bitsilli, '*Iakor''*, *Sovremennye zapiski*, no. 60 (1936), pp. 460–5. Aldanov, 'O polozhenii emigrantskoi literatury', pp. 400–9. V. Varshavskii, 'O proze "mladshikh" emigrantskikh pisatelei', *Sovremennye zapiski*, no. 61 (1936).
20. Vladimir Markov, *Modern Russian Poetry* (Indianapolis–New York, 1966), p. xv.
21. Petra Couvée (ed.), *Anna Prismanova, Collected Works* (The Hague, 1990), p. xxiv. This recent book is part of an extraordinary and timely publishing venture of works by Russian *émigré* writers. Excellently edited, annotated and introduced by Petra Couvée it will enrich the heritage of Russian poetry. Our thanks go to Dr Jan Paul Hinrichs, chief editor of *Russian Emigré Literature in the Twentieth Century – Studies and Texts*.
22. Raeff, *Russia Abroad*, pp. 114 and 213, n. 11.
23. Vera Sandomirsky-Dunham 'The strong-woman motif', in Cyril E. Black (ed.), *The Transformation of Russian Society* (Cambridge, 1960), pp. 459–83. In this challenging article, Sandomirsky-Dunham uses George Fedotov's ingenious term the 'Builder', describing a 'constructive' mover of history, as against the 'Radical' (Bazarov, Rakhmetov) and the 'Passive' (Oblomov, Karataev).
24. For example, M. Aliger 'Vasha pobeda', *Znamia*, no. 11 (1946), p. 23; also Antonina Koptiaeva's *Ivan Ivanovich* (Moscow, 1951).
25. The memorable works of Akhmatova, Chukovskaia, Ginzburg and N. Mandel'shtam can be supplemented by a long list of similar memoirs in prose and in poetic form by *émigré* women writers.
26. This term – 'double-shift-syndrome' – is adopted from Helena Goscilo's remarkable introduction to *Balancing Acts* (Bloomington, IN, 1989), p. xxii. The term describes the typical working day of a Soviet woman, who goes out to work, shops, cooks, puts the children to bed, mends the family's clothes and does the housework, with little or no participation by the husband.
27. Among the most noteworthy writers dealing with those motifs are Liudmila Petrushevskaia, also a prolific and successful dramatist, Natalia Baranskaia, I. Grekova, Maia Ganina, Liudmila Uvarova, Viktoriia Tokareva (in fact almost all the writers included in Goscilo's *Balancing Acts*). They can be complemented by such *émigré* women as Ruth Zernova, Liudmila Shtern, Marina Rachko and others.
28. N. Berberova, E. Zhiglevich, T. Goricheva, Z. Iur'eva, M. Rozanova, V. Pirozhkova, N. Gorbanevskaia, V. Sinkevich have been or are presently editors-in-chief or co-editors of the most important *émigré* publications.
29. Raeff, *Russia Abroad*, p. 197.
30. Ibid.

31. Ibid.
32. Boris M. Eikhenbaum's remark of the 1940s is quoted in Goscilo's 'Introduction', *Balancing Acts*, p. xiv. Interestingly, Khodasevich, when reviewing Zinaida Gippius' memoir *Living Faces*, does not claim this genre especially suited for women's writing; he rather insists on its compelling universal value for our troubled times. *Sovremennye zapiski*, no. 25 (1925), pp. 535–41.
33. Goscilo, 'Introduction', p. xiv.
34. Henryk Baran, 'Structuralism and semiotics', in Victor Terras (ed.), *Handbook of Russian Literature* (New Haven, 1985), p. 451.

8 Victim or villain: prostitution in post-revolutionary Russia

Elizabeth Waters

One of the posters produced in the early 1920s by the Moscow Provincial Soviet of Trade Unions shows a grim industrial town, and a crowd of downtrodden women shuffling from left to right, shawls round their shoulders, kerchiefs over their heads; in the foreground a group of plump men of the bourgeoisie stand and leer. Its central characters are a young man and a young woman: he, disproportionately large, holds in his left hand a hammer, sign of his membership of the proletariat; she, small-scale and dejected, is clearly in need of assistance – and indeed, the worker is holding out his free arm to her in a gesture of fraternal solicitude. The text reinforces this visual image of the prostitute as victim: 'By destroying capitalism the proletariat destroys prostitution. Prostitution is a great misfortune for humanity. Worker take care of the woman worker.'[1] The date of publication was 1923, two years after the introduction of the New Economic Policy;[2] the country was still recovering from the economic and social chaos of revolution, civil war and famine, and for the working class faced with a housing crisis, low wages and high unemployment, life was hard. It was particularly hard for women, many of whom had to support themselves and their families in conditions of a shrinking job market. The alarming level of redundancies among the female labour force appeared, albeit as a minor item, on party and trade union agendas. Economists, such as G. S. Strumilin, sympathetic to goals of sexual equality, argued that women were losing jobs in the industrial restructuring because they lacked sufficient qualifications, hence education and training must be the long-term answers. As a short-term measure, it was suggested that protective legislation be reduced, to encourage employers to keep women on in the labour force; speaking from the platform of the Sixth Trades Union congress in 1924, one woman declared that it was better to work nights than to have to go out on the streets.[3]

A speech made in the late 1920s to the Central Council for the Struggle Against Prostitution, by L. E. Motylev of RSFSR Gosplan, characterized the prostitute as socially dangerous, deserving of punishment. Everywhere, it warned, class enemies and alien elements were waiting to thwart the good intentions of the proletariat, but the proletariat, vigilant and progressive, was fighting back. Ten labour camps especially designed for 'hardened' prostitutes were being set up, it reported.[4] The year was 1929. The five-year plan had been in operation for several months, and its targets were escalating; newspapers warned of wreckers and saboteurs, of rightists and deviationists; quotations from the writings of I. V. Stalin were appearing more and more frequently in the press. The urgency of socialist construction was the talk of party propagandists and 'the drawing of women into production' a constant refrain.

These two statements – the visual and the verbal, the poster and the speech – exemplify a definite shift in approaches to prostitution over the decade. In the early NEP period, the prostitute was counted among the downtrodden and the exploited; by the era of the first five-year plan she was more frequently placed with the wreckers of industrialization, a conscious and culpable opponent of socialist construction. It is not hard to see how this shift was related to broader economic and political changes. With the emergence of the 'administrative-command system', policies on social issues adapted to the new environment, and accordingly policy on prostitution abandoned the liberal approach inherited from European social democracy. There was undoubtedly a break between the Bolshevik and Stalinist treatments of prostitution. But it was not absolute and requires a number of qualifications. The Bolsheviks in the pre-revolutionary period were unenthusiastic exponents of the orthodox social-democratic teaching on prostitution; after October, during the Civil War, when party discussion picked a schizophrenic path between libertarianism and authoritarianism, provisions for house communes and enlightened sex education figured in government policy at one and the same time as the notion, alien to orthodoxy, of the punishability of the prostitute; and, at the end of the twenties, at the same time as Motylev was demanding the incarceration of prostitutes in camps, others were busy rescuing them from the streets. Furthermore, there is another set of discontinuities in the treatment of prostitution, that connects more with a broader Western process of modernization than with the specific Soviet historical dynamic. The early twenties saw a redefinition of the social significance of prostitution, as class and sexuality occupied a less prominent place in analysis, and instead the woman's relationship to the world of work moved into sharper focus.

The characterization of the prostitute as victim was firmly established in orthodox European social democracy in the second half of the nineteenth and the early twentieth centuries. Women's bodies, bought and sold on the market, provided a telling example of the inhumanity of capitalism in general and of the oppression of the female sex in particular. Socialist writers saw prostitution as the product of women's inequality, not of moral failings and pathological personalities; they saw the prostitute as the blameless victim of an unjust social system. In contemporary society, they argued, all women were forced to sell themselves: marriage sanctified by the church and confirmed by the law was, in essence, a variation of prostitution. Only the advent of socialism would give women equality and independence, and would save them from loveless marriages and from the streets.[5]

Pre-war Russian social democrats had paid little attention to prostitution in their theoretical writings, and the subject did not feature with any frequency in their campaigning. The fight against regulation (before 1917, prostitutes had been compelled to register with the police, to forfeit their internal passports in exchange for the notorious 'yellow ticket', and to submit to medical check ups) was left, by and large, to the liberals, the philanthropists and the feminists.[6] Individual socialists attended the All-Russian Congress on the Struggle against the Trade in Women and Its Causes, held in St Petersburg in 1910,[7] but involvement in such reformist political ventures was thought to be of small importance, if not a waste of time. When Lenin reported in *Rabochaia pravda* on the 5th Congress on the Struggle Against Prostitution held in London in 1913, he stressed the hypocrisy and ineffectiveness of philanthropic efforts, without promoting alternative socialist action.[8] For the Bolshevik leader, such matters as prostitution were always peripheral to classes and means of production, to those institutions responsible in his view for generating the industrial struggles of the working class, and in turn providing the motor for social development. This belief in the essential marginality of sexual politics comes through in the conversations he had after the revolution with Clara Zetkin, the long-time leader of the German social-democratic women's movement and convert to the Third International: Lenin expressed surprise, she reported in her *Reminiscences*, that a communist woman in Hamburg is organizing prostitutes; surely, he asked, there are other working women in Germany who would be better recipients of her attention.[9]

To ignore is not necessarily to reject. The Bolsheviks prior to 1917 wrote little and campaigned rarely on prostitution, but there was nothing in their record to suggest they had fundamental disagreements with the social-democratic analysis. In the immediate post-1917 period, however, the party spoke and acted in ways that went beyond and against this orthodoxy.

Aleksandra Kollontai, the Bolshevik feminist, in a speech to the 3rd All-Russian Conference of Heads of Provincial Women's Departments in 1920, repeated the traditional social-democratic views: legal wives sold themselves just as much as prostitutes, and to penalize prostitutes simply because they exchanged sex on a short-term rather than a long-term basis, and slept with many men rather than one, would be grossly hypocritical. However, prostitutes could, she considered, be punished as labour deserters, if they refused to engage in socially useful labour.[10] Kollontai was not alone in making this argument. The Interdepartmental Commission on Prostitution, set up during the Civil War with representatives from various party and government institutions to develop an analysis of prostitution and formulate policies to combat it, took the view that prostitution *per se* was not punishable, but proposed the despatch to the camps of women who refused to engage in socially useful labour. Hardened prostitutes should be dealt with, it was suggested, by those government bodies responsible for the struggle against labour desertion.[11] Previous socialist writing had not foreshadowed such an argument, the assumption being that while prostitution was inevitable as long as the bourgeoisie remained, it would under socialism fade away. Transitional strategies, appropriate for a society that had overthrown the rule of landlords and capitalists, had never been discussed; the construction of socialism in an underdeveloped country, one plunged moreover into a debilitating civil war, had never been envisaged.

It might be reasoned that orthodox socialist analysis contained within itself the seeds of this deviation, that the belief in prostitution's inevitability under capitalism encouraged a fatalism that paralysed action, and that a lack of transitional strategies made orthodox social democracy vulnerable to hijack by authoritarianism. But Bolshevism provided the source for tolerant as well as repressive treatments – tolerance during the NEP period and repression during the Civil War and during and after the first five-year plan – so flawed ideologies cannot offer a total explanation for policies on prostitution.

After the introduction of NEP, talk of prostitutes as work shirkers ceased, and the labour camps were for the most part closed. With industrial rationalization and rising unemployment, the concept of 'labour desertion' no longer made sense. Thousands of women, with no job and a family to support, took to the streets. One observer remarked:

In our transitional time, woman's body is still a marketable commodity. It is sought out on the streets, and the boulevards, in theatres, at restaurants and railway carriages. Everywhere we meet men, hungrily eyeing women to see if their love is for sale. A woman knows that if all other sources should be exhausted, there is still one which will not change and without fail will secure her a livelihood.[12]

It took time though for the Bolsheviks to adjust, psychologically, to economic and political retreat, and to the accumulating social problems, including prostitution, that were too deep and numerous for easy and immediate solution. Thus, Aleksandra Kollontai's short story, *Sisters* – about a woman whose estranged husband had once brought a prostitute to their home and who wonders whether she too, now redundant and alone, will be forced onto the streets – was criticized by *Kommunistka*, the communist women's journal, for not showing the power of organization and of comradeship to keep women away from prostitution. The journal published the story, but with a note from the editors setting out their disagreements – would not it have been better to have had a working woman as heroine and why did the central character fail to turn to the welfare organizations? The editors made no mention, perhaps did not notice, that Kollontai drew her anti-hero, the husband and client, as an 'oppressor' – he is a *communist* businessman, it is true, but works for a trust, rubs shoulders with the Nepmen and has acquired their habits, even to the point of using perfume, something which for Kollontai was a symbol of alien class allegiance and unhealthy attitudes and lifestyles. *Sisters*, like the Moscow Trade Union poster, and also published in 1923, raised the theme of the economically powerful male who sexually exploits the downtrodden female.[13] A popular pamphlet by G. I. and Ia. Lifshchits, published some time before, had taken the similar view that prostitution was maintained by the decadence of the exploiting classes, and contrasted the vices of the oppressors with the healthy sexual lives of proletarians. 'Prostitution cannot be a proletarian matter, because it presupposes the existence of clients from a higher social class than the prostitutes themselves.'[14]

Preoccupation with class and morality was an important characteristic of the traditional social-democratic approach. August Bebel and other socialist writers had underscored the victim status of the prostitute by constant reference to the decadence of the ruling class, from which the prostitutes' clients were allegedly recruited. They were not the first to make the connection between class and sexuality; it was in fact a leit-motif of public discourse on prostitution in the nineteenth century. The socialists did, however, give the matter their own particular ideological twist: whilst mainstream commentators concentrated on the loose behaviour of the lower orders, particularly their women, the socialists inveighed against the decadence of the upper classes, especially the males, whom they pictured as rapacious beasts, in a sexual as well as an economic sense. Capitalism was seen as a threat to the sexual as well as the economic integrity of the proletariat; prostitution stood for the violation both of the women and of the working class.

In the 1920s, this theme was no longer a major one. The upper-class ravager who lured young proletarian girls to a life of depravity had ceased to be a believable character; during the Civil War there were no suitable contenders, and the Nepmen, later in the decade, had neither the numbers nor the style to qualify for the role. During the Civil War, the contrast between idleness and industry remained central to the presentation of prostitution, but for the most part the woman was now the guilty party. Focus was on the prostitute as work shirker rather than the client as sexual oppressor, on the woman as active agent rather than passive object, on what she herself failed to do, not what was done to her.

This is not to say that the sexual subtext to the discussion of prostitution disappeared completely. Metaphors of pollution, no doubt a reflection of uncertainty about sexual identities and moral norms, were from time to time employed in the literature. Prostitution was a 'disgraceful spot' and every measure must be taken to wash it away. There was talk of 'the slime of the dreadful marsh' and of 'foul vice-ridden bodies'.[15] On the whole, though, the writings of the twenties on prostitution eschewed such language, as authors strove for a correctly scientific manner. Another reason for the desexualization of the debate on prostitution in the 1920s was that the 'sexual question' had found itself a place in public discussion on the family and morality.

With the introduction of NEP, women could hardly be blamed for work shirking, but their agency, now understood as a force for positive rather than negative behaviour, continued to be given emphasis. The image of woman as strong and self-reliant, promoted in the twenties by the women's department (Zhenotdel) and the women's press, did something to erode the conventional portrayal of the prostitute as passive victim. More importantly, wider social changes, specifically in the organization of prostitution, were reducing its plausibility.

Women, according to the Zhenotdel, should help each other, and should cultivate independence and a sense of dignity. In one short story published in Rabotnitsa, Lenka loses her job and, not being able to find another, takes to the streets. One day she meets a woman friend, who helps her return home where she will be able to lead an honest life.[16] In another story, the young woman sleeps with men in exchange for money to buy fashionable clothes, until a pregnancy and bungled abortion bring her to her senses. She realizes how awful she has been, and how much more fun she will have spending her time with the other women down at the club.

The government policy of deregulation and non-punishability arguably made it easier for women to abandon prostitution. Those who decided to stay had no need to fear the 'yellow ticket' or excessive police harassment, and were more likely than before to work independently, less likely to seek the protection of a pimp or a brothel. 'Apartment' prostitution became widespread in the twenties. In Kazan eight women rented a six-room flat together, on their own, without a madame, sharing responsibilities.[17] (Revolutionary ideology had unexpected effects!) Though 'dens of vice' still existed, they were, unlike the pre-revolutionary establishments, usually modest in size, an informal arrangement between two or three women and a landlady, who was more likely to be an impoverished widow than a wily Nepwoman. Prostitution in the 1920s was women's business, not big business. In England, according to Judith Walkowitz, the regulation introduced by the Contagious Diseases Act in the 1860s had served to turn prostitutes into an 'outcast group'.[18] In Soviet Russia, in the 1920s, the process was in reverse; the mechanisms which in the past had served, admittedly not always successfully, to keep prostitutes apart and isolated from society, were removed, and as a result the women became more integrated into their communities.

Assimilation was also assisted by the changing social composition of the profession. As the number of women residing in the urban areas grew, so did the pool of city women from whom prostitutes were recruited. It was no longer unusual for prostitutes to be urban born, or at least to have had several years' residence in the city and be well versed in its ways. A Kazan study found that 40 per cent of its sample were members of trade unions and 50 per cent were registered at the labour exchange.[19] Also, prostitutes were more likely than before to be married and to live in fairly permanent relationships with men, another pointer to their acceptance within their communities. A survey undertaken by Moscow State University found that of the 114 women who answered a question on marital status, 9 had registered husbands and 53 lived in common-law marriages;[20] 80 per cent of the Kazan sample were married.[21]

If the prostitute as casualty of class exploitation and marginalization no longer had the same resonance as before 1917, the notion of victim was not entirely abandoned. Women were disadvantaged in the economic sphere, which provided them with too few opportunities to earn a living wage and develop their potential, and in marriage, which enslaved them and doomed them to inequality – or such were the views of the Zhenotdel, the unions, and most importantly, of the medical profession. Most importantly, because in the 1920s the doctors were more active than any other party or professional group in the production of commentary and analysis of prostitution and in the campaign against it. It was venereologists who organized local 'days' and 'weeks of action', held meetings, published pamphlets; they also fought for welfare measures to help women in need. The medical profession condemned repressive measures against prostitutes, its anxiety about the spread of venereal disease outweighed by belief in individual freedom. A leaflet produced by the State Institute of Venereology warned prostitutes that sexually transmitted diseases were an inevitable occupational hazard, adding in the politest of tones that 'if you like' the authorities will try and find you work.[22] Repeatedly the doctors made the point that the struggle was not against prostitutes but against prostitution, that prostitutes were the victims of circumstance and should not be punished.[23]

Legislators, also, held to the principles of non-punishability.[24] The Criminal Code introduced in 1922 made provision for prosecution only of individuals who forced women into prostitution or lived off 'immoral' earnings. (Articles 170, 171).[25] The law may have established the principle of unpunishability, but the law enforcement agencies did not always take heed. The Commissariat of Internal Affairs, Narkomindel, had a reputation for favouring a tough approach to prostitutes. In the wake of the revolution it canvassed the reintroduction of regulation. In mid-1922, it developed a proposal for the organization of a 'Moral Militia', a special task force charged with arresting brothel owners, fining clients, and, under certain circumstances, publishing their names.[26] No sooner did these plans become known than they were subjected to sharp criticism: Petrograd Gubispolkom's Interdepartmental Commission on the Struggle Against Prostitution said they amounted to the reintroduction of regulation; *Izvestiia VTsIK* was of the same opinion, and also warned that publishing the names of clients drove prostitution underground and made more difficult the fight against venereal diseases.[27] The proposal was put to one side, but even without these extra powers, the militia contrived to win itself a reputation for heavy-handed interference. Some of its members were in agreement with official policy on prostitution – there were even those who in their enthusiasm to do good works forced clients to marry the prostitutes they had visited – but the majority appears to have opted for measures of repression. There were reports of raids on houses of ill-repute, and of prostitutes receiving fines and rough treatment.[28] According to one report, the picture in 1923 was 'literally the same as we saw in the old world, the old system of the oppression of women'.[29] Although this would seem to be an exaggeration, directives issued by the authorities in the mid and late twenties suggest that something of the 'old world' continued to survive. A typical directive had this to say:

Bearing in mind that a woman engaging in prostitution has taken this path because of unfortunate material or living conditions, all militia workers who have dealings with such a woman in the course of their work, must observe all the rules of polite and correct conduct and in no circumstances allow themselves to behave in an offensive manner.[30]

Judges as well as militiamen tended to treat prostitution as if it were a criminal offence. During the Civil War, despite the nice distinction made by the Interdepartmental Commission between selling sex (which was not punishable) and shirking work (which was), courts in Moscow, close to the hub of things, appeared to be unaware of official policy; at any rate, they handed down sentences 'for prostitution'.[31] This practice continued, the legal press admitted, even after the introduction of the 1922 legal code.[32] The Tomsk newspaper *Krasnoe znamia*, in 1923, mentioned the appearance in court of two young prostitutes along with their landlady, and reported that the defendants were all sentenced under Article 171 to three years' imprisonment with confiscation of property. The sentences, however, were provisional – the two young women, peasant migrants, were reckoned to be insufficiently politically conscious to understand the nature of their crimes (while the landlady was let off because she was proletarian).[33] This suggests that, even when the law was misunderstood, the view of the prostitute as victim prompted leniency.

To what extent was this view shared by 'unofficial' society? Of the opinions of the prostitutes themselves there is little evidence available, and it is not easy to interpret, since it comes to us as it was reported to, and by, the experts and the authorities. In these exchanges, the prostitutes were clearly in subordinate and disadvantaged positions, and reacted to their powerlessness by being truculent and uncooperative, or by seeking approval and giving 'acceptable' answers: just as women who wanted state abortions were inclined to give 'economic need' as their motive, knowing that such an answer was more likely to get them the permission they desired, so prostitutes might well be tempted to explain their 'fall' with a story of victimization, in the knowledge that this would win them sympathy. Their response to the questionnaires suggests that they were capable of making the same connections as the experts and the authorities between orphaned childhood, early initiation into sex, unemployment and prostitution. They might well have agreed that they had been unlucky in life; few though appear to resemble the downcast, downtrodden women of the Moscow Trade Union poster. Prostitutes come across in this material as women who know their mind and have made their own choices: victim of circumstance, yet mistress of their own fate.

They were not cowed by social scientist, doctor or militiaman, whom they frequently shocked with their cheeky manners and penchant for obscenities. If they were short-tempered and quarrelled with each other, they also showed solidarity in the face of adversity, helping each other out in time of need. They organized their own trade, dividing the streets into pitches, and operated something like a closed shop. In Saratov, in the early twenties, prostitutes, presumably influenced by the military terminology that was so widespread during the Civil War, referred to their streets as 'fronts',[34] an expression which also captures the typical attitude of the women to their trade: it was a job, not pleasant perhaps, but a way to make ends meet. They were not in it, apparently, for the sex – the vast majority professed to view intercourse with indifference, if not revulsion. They did not, however, reject men, and regarded the security of monogamy as highly desirable. The doctor who reported that prostitutes wanted to be with one man, 'but not for longer than 1–3 months',[35] seems to have had an unrepresentative sample; other surveys report 80 per cent of the interviewees wanting to marry and have children. The evidence suggests that many of these women realized their dreams. One 22-year-old confessed:

'I had relations with many men, they all filled me with repugnance. I drank a lot so as not to think about the future. Then I met this communist and in the years since that time he has not held my past against me. I was terribly miserable. Now I am terribly happy.'

A second ex-prostitute had this to report: 'Now it's six years I've been married. My husband loves me and has forgiven everything; the only sorrow is that we have no children.'[36]

It was argued by some experts that as a communist morality developed, and as the place of prostitution in the oppression of the female sex was understood, popular attitudes would change. A number of women interviewed in Kursk in the mid-twenties said they would rather die than engage in prostitution, and their strong feelings on the subject were allegedly motivated not by fear of the social ostracism suffered by the 'fallen woman', but by a sense of their human dignity.[37] Men, too, it was claimed, were beginning to see prostitution as a shameful and exploitative institution; according to the venereologist, V. M. Bronner, a leading expert in the field, the number of men to visit prostitutes was declining: while in 1924, nearly one-fifth of patients at the first Moscow VD clinic had caught the disease from prostitutes, by 1930 the figure had fallen to under 10 per cent.[38]

Not all the evidence was as positive. Students in Orenburg, asked whether brothels were necessary, answered in the affirmative, the female as well as the male contingent, arguing that men had to satisfy their sexual needs.[39] Another survey, conducted in 1925, found that one-fifth of young people considered prostitution to be both necessary and desirable.[40] 'What is one to do?' wrote one young man, clearly close to despair. 'Marriage is not an option; it is forbidden to visit a prostitute; casual sex is fraught with the possibility of alimony and disgrace.'[41] Young men who could not afford to support a household, and who did not want to pay alimony, finding no answer to this question, tended to ignore the injunction to pass by the prostitute on the other side. One in four still had their first sexual experience with a prostitute, and 40 per cent of male students paid for sexual services,[42] as did many older urban males, married and unmarried. None of these categories appears to have worried unduly that their communities would censure them for their actions.

It would be a mistake to imagine that the same level of tolerance was shown to the women as to the men. The double morality was still strong, and while young men who had no sexual experience were made fun of, promiscuous women – and the prostitute was in common parlance the slut (*bliad'*) – could expect a certain amount of public harassment. Nevertheless, the survey material indicates that many workers saw prostitution as offering a sensible solution to the problems confronting women as well as men: not only did it provide an outlet for male sexual appetites without the responsibilities and expense of marriage, it also gave poor and destitute women a source of income. Widows in working-class Leningrad, it was said, engaged in prostitution without anyone thinking them worse for it.[43]

In 1930, medical workers in Stalingrad reported that the questions asked at public lectures revealed resentment against prostitutes for the fine clothes they wore, and ignorance of the economic factors pushing women to sell themselves. In all probability, recent migrants from the countryside made up a large percentage of these audiences, and no doubt further research will show how peasants brought with them to the towns conservative attitudes on family and morality, and on prostitution. What is already clear is that towards the end of the twenties the militia's advocacy of repressive measures against prostitutes became more influential.

In 1926, the January issue of *Administrativnyi vestnik*, the journal of

the Commissariat of Internal Affairs (NKVnudel), published an article
on the struggle against prostitution. The author, D. M. Levin, presented
an historical survey of the campaign, and made the point that Soviet
power fights prostitution not prostitutes, listing the measures that must
be taken to improve the status of women. All this was uncontroversial.
He added, however, that prostitutes posed a dangerous threat to
society, and he suggested that a commission should be set up to examine
the cases of women suspected of prostitution. Confirmed prostitutes, he
argued, should be exiled to sparsely populated areas so that there would
be no opportunities for them to practise their old trade in the new
environment.[44] In the early twenties, such propositions had been
greeted by an immediate outcry of protest, this time round their reception was respectful and warm. There had always been those who had
spoken out for harsh measures against the clients, who had argued that
the names of men who visited prostitutes should be published and that
they should be deprived of their right to vote; now the prostitute herself
was also targeted. In 1929, the women's magazine *Delegatka* published
an account of how three men had followed a prostitute and her client
from the Berlin restaurant in central Moscow to the Sandunov baths,
had apprehended them and taken the couple to the local militia pre-
cinct. The militia was, in this instance, reluctant to take action: 'These
citizens have not caused a breach of the peace. We have no instructions
on such matters'; *Delegatka*, on the other hand, did not hesitate, and
published the names of both the client and the woman.[45]

At the same time, the Zhenotdel and the welfare organizations were
stepping up their 'rescue' activities. Industrialization was bringing to the
big cities large numbers of young women with few contacts and little
money, who were likely, it was feared, to fall into the temptation of
prostitution. The number of places in Moscow's sheltered workshops
more than doubled between 1928 and 1930.[46] 'Social patronage' centres
were set up at key locations, such as city railway stations. The Kazan
station in Moscow was hung with posters. 'Needy and homeless
women!', they read, 'Turn for advice or help to the centre of social help
at the Kazan station and to the Patronage Secretariat, 4th Mesh-
chanskaia, 15, tel 5-03-23 between 12 and 2 daily. Social patronage
defends your rights and helps you return to a life of work and social
utility.'[47] The women who ran the centre did not simply wait around to
be approached; in the evenings they patrolled the toilets and buffet,
doing their best to persuade women to return to a 'working life'. Conferences of former prostitutes who had successfully made this transition
were held in Moscow in 1931 and 1932.[48]

Impatience had been growing for some time, nevertheless, with women who refused to be reformed, who disobeyed and discredited the workers' state. The two views of the prostitute, as victim and villain coexisted for a while, the contradictions of subscribing to both, partially resolved by the division of prostitutes into the good and the bad, into those who could be returned to the fold and those who were beyond rescue. An article in one medical paper had this to say:

Talking about prostitutes and prostitution we do not at all have in mind that expensive vice, which with a wave of vulgarity sweeps across the central streets of our large towns. With prostitution of this sort we can and must fight with administrative actions – exile to places far from the large centres, with strict isolation, etc. Here we are talking about working women or peasant women, who cannot cope with the heavy struggle against economic factors: hunger, need and unemployment.[49]

D. M. Levin made the same distinction between prostitutes 'who had not yet been smeared by the slime of the dreadful marsh' and could easily be returned to the 'labouring family' and the other recalcitrant ones, who were beyond redemption.[50]

The prostitute offended not because she represented decadence and vice, but because she failed to conform, to fit into the collective. She was work shirker not sexual deviant. The title of a book on prostitution published in 1929, *Off the street into production*,[51] is expressive of the industrial focus of this period and of the faith in the power of participation in the work process to cure all ills. Il'f and Petrov's novel *The Golden Calf* implied that industrialization did succeed in reducing the level of prostitution. On his visit to a Central Asian town, their hero, Ostap Bender, discovers that the local high life is being eliminated: the native bazaar is about to be demolished to make way for a hospital and a cooperative centre; where there was once 'By Moonlight' there is now a 'factory-kitchen' selling non-alcoholic beverages, which has 'plates . . . washed by an electric machine' and a graph showing that stomach ailments 'have fallen sharply'. The prostitution graph 'has also dropped sharply', notes Ostap's local guide.[52] The experts were in agreement. 'The basic preconditions for the solution of [this problem]', wrote V. M. Bronner in 1931, 'the liquidation of unemployment, the mass drawing of women into production, the growth of the living, material and cultural level of workers and the broad labouring masses, already exist.'[53] If in 1929 there were reported to be 3,000 prostitutes in Moscow, by 1931 the number was said to be down to 400. In Tula the drop over the same period was from 500 to 24.[54]

One would have expected on the contrary, a spectacular rise. The over-ambitious industrialization projects of the five-year plan, and the forced collectivization, had thrown the country into turmoil: mass migration, poverty and hunger were the norm. So were these figures wishful thinking? Did the talk of the 'liquidation' of prostitution mask a rise in its incidence, just as the rhetoric of factory discipline went hand-in-hand with work-place chaos? It would seem probable that, as during the 1914–21 era of world war and civil war, when families were separated, uprooted, and deprived of the means of livelihood, the number of women exchanging sexual favours for bread and shelter was on the increase, but that prostitution, defined as commercial sex engaged in on a permanent basis, declined dramatically. For a government that had the political will and wherewithal to collectivize 25 million peasant households in a matter of months, the 'liquidation' of a few thousand prostitutes cannot have seemed a very difficult task. This 'victory' was achieved through the break-up of working-class communities, and the marshalling of public opinion behind a more rigid moral code; Motylev's designation of the prostitute as a socially-dangerous element deserving punishment had triumphed.

The revolution of 1917 confirmed the right of politics and sexuality to a place in public discussion, and by the same token conferred marginal status on the debates about prostitution, an issue which previously had acted as a conduit for anxieties about social change and sexual identities. Bolshevik ideological commitment to welfare and the emancipation of women, nevertheless, kept it in the public eye, although it did not ensure a consistent treatment. Socialist teachings on prostitution had been scattered and fragmentary. 'Orthodoxy', set down most famously by August Bebel in his *Woman and Socialism*, exercised little influence on pre-revolutionary Bolshevism, and in the early years of the Soviet period was easily suppressed by the spirit of 'war communism': by the desire to establish control, and the confidence that to punish in the name of the revolution those social groups who were extraneous to the proletarian struggle was both possible and necessary. In the NEP period, it came into its own. Members of the medical profession rather than party officials were most prominent in the campaign against prostitution; they worked, though, with apparent conviction within the political ideology of the moment, preaching tolerance and the elimination of prostitution through full employment and welfare, equality and emancipation, aiming to provide opportunities for women so that they would not need to choose prostitution. With the introduction of the five-year plan and the pressure for immediate and full-scale industrialization, talk of residual class antagonisms, which had earlier explained the existence of prostitution and legitimated the struggle for women's liberation, ceased; in consequence the prostitute lost her victim status and, recategorized as villain, was marked out for 'liquidation'.

174   *Elizabeth Waters*

   In the Western world, this century, the reordering of political and sexual discourse, a result of a decline in the rhetoric of class antagonisms and the emergence of scientific and public debate on sexuality, has redirected attention away from prostitution. Rescue work has been replaced by welfare, and prostitution redefined as a medical problem, the moral approach giving way to a matter-of-fact pragmatism. In the Soviet Union, this process was interrupted by the repressive policies of the early thirties. The official file on prostitution, closed by the rise of the Stalinist system, has only recently been reopened, after a silence of more than fifty years, by glasnost and perestroika.[55]

Notes

1. Lenin Library Poster Collection: P2 X, no. 818; the poster is reproduced in *Seht Her, Genossen! Plakate aus der Sowjetunion* (Harenberg, 1982), p. 153.
2. During the twenties, posters were an important method of communicating social messages on such topics as cleanliness, literacy and atheism. Because female illiteracy was high, posters on 'women's issues' were particularly common, though prostitution was not in fact a major theme.
3. *Shestoi s"ezd vserossiisskogo soiuza professional'nykh soiuzov* (Moscow, 1924), p. 223.
4. L. E. Motylev, 'Ob otrazhenii bor'by s prostitutsici v piatiletnem plane', *Venerologiia i dermatologiia*, no. 7 (1929), pp. 87–95.
5. For an influential exposition of the socialist view, see A. Bebel, *Zhenshchina i sotsializm* (Moscow, 1923). On the theories and policies of the German SPD see W. Thönnessen, *The Emancipation of Women. The Rise and Decline of the Women's Movement in German Social Democracy 1863–1933* (London, 1973).
6. For a discussion of the campaign against regulation see L. Bernstein, 'Sonia's Daughters: Prostitution and Society in Russia' (PhD dissertation, University of California, 1987).
7. *Trudy pervogo vserossiiskogo s"ezda po bor'be s torgom zhenshchinami i ego prichinami 21–25 aprelia 1910* (St Petersburg, 1911). On the Congress see L. Edmondson, *Feminism in Russia, 1900–1917* (London, 1984), pp. 145–6. The Mensheviks, it should be noted, gave more attention in their writings than Bolsheviks to prostitution, and were more involved in the campaign to abolish regulation.
8. V. I. Lenin, 'Piatyi mezhdunarodnyi s"ezd po bor'be s prostitutsiei', *Polnoe sobranie sochinenii*, 5th edn, vol. 23, pp. 331–2.
9. C. Zetkin, *Reminiscences of Lenin* (London, 1929), p. 51.
10. A. Kollontai, *Prostitutsiia i mery bor'by s nei (Rech' na 111 Vserossiiskom soveshchanii zaveduiushchikh gubzhenotdelami)* (Moscow, 1921).
11. 'Tezisy po bor'be s prostitutsiei, vyrabotannye mezhduvedomstvennoi

komissiei po bor'be s prostitutsiei', *Materialy mezhvedomstvennoi komissii po bor'be s prostitutsiei* (Moscow, 1921), pp. 4–7; 'O merakh bor'by s prostitutsiei, Tsirkuliar no 93', in *Materialy*, pp. 8–13; see also I. Gel'man, 'Prostitutsiia i mery bor'by s neiu', *Voprosy sotsial'nogo obespecheniia*, no. 2 (1921), p. 59.

12. Zal'tsman, 'O merakh bor'by s prostitutsiei i venerizmom v gorode Smolenske', in *Prostitutsiia i mery bor'by s nei* (Smolensk, 1925), p. 31.

13. A. Kollontai, 'Sestry', *Kommunistka*, nos 3–4 (1923), pp. 23–6.

14. G. I. and Ia. I. Lifshchits, *Sotsial'nye korni prostitutsii* (Iaroslavl, 1920), p. 21.

15. See for example G. I. and Ia. I. Lifshchits, *Sotsial'nye korni. Prostitutsiia i mery bor'by s nei* (Smolensk, 1925); and D. M. Levin, 'K voprosu o bor'be s sotsial'no-paraziticheskom elementom', *Administrativnyi vestnik*, no. 12 (1925), passium.

16. E. Anurova, 'S raznykh dorog na odno', *Rabotnitsa*, no. 19 (1924), pp. 17–18.

17. S. Ia. Golosovker, *O prostitutsii* (Kazan, 1925), p. 9.

18. Judith R. Walkowitz, *Prostitution and Victorian Society. Women, Class and the States* (Cambridge, 1980). For a discussion of the extent to which prostitutes in pre-revolutionary Russia constituted an 'outcast' group, see B. A. Engel, 'St Petersburg prostitutes', *Russian Review*, vol. 49 (1989), pp. 21–44.

19. Golosovker, *O prostitutsii*, p. 6.

20. D. P. Rodin, 'Iz dannykh o sovremennoi prostitutsii', *Pravo i zhizn'*, book 8–10 (1926), p. 100.

21. Golosovker, *O prostitutsii*, p. 6.

22. N. Rossiianskii, 'Bor'ba s prostitutsiei i venerologicheskie dispansery', *Venerologiia i dermatologiia*, no. 2 (1924), p. 79.

23. A. Ia. Gutkin, *Zadachi sovremennogo obshchestva v bor'be s prostitutsiei* (Orenburg, 1924), p. 6; M. Barash, *Prostitutsiia* (Moscow, 1925), p. 4; L. M. Vasilevskii, *Prostitutsiia i rabochaia molodezh'* (1924), p. 20.

24. There was little discussion in the legal press about prostitution at the time of the drafting of the 1922 Criminal Code. L. Eratov in *Ezhenedel'nik sovetskoi iustitsii* argued that though prostitution was in principle punishable, in practice the campaign against this evil should be fought by social rather than legal measures. See 'Nakazuema li prostitutsiia?' no. 4 (1922), pp. 4–6.

25. The references to prostitution in the Code were as follows:
Article 170: Constraining a person from selfish or other personal motives to engage in prostitution, by the use of physical or psychological influence is punished by deprivation of freedom in strict isolation for a period of not less than three years.
Article 171: Procuring, the maintenance of dens of vice, and the recruitment of women to prostitution are punished by deprivation of freedom for a period of not less than three years with the confiscation of all or a part of property.
    The 1926 Criminal Code combined the two articles (as Article 155) and replaced the minimum sentence with a maximum sentence of five years. See

Ugolovnyi kodeks RSFSR redaktsii 1926 (Moscow, 1926), p. 40. This was in line with a general tendency to give judges greater discretionary powers and encourage shorter sentences.

26. S. G. Bykov, Prostitutsiia v gorode Saratove i mery bor'by s nei (Saratov, 1922), p. 21.

27. A. Prigradov-Kudrin, 'Militsiia nravov', *Izvestiia VTsIK*, 18 June 1922. Clara Zetkin wrote an influential attack on the proposed Moral Militia. See 'Protiv militsii nravov', *Izvestiia*, 8 July 1922; reprinted in V. M. Bronner, 'Bor'ba s prostitutsiei v RSFSR' in *Prostitutsiia v Rossii* (Moscow, 1927), pp. 90–4.

28. S. G. Bykov refers to the 'excessive zeal' of the militiamen, see *Prostitutsiia v gorode Saratova*, p. 21. M. Sheinin talks of the chaotic state of the legal process. Prostitutes, he says, were put in concentration camps, sentenced to terms of forced labour, were made fun of, shown contempt. See 'Opyt raboty Vitebskoi komissii po bor'be s prostitutsiei', *Voprosy sotsial'nogo obespecheniia*, no. 2 (8) (1922), p. 13.

29. L. A. and L. M. Vasilevskie, *Prostitutsiia i Novaia Rossiia* (Tver, 1923), p. 72.

30. B. V. Tsukker, *Prostitutsiia i ee prichiny* (Moscow, 1927), p. 41.

31. See TsGAOR goroda Moskvy, f. 1488, d. 61–3; f. 1188, d. 30.

32. M. Strogovich, 'Bor'ba s prostitutsiei putem ugolovnoi repressii', *Ezhenedel'nik sovetskoi iustitsii*, no. 37 (1925), pp. 1212–4.

33. *Krasnoe znamia*, 4 July 1924.

34. See Bykov, *Prostitutsiia v gorode Saratove*, p. 11.

35. Golosovker, *O prostitutsii*, p. 7.

36. S. V. Trakhtenburg, 'Polovaia zhizn' zhenshchiny', *Venerologiia i dermatologiia*, no. 4 (1926), p. 633.

37. V. Bronner, 'Iskorenim prostitutsiiu', *Kommunistka*, no. 8 (1928), p. 21.

38. V. M. Bronner, *Prostitutsiia i puti ee likvidatsii* (Moscow, 1931), p. 29. It is impossible to say, of course, how honest people were in framing their replies.

39. Gutkin, *Zadachi sovremennogo obshchestva v bor'be s prositutsiei*, p. 13.

40. Golosovker, *O prostitutsii*, p. 5.

41. O. Z. Shapiro, 'Opyt izucheniia zaprosov i interesov auditorii v voprosakh sanitarnogo prosveshcheniia', *Venerologiia i dermatologiia*, no. 6 (1929), p. 84.

42. Vasilevskie, *Prostitutsiia i Novaia Rossiia*, pp. 45–6.

43. B. Rein and L. Zheleznov, *S ulitsy na proizvodstvo* (Moscow, 1929), p. 10.

44. D. M. Levin, 'Bor'ba s prostitutsiei', in *Administrativnyi vestnik*, no. 1 (1926), pp. 34–5.

45. 'Po goryachim sledam' *Delegatka*, no. 17 (1929), p. 12.

46. V. Bronner, *La Lutte contre la prostitution en URSS* (Moscow, 1936), p. 43.

47. D. I. Lass, *Po puti k likvidatsii prostitutsii* (Moscow, 1931), p. 22.

48. Fannina W. Halle, *Woman in Soviet Russia* (London, 1933), pp. 244–53.

49. *Meditsina*, no. 16 (1925), p. 11.

50. Levin, 'K voprosu o bor'be s sotsial'no-paraziticheskom elementom', p. 55.

51. Rein and Zheleznov, *S ulitsy na proizvodstvo*.

52. I. Il'f and E. Petrov, *Zolotoi telenok* (Moscow, 1961), pp. 343–4.

53. Bronner, *Prostitutsiia i puti ee likvidatsii*, p. 3.
54. *Ibid*, p. 30.
55. For discussion of the recent debate about prostitution in the Soviet Union see my 'Restructuring the "Woman Question": prostitution and perestroika', *Feminist Review*, no. 33, 1989, pp. 3–19; and 'Changing attitudes to prostitution in the Gorbachev era' in J. Riordan (ed.), *Soviet Social Reality in the Mirror of Glasnost* (London, 1991). Prostitution in the 1920s has been examined in G. A. Bordiugov, 'Sotsial'nyi parazitizm ili sotsial'nye anomalii? (Iz istorii bor'by s alkogolizmom, nishchestvom, prostitutsiei i brodiazhestvom v 20–30e gody)', *Istoriia SSSR*, no. 1 (1989), pp. 60–73; and A. S. Meliksetian, 'Prostitutsiia v 20-e gody', *Sotsiologicheskie issledovaniia*, no. 3 (1989), pp. 71–4.

9   Young women and perestroika

Sue Bridger

During the six years of Mikhail Gorbachev's attempted perestroika, the official approach to issues of concern to women has been markedly different from that relating to many other areas of social, political and economic life. At a time of radical change and questioning of the legacy of the past, policy on women has been characterized by a renewed commitment to programmes instituted during the 'period of stagnation'. Legislative change on benefits, leave and the provision of part-time work has been designed to assist women to spend more time with their children and to promote further the 'strengthening of the family' begun under Brezhnev. In the area of family policy and women's roles in society, glasnost has provided a ready platform for conservative as well as radical voices. As economic reform begins to affect Soviet workers, however, government policies on the family may not necessarily prove to be the boon to women that their promoters promise.

The policy of glasnost has, of course, not only encouraged debate but has turned the spotlight on to areas of women's experience previously untouched by the Soviet media. Difficult and dangerous working conditions, prostitution and the treatment of abortion and childbirth have all come under scrutiny. Sex has ceased to be a taboo subject as censorship has been relaxed and attitudes have liberalized. Many of the issues raised are inevitably of concern to women of all ages, yet others affect young women disproportionately. The question of sex education, unplanned pregnancies, divorce and the employment problems of women with young children are issues of major concern to young women in particular. As a group, young women, and especially young mothers, are a prime target of both benefit changes and government sponsored campaigns on the family. This chapter attempts to assess the impact on young women both of the liberalization of Soviet society and the combination of legislative and economic change.

For the purposes of this chapter the broad definition of youth as the 15–30 age-group characteristic of much Soviet writing is applied. As there are some 30 million young women within these parameters it

178

would be presumptuous to suggest that the argument presented here
constitutes a definitive view, especially in a society as diverse as the
USSR. The material is, for example, overwhelmingly based on Russian
sources. Nevertheless, it is hoped that the chapter will at least serve to
highlight both positive and negative aspects of some significant trends
affecting young women in the USSR during perestroika.

Sex education and information

In 1984 a course entitled 'The Ethics and Psychology of Family Life' was
introduced into the Soviet school curriculum. Its appearance marked
the culmination of the style of demographic policy instigated under
Leonid Brezhnev. The aim of 'strengthening the Soviet family', as it was
described in the 1981 decree extending maternity benefit, was to be
promoted through an increase in literature, propaganda and instruction
about family life. During the 1970s, concern over the falling birthrate in
European areas of the USSR led not only to a series of legislative
measures aimed at directly encouraging women to have more children
but also to a closer look at the institution of the family itself. The
instability of the Soviet family as typified by the high incidence of
divorce came to be seen as a major factor in both disrupting a woman's
childbearing years and also promoting a sense of insecurity which made
her psychologically ill-prepared to consider producing more than one or
two children.[1]

The pronatalist campaign which followed from this drew heavily upon
the work of Soviet educational theorists in order to encourage a change
in attitudes towards personal relationships and family life. From the
1960s the view had been propounded that only a form of upbringing
sharply differentiated by gender was capable of producing stable
families. The work of such writers as Khripkova and Kolesov not only
ascribed to the two sexes a range of differing characteristics which were
deemed 'natural' but also insisted that girls and boys should be treated
in such a way as to emphasize these 'natural' differences, thereby producing 'real men' and 'real women': by extension, it was implied, the
attraction of opposites would inevitably produce harmonious, long-last-
ing and fertile marriages.[2]

The basis of the 'Ethics' course lay firmly in work of this type. The
authors of its approved textbooks explored the nature of friendship and
attraction, drawing heavily on the classic works of Russian literature.
They explained the need for give and take in marriage, a sound
approach to the family budget and the importance of tolerance in relationships with parents and in-laws. They also expounded the by then

accepted view on the essence of femininity and masculinity and their importance in personal relationships. What they did not do was tackle the question of sex. Within a year of the course's introduction a change of national leadership and the beginnings of glasnost were encouraging criticism of it as being divorced from reality.

It would be misleading to suggest that the course was not or could not be used as a basis for sex education or for a discussion of those aspects of personal relationships of most concern to young people. Numerous examples have appeared in the media of talented teachers using the course in just this way, inviting local doctors in to speak, using information from sociological surveys and the writings of psychologists. Nevertheless, the avoidance of sex education in the official syllabus has led to accusations of both superficiality and hypocrisy.[3] On a practical level, the problem has been compounded by a lack of training and, not surprisingly in a country where sex has for so long been a taboo subject, embarrassment in those expected to teach the course. As the weekly, *Sobesednik*, put it in a forthright article on young people and sexually transmitted disease:

Here in the clinic on the main street of Tyumen, all we heard from the doctors is how stunned they are by the teenagers' low level of knowledge about sex. But what can you expect when most adults are not well-versed in the subject, to put it mildly. Tenth-form students laugh openly at the subject, 'The Ethics and Psychology of Family Life'. The teacher – some 'upright old auntie', as the school students call her – tells them about the family from some thick pre-perestroika textbook ... and enthusiastically quotes the poets. But 'auntie' doesn't tell them what to do to avoid getting pregnant.[4]

The article quoted above is illustrative of the changing social climate in the USSR since 1985. From cautious beginnings, the press, and especially youth publications such as *Sobesednik*, have broken taboos on printing information about sex in a widely available form. With the discovery that the demand for this information was colossal, articles have become increasingly bold in the range of subjects tackled: discussions of masturbation, impotence, frigidity, orgasm and homosexuality have all appeared since 1988.

The appearance of information on sex has not, however, been produced by a change in government attitudes towards marriage and the family. Concern over the birthrate continues to be regularly expressed, whilst 'strengthening the family' remains a priority. In line with many of the social developments which have taken place since 1985, the opening up of discussion and information about sex can be viewed as an attempt to inject some realism into an issue of public concern.

The new honesty about sex, though widely welcomed by young

people themselves, has created a considerable stir in the older generation. The demographer, Viktor Perevedentsev, reviewing letters to the
weekly, *Nedelia*, observed how sharply polarized attitudes had become.
On the one hand, were letters, especially from doctors, urging further
liberalization and more information; on the other, shocked responses
from some readers denied any need for sex education – 'they'll find it all
out for themselves when they get married' – and blamed the rising tide
of immorality on modern films, free abortion and female emancipation.[5]
Views of this type have been regularly printed in response to the wave of
articles on sex, yet taboos are still being lifted. The new realism continues to prevail as it produces not only previously suppressed information but also reveals the fruits of ignorance: the often tragic
consequences for young women of the years of silence.

Young women and sexual relationships

The urgent need for sex education was expressed in one of the letters to
Nedelia reviewed by Perevedentsev. Its author, a woman school doctor
from Moscow, wrote, 'I can state with certainty that there are plenty of
young lives crippled by the age of fourteen through an ignorance of
ethics, psychology and anatomy.' She went on to urge that separate
gynaecological clinics be opened for under-age girls 'because you won't
get them to stand in queues with adults'.[6] The reaction of much of the
adult world to young women seeking advice on contraception or facing
an unplanned pregnancy has been well-documented in the press. Fif-
teen-year old 'Ira', writing to *Sobesednik* from Moscow described her
attempt to get contraceptive advice, 'The doctor was an old guy who
practically fell off his chair when I explained that I wanted a consul-
tation. He advised me to come back with my birth certificate and
my parents. He also "advised" that my father should give me a good
hiding . . .'[7]

Outside the capital, matters do not improve. After the death of a
student from a botched illegal abortion, women's council members
attempted to arrange a series of lectures by doctors at the Arkhangelsk
Pedagogical Institute. The doctors were not allowed in by the college
authorities because it was thought undesirable for 'the students' moral
well-being to be damaged by unnecessary information'.[8] Similar
attitudes have been reported from schools faced with cases of teenage
pregnancy. Shocked reactions on the part of the school authorities have
led in some cases to the involvement of the police and local officials in
investigations of alleged immorality.[9]

In reports such as these, the most striking feature to the Western eye is perhaps the utter lack of medical confidentiality for the young women involved. Whilst reliable contraception may be very difficult to obtain for women of all fertile age-groups in the USSR, for girls under eighteen the situation becomes virtually impossible. Officially unable to receive contraceptive advice without parental consent, they run the risk of becoming the subject of local gossip if they approach an unsympathetic doctor who takes a strongly moralistic line. A letter printed in *Sobesednik* underlines the point: 'Fifteen and sixteen-year old girls are frequent visitors to my home. I, a metalworker, "prescribe" and sell them contraceptives. They ought to go to the women's clinics but they are afraid of gossip since the doctors tell the whole town about their young patients.'[10] Worse still are the enforced gynaecological examinations which may be arranged by schools and which have come to light in young women's letters to the press.[11] Checking on virginity in this way is no doubt intended to instill fear and to provide for punitive action to be taken against transgressors. Journalists have remarked on the massive invasion of privacy which this involves, though the breathtaking degree of sexism implied has so far passed without comment.

Perusing accounts such as these leaves the reader in little doubt that for many in positions of authority, when faced with unplanned teenage pregnancies the preferred action is a nice quiet abortion. Providing contraceptive advice implies admission of the realities of under-age sex. Hustling the girl involved away for an abortion allows the silence to remain unbroken, the pregnancy, if it comes to light at all, to be regarded as a regrettable but isolated incident of immorality. For those who embark on sexual relationships, the lack of contraceptive advice is compounded by the more general lack of sex education. Information about the menstrual cycle or the withdrawal method evidently comes as a revelation to many girls involved in sexual relationships. In the prevailing moral climate, buying condoms – even were they not in such catastrophically short supply – becomes unthinkable. As one twenty year-old man neatly summed up the situation, 'Public opinion being what it is I can't bring myself to go into a chemist to buy a condom. If I was selfless enough to go through that I wouldn't need the condom.'[12]

Abortion, the silent solution for the school and the family, is likely to be a major trauma for the girl involved. Since 1987, press articles have revealed the gruesome realities of abortion for Soviet women: the poor conditions in abortion wards, the lack of anaesthetics and the punitive attitudes of medical staff.[13] In its attempts to dissuade women from having abortions – in the past, in the hope that they would bear more children, and today, in the hope that they will use contraception –

journalists and doctors writing in the popular press have threatened women with dire consequences: pelvic inflammatory disease, future miscarriage, secondary infertility. Whilst multiple abortions in the conditions of current Soviet medicine have undoubtedly produced all of these phenomena and more, the fear engendered by this method of propaganda becomes a further burden for young women to bear:

I had an abortion at sixteen. After that I lived with the fear that I wouldn't be able to have children. I was obsessed by this idea until my daughter was born. That pregnancy at the age of sixteen was the first thing that made me think seriously about anything. I had no help at all from my parents. It was a subversive subject at school. My youth is a miserable memory. I regret the lost years.[14]

It must be said, however, that the trauma of abortion or the fear of an unwanted pregnancy is not enough to dissuade many young women from becoming involved in sexual relationships. Many of the letters to the press from young women describe sex as a natural culmination of falling in love and view it as acceptable within the bounds of a single and special relationship. Yet it is equally clear that, for others, casual sex has become a way of life long before they leave school. Throughout the 1980s Soviet writers have indicated that the age at which young people embark on sexual relationships has fallen significantly. By 1989, the head of the Tyumen STD clinic cited above was stating that most young people were having sex by the age of fourteen or fifteen, 'whether we like it or not'.[15]

Judging by letters to the press, promiscuity in girls often seems to be linked to their involvement in youth groups. The role of girls in gangs and youth groups is an aspect of Soviet youth culture which has received relatively little attention. Many of the groups which have received publicity in both the USSR and the West – the Afgantsy, the Liubery, the neo-fascists, the Kazan street gangs, the bikers and heavy metal fans, even the rock music community – are either an exclusively male preserve or are overwhelmingly male-dominated. It should not be assumed, however, that young women are not involved in youth groups or gangs, but their attitudes and their role within them have received little consideration and emerge largely through their own letters to the press.

Most of these letters describe the initial excitement at belonging to a youth group, the pleasures of feeling beyond parental control and the hedonism of a culture which in no way conforms to accepted standards of behaviour. Yet several of the published letters also describe how they are expected to provide sexual favours for the males in the group and not infrequently express considerable distress at being unable to extricate themselves from the group's influence. 'I could howl at the pointlessness of my life . . . I'm surrounded by scum and riff-raff – but then that's what I am too. Only I'm still capable of thinking about life whilst they've forgotten how. All they do is preach free love and practise it.'[16]

As the letters make clear, ending casual sexual relationships may not be simply a matter of walking away and finding new friends. Several of these letters, from girls as young as thirteen, describe threatened or actual rapes and beatings when they try to leave the gangs; some say that they are afraid to write their address.[17] Rape and violence from men remain the major areas of women's experience which are still largely untouched by glasnost. Where casual sex is discussed at all it is accompanied by dire warnings about sexually transmitted disease, infertility – 'a woman who has had seven sexual partners will usually become infertile'[18] – and, more recently, AIDS. There has been virtually no discussion of how girls who are still at school are supposed to deal with the forces at work in male-dominated gangs. On the basis of the small number of letters published on the subject it would clearly be naive to assume that young women are always willing participants in casual sex. Whether typical or not, the writers of these letters evidently get less out of the experience than they care to admit to their immediate circle.

Liberalization and the exploitation of women

The liberalization of attitudes towards sex has not been limited to the provision of information. The lifting of taboos has led to a growing use of nudity and semi-nudity in the official media and the arts. In the overwhelming majority of cases it is predictably the female body which is on display. The use of female nudity to entertain, titillate and sell products, so familiar to the Western public, is increasingly in evidence in the USSR. Indeed, the Soviet media have moved extremely rapidly from a position in which nudity was only just acceptable to one in which it is becoming almost compulsory. The playwright, Mikhail Roschin, recently described how his play, 'Valentin and Valentina' caused a huge scandal when first staged in 1971 because of a brief nude scene involving the two lovers of the title. 'Now there's not a single show without a naked body, especially the naked body of an actress. If you don't have that it's not considered a good show.'[19] Young women, having the requisite physical beauty, are inevitably most in demand to play the parts required by this new fashion.

Just how closely related the liberalization of attitudes to sex education is to the exploitation of female nudity can be seen from a perusal of the youth magazine, *Sobesednik*. The magazine which has published some of the most thoughtful and informative articles on sex has also been the constant champion of the beauty contests which have burgeoned in the USSR since 1988. By 1990, full-page photographs of female nudes were being sponsored in the magazine by commercial centres, advertising agencies and even rock bands. In addition, female nudity was being used to illustrate articles not only on sex but also on less likely topics such as ecology.

Five years of liberalization have brought some very visible changes to the Soviet environment. In Moscow and Leningrad at least, video salons have pornographic films on show whilst, on the commercial TV channel 2×2, bare breasts are evidently *de rigueur*. Erotic art shows and the more grandiose 'Festivals of Erotica' are, despite their pretensions, evidently the nearest thing to a strip show currently available. Even the state newspaper kiosks are selling 'erotic horoscopes' and pocket calendars complete with female nudes.

As yet, however, most women appear unconcerned about the sexual exploitation involved. The well-known commentator on women's issues, Larisa Kuznetsova, recently complained that, in response to articles critical of the new trends on moral grounds, not a single letter had been received in response from a woman condemning soft porn for its portrayal of women.[20] This should not perhaps be so surprising in a country in which home-grown feminism has been suppressed and Western feminism derided. To be fair, even with a relatively unhampered women's movement, it has taken British feminists some twenty years to work up a head of steam on the issue of pornography even though images demeaning to women have been on public display throughout the entire period.

Amongst the flagships of perestroika, it is not only *Sobesednik* which has proved to be rather less than radical in its attitudes towards beauty contests and glamour modelling. The live television programme *Vzgliad*, well-known for its forthright interviews and investigative journalism, has been happy to show clips from regional beauty contests with contestants disco-dancing in bikinis for the judges' approval. *Moscow News* splashed the picture of the first Moscow beauty contest winner across its front page complete with vital statistics.[21] In line with the majority of the Soviet media, *Moscow News*' criticism of beauty contests has been largely confined to their poor organization and the dubious role of commercial interests.

The tenor of much of the Soviet journalistic coverage gives the impression of a nation entranced by the spectacle of young women indulging in a moment of glamour as a long-awaited respite from the image of woman as construction worker or tractor driver. Indeed, the secretary of the Moscow Komsomol Committee which invested no less than 40,000 roubles in the 'Moscow Beauty' competition declared that the contest was about 'saving women from urbanization, from being lost in the crowd and raising the prestige of women in society'.[22] Interestingly, two of the most forthright pieces of criticism have come from men who have lived in the United States. One of them, the TV journalist, Vladimir Pozner, commented:

There's a word which is very common in America these days – not 'exploitation', but 'sexploitation'. Beauty contests are sexploitation. The men sit there and ogle beautiful women ... Yet they present beauty contests to us as if they're something so wonderful, such a discovery ... And women don't shout about it but regard it as perfectly acceptable. They should be boycotting these contests, going out with placards and protesting.[23]

Some writers in the Soviet press have suggested that the fascination with nudity, erotica and beauty contests merely reflects the swing of the pendulum after the years of prudishness and enforced silence on sex. In due course, the argument runs, people will become bored and look once more for genuine artistry rather than cheap thrills. 'All you have to do is flood the market with "forbidden fruit" and these fruits cease to be interesting'.[24] Unfortunately, as the rather longer experience of the West has shown, waiting for boredom to set in as a means of combatting the sexual exploitation of women may mean a very long wait indeed.

To the Western observer, much of this is curiously reminiscent of the 1960s. The liberalization which took place in that decade was perceived by young men and women alike as a breath of fresh air after the prudishness, moralizing and heavy emphasis on marriage and the family which had characterized the 1950s. Yet in a profoundly patriarchal society, the terms of the liberalization which took place were inevitably set by men. In the new morality of the sixties, men called the shots and women were expected both to accept and enjoy the sexual manipulation which followed. Like British women in the sixties, Soviet women today have no developed, autonomous women's movement with which to combat their own exploitation. Like British women then, they too are now enjoying greater freedom without looking too closely at what it might imply. Yet, unlike their British counterparts, they have other, more compelling reasons to embrace wholeheartedly something new.

In the case of beauty contests, in particular, winning a prize offers the tantalizing prospect of travel abroad – enough to tempt contestants from a wide range of educational and occupational backgrounds. In addition, the distant possibility of a career in glamour modelling or even the cinema through success in a contest, promises an undreamed-of chance to escape a humdrum existence. Parading along a catwalk in a revealing swimsuit may seem a very small price to pay when set against the realities of many women's working lives. The contrast between the new images of femininity and the old images of the woman worker appear all the more stark in the light of the information on working conditions so recently held up to public scrutiny.

Women at work

International Women's Day 1990 was greeted on Soviet television by a lengthy discussion programme entitled 'It Isn't Easy To Be A Woman'. For one and a half hours the panel of experts and studio audience talked heatedly and obsessively around the one central issue of whether or how much women with children should be involved in paid work. That this should have been seen as a burning issue five years into the Gorbachev period of reform says a great deal both about the changes which have taken place since 1985 and about the stranglehold which the propaganda and practices of the past exert upon current thinking both by and about women in the USSR.

During the Brezhnev years over 90 per cent of Soviet women of working age were either in employment or were studying. Although the encouragement of part-time and flexi-time working for women with young children had been discussed since the 1960s, very few women were involved in such schemes prior to 1985. The overwhelming majority of Soviet women worked full-time with an average total break of only 3.6 years for childbearing.[25]

Soviet statistics on women in employment habitually presented the high level of women's involvement in the workforce as an achievement of socialism, a measure of women's emancipation. The numbers of women with higher degrees or employed in medicine and education were used as a yardstick of social progress. Less palatable statistics on female employment were omitted, as indeed was any reference to the fact that medicine and education are notoriously badly paid sectors of the economy. In the press, articles on female employment stressed the detailed health and safety provisions of Soviet employment law and the achievements of individual women workers. Against this background, letters of complaint could be viewed as revealing unacceptable exceptions to good practice to be set right by the intervention of Communist Party officials with the help of campaigning journalists. The realities of women's working conditions, levels of pay and promotion prospects were not thoroughly discussed in the Soviet media until the policy of glasnost began to permit uncomfortable truths to be aired.

At the National Women's Conference in July 1987, the outgoing chair of the Soviet Women's Committee, Valentina Tereshkova, quoted the latest employment statistics showing that women made up between 30 and 50 per cent of the workers engaged in heavy physical work in the timber, paper, glass, food and other light industries. In construction, 26 per cent of heavy physical work was done by women.[26] Since 1987 a series of press and journal articles has looked at the question in some depth. The proportion of women employed in work described as heavy or harmful has been found to be falling only very slowly, a phenomenon closely related to the question of female earnings.

In health, education, culture and the service sector where women predominate, earnings are significantly lower than the national average. Over the past two decades the differentials between average pay in these sectors and in industry have actually increased. Work in education on average pays only 71 per cent of the industrial average, whilst the cultural sector pays only 53 per cent. However, in every branch of industry, women's average gradings at work – and, hence, their level of pay – are lower than those of men. At the 1987 Women's Conference, Tereshkova noted that, during the previous five years, the number of women workers gaining a higher grading had fallen by an average of 1.5 per cent. Around 40 per cent of women workers are engaged in unskilled or semi-skilled and predominantly heavy manual work for which little or no training is required. Across the economy as a whole, women still receive only 73 per cent of male average earnings.[27]

Sociologists have ascribed this phenomenon primarily to the influence of the 'double shift'. The time spent on housework and child care in the USSR is estimated to be only 18 per cent less overall than the total working time in production. Women spend more than double the time spent by men looking after home and family.[28] Surveys have shown that women's educational levels and qualifications are, on average, higher than those of men up to the age of twenty. By the age of thirty, however, the discrepancy in work gradings between men and women is already in evidence. While young women are away from work having children and, on returning, are still heavily involved in housework and child care, men's skill levels continue to rise. The more children women have, the further they lag behind men at work. Legal provisions for training women with young children during working time on guaranteed average pay are very little used in practice. In consequence, women have great difficulty once they have had children in moving beyond their previous grading.[29] In addition, the pressures of child care may lead women to look for easier, lighter work nearer home or in an enterprise which can offer child care facilities yet which may not be particularly to their liking or correspond with their levels of skill.

Since 1987, readers' letters to the press have made it clear, however, that the 'double shift' is not the only factor involved. Women have described being continually passed over for promotion in favour of men who have less experience or have even been their assistants. Sometimes the discrimination is quite blatant:

The site foreman told me straight out, 'You know enough to be on the sixth grade but they won't give it to you because you're a woman.' Recent events have completely borne this out. My husband and I went on a training course together . . . got the same exam results and then they raised his grade but they didn't raise mine.[30]

Zoia Pukhova, replacing Valentina Tereshkova as head of the Soviet Women's Committee, has been forthright in her criticism of current attitudes to women in employment. She clearly sees such examples as part of a well-developed pattern, describing the habit of giving higher gradings to men where women have identical skill levels as an 'established practice whereby managements keep down the wage bill'.[31]

The difficulties women experience in gaining higher gradings means that doing heavy or harmful work may be the only way to obtain a significant increase in earnings. For the same reason, the benefits which may also accompany this type of work, such as earlier retirement, better pensions and extra holidays, are also likely to be more attractive to women than to men. As a result, women themselves may be strongly opposed to being redeployed on to light work.[32]

Against this background, the debate on whether or not mothers of young children should go out to work becomes more understandable. Looking honestly at what women actually do at work has produced a groundswell of opinion that such conditions are not acceptable. In response, some writers have concluded that the answer is to increase mechanization, raise penalties for the infringement of health and safety legislation and develop trade unions capable of protecting workers' rights.[33]

More frequently, however, the removal of women, especially mothers, from work in difficult conditions has been the favoured option. From this line of argument it is but a short step to seeing motherhood as women's primary duty and major sphere of work. Because women suffer from low pay and are trapped in low-skilled work in poor conditions, because child care provision, health care and public services are inadequate, therefore, 'it is obvious that in these conditions we must rethink the stereotypes which have developed and realize that, for the future of the country and of socialism, the most important form of creative work for women is the work of motherhood.[34]

The revelations brought by glasnost have become grist to the mill in the continuing government attempts to raise the birthrate in the European USSR. Party policy under Gorbachev has been to maintain and develop the Brezhnev line on 'strengthening the family' by extending maternity leave and increasing provision for part-time working and homeworking. Under perestroika, however, government thinking has embraced both conservative views on women as mothers, and pronouncements that women must be more actively involved in politics and in decision-making at all levels. Mikhail Gorbachev's own speeches and writings have contained elements of both. In his book, *Perestroika*, he wrote of the need to allow women to 'return to their purely womanly mission', whilst at the 19th Party Conference in 1988 he spoke of the need to open up a 'wide road' for women into government posts.[35]

The media debate surrounding these apparently contradictory views of women's roles has achieved something of a synthesis of the two by promoting the concept of 'choice' for women. Whilst some women may 'choose' to have a career – and the implication is usually that these will be relatively few – others, or indeed most, may 'choose' to stay at home with their children. The fact that it was this very concept of 'choice' which dominated the studio audience response in the television programme on International Women's Day 1990, bears witness to the appeal of this message for Soviet women.

In the past, runs the argument, women had no choice at all. They were constrained to work full-time, to endure the conditions now so graphically described in the press, to bear children and care for them, juggling the demands of work and home and somehow or other coping despite the queueing, the absence of labour-saving devices, the lack of male assistance. Now, this view continues, young women who have watched their mothers and grandmothers sacrifice themselves on the altars of production and reproduction have no wish to repeat their experience. Having a choice, for young women, means being able to fit in the demands of child care and housework around a less demanding work regime, at least whilst children are small. It means that spartan living conditions and the constant shortages can be coped with as a legitimate part of the working day rather than as a stress-filled series of chores at the end of a full-length shift. It means having time to play with the children rather than simply feed them and put them to bed. Most of all, perhaps, it means having some time to themselves, leisure to take things at a somewhat slower pace, time to be amused by the frivolities of fashion and beauty contests, perhaps simply to get a bit of enjoyment out of life.

From this perspective, the encouragement of part-time working and homeworking appears not as a retrograde step threatening female emancipation, but as a blessed release from the rigours of the Stalinist past. Throughout this line of argument, of course, the question of what men are contributing to the family is glaringly conspicuous by its absence. As a result, the increased leave provisions, entitlement to part-time work and the attitudes to women's employment which are being fostered have ensured that, as economic reform puts pressure on Soviet enterprises, women are the first to be hit.

'Back to the home' and the economic reform

The development of attitudes favouring a reduction in women's involvement in the workforce has already had a considerable impact in an era of economic change. Paradoxically, as the concept of 'choice' in employment for women gains currency, women are, in practice, finding their choices more and more constrained.

During the 1980s, maternity leave was twice extended. By 1990, part-paid leave stood at eighteen months with an option to take additional unpaid leave until the child reached the age of three. Whilst the new maternity leave provisions and a shortage of nursery places mean that women are likely to be absent from work for long periods when having children, further measures introduced since 1985 create additional problems for their employers. In 1987, paid leave to care for sick children was extended from seven to fourteen days in each case of illness. Although this benefit is available to both parents, in practice the leave is taken almost exclusively by the mother. The high incidence of sickness amongst children in state nurseries and consequent loss of working time by their mothers may lead women to conclude that, on balance, it would create less stress for themselves, their children and their colleagues if they simply stayed at home. A further legal innovation in 1987 provided that part-time work paid pro rata must be given on request to pregnant women, women with children under eight or women caring for another member of the family. Failure to comply with this requirement is now punishable by law.[36]

What is not, however, punishable by law is sex discrimination in employment. With the advent of cost accounting and self-financing in Soviet enterprises, women have borne the brunt of blatantly discriminatory practices in redeployment and redundancy. The increased leave provisions and the entitlement to part-time work have become a contributory factor in this phenomenon, making women appear a costly and troublesome sector of the workforce. Where the workforce is predominantly female, young mothers become the target of cost-cutting exercises and may find themselves facing constructive dismissal, as in this letter from textile workers in Ivanovo Region:

There are a lot of young women with small children in our collective. Most of them would prefer to work part-time but this doesn't suit the management. They give us a full day's quota of work even though we're only working four hours, knowing perfectly well that it can't be done. The management is simply forcing us to resign. The director even said, 'They've turned the place into a children's nursery – we can do without workers like that.'[37]

Although examples have appeared in the press of successful retraining schemes and relatively painless transitions from one form of work to another, it is clear that in many cases women are simply dismissed with little or no concern for their future employment. Zoia Pukhova reported in 1988 how letters complaining of female redundancies had been arriving at the Soviet Women's Committee in increasing numbers from all over the country.[38]

In July 1989 *Rabotnitsa* magazine for the first time devoted an entire article to the problem of female unemployment. Taking the example of one industrial town in Moldavia, the journalist, Nadezhda Menitskaia, found a wave of redundancies had pushed up the numbers looking for work by 25 per cent during 1988. In the absence of published statistics and prognoses, rumours fuelled the fear of further redundancies. Here, as in other examples which have appeared in readers' letters, it is evident that the attitudes which make women with young children prime targets for redundancy also make them the least likely to be offered alternative work.[39]

Official pronouncements on the state of the USSR's economy give little cause to halt rumours of redundancies. With the aim of increasing labour productivity by 250 per cent, the Soviet Union aims to redeploy some sixteen million 'surplus' workers by the year 2000, 3 million of them by the end of 1990. In all, around a quarter of the Soviet workforce – some 32 million workers – are regarded as being in redundant posts. Where considerable labour shortages have developed, they are often in sectors of the economy which have become profoundly unattractive to women, notably in agriculture.[40] Young women have been leaving the land in droves over the last twenty years in silent protest at appalling working conditions on state and collective farms. Reports from the countryside suggest that the financial pressures and lack of small-scale mechanization faced by the new cooperatives and family-based agricultural units may, if anything, have made conditions worse.

Given a choice between returning to the farms or to the kitchen sink it seems likely that times will need to get much harder before young women will opt for the former. Nevertheless, with the transition to a market economy, it seems unavoidable that the notion of 'choice' for women will be consigned to the rhetoric of perestroika. The impact of unemployment is, in effect, being cushioned by fostering the notion that home is the only right and proper place for women with children to be.

The financial effect of change

Economic change, when taken together with changes in leave entitlements, appears likely to have a considerable impact on the lives of most young women in the USSR. The extension of maternity leave, the encouragement of part-time working and homeworking and the impact of redundancies cannot but reduce women's average earnings and disadvantage them still further by comparison with men. Time away from work not only diminishes earnings directly but inevitably affects career development and promotion, compounding the effects of the 'double shift' on women's pay prospects.

In 1989 the Soviet press began to investigate the question of poverty in the USSR. Figures from the States Committee for Labour and Social Issues put 41 million Soviet citizens below the poverty line in 1988. Since then, economists have suggested that inflation and shortages have already added considerably to this total.[41] One article in *Rabotnitsa* examined the financial difficulties of families with young children living on the husband's salary and maternity benefit and went on to castigate the levels of benefit as much too low.[42]

The longer the period of maternity leave and the more difficulties women with young children experience in finding and keeping employment, the longer the periods of financial difficulty will inevitably become. Examples of family budgets appearing in the press show major difficulties in buying clothes for both parents and children, even where the husband appears to be on a better than average wage. Where earnings are less substantial, problems buying food are the inevitable consequence, a trend exacerbated as state shops empty and a varied diet is only available at market prices.[43]

If making ends meet is a headache for young mothers with husbands in employment, the problem is amplified considerably for single women with children. There were some 550,000 unmarried mothers in the USSR in 1988, over 10 per cent of children each year being born outside marriage, though this by no means represents the sum total of single mothers.[44] To these should be added the growing numbers of divorced women bringing up children alone, with or without adequate maintenance from former husbands. Studies of marital breakdown from the early eighties charted the significant increase in divorce rates amongst young people which had taken place over the previous decade. By the mid-1980s, sociologists were reporting that around a third of all divorces were taking place in marriages of less than four years' duration. V. A. Sysenko, writing in 1983, observed that the figures 'bear witness to the fact that divorce is primarily a youth problem'.[45]

The factors involved in the breakdown of young marriages include overcrowded housing, conflicts with parents and in-laws, lack of money and sexual difficulties as well as the well-charted problems of heavy drinking and infidelity. Yet a crucial underlying factor in divorce is to be found in young people's reasons for marrying and their expectations of married life. The wave of pronatalist propaganda which emanated from the Brezhnev era and has survived into the age of perestroika, has put considerable pressure on Soviet young people to regard early marriage as both acceptable and desirable. Much of the writing which has appeared in the popular press over this period has peddled the image of the ideal young family: the vigorous and devoted young husband and father as the 'supporter and defender' of his adoring wife and 'helpmate', who is at once the mother of his children and the 'guardian of the family hearth'. It is an image of a strong and sexually exclusive lifelong partnership in which love conquers all and children grow happy and confident in their parents' all-embracing care.

The promoters of the vision have urged young people not to put off the joys of marriage and parenthood and have warned of the perils of loneliness which await those, particularly women, who do. This promotion of early marriage allows for few positive images of the single state and young people have been left in no doubt that being unmarried is a pitiable condition, caused by 'their own stupidity, egotism and an underestimation of the role of the family in an individual's life'.[46]

By 1985 the average female age at marriage across the USSR was twenty-two, yet surveys were showing that teenage marriage was commonplace in European areas, and not merely in the major cities. A survey of young families in towns and cities of the Urals from this period found that three-quarters of women had married between the ages of eighteen and twenty-two.[47] For a significant proportion of young women pregnancy evidently precipitates their decision to marry at an early age. A 1981 study in the city of Perm found that almost 62 per cent of women were pregnant on marriage; in the case of 16–17 year old brides the figure rose to 96 per cent. Similar results have been recorded in Leningrad and other major cities.[48] Ignorance about sex and the frequently insuperable difficulties for young people in gaining access to contraception thus bring further casualties in their wake by pushing young women into hasty and potentially unstable marriages. The result for increasing numbers of young women is a short-lived relationship and the long-term poverty of single parenthood.

Supporting a child alone may turn out to be a far from temporary phase. Only 40 per cent of divorced women remarry, half the rate of remarriage amongst divorced men. By 1990, Moscow-based computer dating agencies, proliferating with the revival of cooperatives, were promising that clients whose expectations were not too high would find a marriage partner within 2 to 6 months, but 'women with children wait for over a year'. Even so, studies of divorce indicate that second marriages have a particularly high rate of failure.[49]

For divorced or single women with young children to support, the effect of change in the Soviet economy seems destined to plunge them further into financial hardship. When mothers of young children are seen as undesirable workers, single mothers become particularly vulnerable. Studies of single parents have found that, where lack of money means a poor diet and inadequate housing, children become ill more frequently.[50] As a result, in the current climate, their mothers become ever less employable. From a town in Belorussia a woman recently wrote to Rabotnitsa: 'I'm turning to you in my misery. I'm a single mother of two children and I've been made redundant for the second time in a year. I live in a small town and it's impossible to get a job. There are 200 people on the books at the labour exchange'.[51] In another example from the same magazine, a single mother described the trauma of seeing her small daughter only once a week at a 24-hour nursery and the child's distress at her departure. 'I lived all week in anxious anticipation of Saturday. I couldn't leave work in the middle of the week because I'd been looking for a job for two years and I was still on a month's probation'.[52]

In the face of current economic realities it seems scarcely surprising that 8,000 single mothers each year choose to put their new-born babies into care rather than take them home.[53] When it looks impossible to survive on state benefit and jobs become harder to find, appealing to sentiment and castigating youthful egotism is evidently not enough to persuade a significant number of young women into a life of scant means and restricted opportunity.

In conclusion: what future for young women?

I'm twenty-eight and a mother of two. The elder one is nine, the younger one is coming up for two. I'm at home with the little one at the moment and nearly every day my elder daughter says, 'It's so good that you're at home!' I can do her plaits properly and give her a meal before school. When she comes home I'm in a good mood (because I haven't been doing my hellish job and haven't got tired). After all, what was it like before? You fly out of work round the shops, buy as much food as you can so you won't have to go again tomorrow, get home from the shops as fast as you can. At home you've got to cook supper and prepare tomorrow's lunch, your daughter's coming out with all kinds of questions which you haven't got time to answer . . . You go on putting up with it all and taking your 'patience' out on your husband or your child. Whereas now . . .! I've amazed myself at how calm I've become.[54]

The sentiments expressed in this letter to the press appear to be highly characteristic of current attitudes amongst Soviet women. Other readers see a lack of cash as the major obstacle to this highly desirable development and propose raising men's wages to allow women to stay at home with their children. Readers, journalists and economists taking up the debate propose continuing maternity benefit until the child reaches school age, or even instituting a new, higher state benefit for women staying at home until their children are perhaps ten or eleven years old.[55]

In April 1990 the Supreme Soviet announced a new range of benefits, which were to be introduced in January 1991. The major change was to raise maternity benefit, payable until the child reaches eighteen months, to the level of the minimum wage. Benefit to unmarried mothers has also been raised to this same level. In future, leave to look after a child to the age of three will be available to any family member and not just the mother. Part-time work entitlements will, however, only apply to the mother, unless the father is bringing up children alone. The right to be given part-time work is to be extended until the child reaches fourteen years of age. In addition, 'a unified system of state benefits for families with children which will take into account family type, income and the cost of living index' is to be developed.[56] Given that most women earn less than their husbands, however, it seems unlikely that many men will opt to take parental leave. As Elena Tolokina, an economist promoting the concept of wages for child care, recently observed, 'Ideally this wage should be paid to the family . . . but in our current situation . . . when it comes to deciding who should leave their job temporarily, the family will still choose the woman'.[57]

There are, of course, pressing social and psychological grounds which will reinforce the economic arguments for most men. The Supreme

Soviet itself remains less than wholeheartedly behind the concept of parental responsibility in its failure to extend part-time and other job-related entitlements to fathers, if the mother is available to take them. As Larisa Kuznetsova noted when raising the possibility of a change in attitudes towards parental obligations in 1988, 'For this we need not merely a new view of things but, however strange it may seem, a new type of man, capable of seeing sexual equality not as something which prejudices a man's rights but as the dialectical development of them'.[58] When the 'new man' remains the subject of much ironical comment in the West after two decades of feminism, it is difficult to be optimistic about his appearance in the USSR where rigid sex-stereotyping on highly traditional lines has been promoted as a wise form of upbringing since the mid-1970s.

In much of the writing on women and child care, the husband appears only as a shadowy figure, apparently waiting in the wings to facilitate and support the movement of women back to the home. Yet this is a colossal and dangerous assumption to make. To become a full-time mother 'requires an important and, these days, fairly rare character – the husband with an appropriate salary and appropriate principles . . . Moreover, a husband like that would at one time have been absolutely sober. But now he's become an endangered species.'[59] The fact that around 70 per cent of divorce petitions are brought by women suggests a high level of dissatisfaction with the role played by men within the family. Over the last two decades, surveys have again and again painted a picture of male inactivity and female exhaustion within the home. Minimal involvement in housework and child care and excessive consumption of alcohol have been the hallmarks of much male behaviour. Despite glasnost, domestic violence still receives scant attention in the Soviet press, yet the USSR would indeed be unique as a society if violence against women and children were not an inescapable consequence of alcohol abuse. Occasional readers' letters and official comments indicate that this is far from being the case.[60]

The most disturbing aspect of the 'back to the home' lobby is the consequence of its argument at a time of economic change. Already women with young children are experiencing difficulty finding work. As the move to the market makes more widespread unemployment a reality, women with young children will be forced back into the home whether or not their husbands' salary and behaviour can provide adequate support. And if there is no husband the economic consequences may be grim indeed. Living on benefits, even equivalent to the minimum wage, in a period of price inflation and shortages, is likely to be extremely uncomfortable. As the economist, Tatiana Koriagina, has warned, 'where there are shortages, it makes no difference 80 or 100 roubles, the needy will simply not be able to buy goods'.[61] It is a prospect which raises the familiar Western spectre of women staying with drunken and violent men because they have nowhere to go and no realistic means of support.

The sexual liberalization which has taken place since 1985 has added a new element of exploitation to women's lives in the USSR: 'in the cinema and television, in books and magazines, women are more and more frequently presented as some kind of living object for the satisfaction of a certain male need', warned a recent *Pravda* article.[62] Police estimate that there are already some 10,000 prostitutes in Moscow alone. A Georgian study from the mid-1980s found 70 per cent of prostitutes to be under thirty, most were divorced and around a half had children. Of these, 40 per cent had two children or more. Most had been in low-paid, low-status jobs. Prostitution was seen as a means of supplementing income, in particular to get hold of consumer goods. By 1990, it was already beginning to look more like a means of survival. In an anonymous letter to the press, a young mother of two children who could not be placed in nurseries because of illness, described her desperation at attempting to live on her husband's wage: 'The children need fresh food but if I buy it the money we've got only lasts half the month. I've sold everything I possessed and now there's nothing left to sell . . . I don't know how to become a prostitute, there's no-one even to ask, but I want to do it, just to earn a bit of money.'[63] With the development of a home-grown porn industry and the coming of the market, greater numbers of young women may discover, like this woman, that only their bodies are still in demand.

In the least pessimistic scenario, shunting young mothers out of the labour force cannot help but reduce or remove their economic independence and significantly cut down their earning power over the course of their working lives. Where child care remains undervalued and is viewed firmly as 'women's work', the move is likely to do little for women's self-image. Familiar Western patterns of problems for women attempting to rejoin the workforce can be envisaged: outdated skills, dwindling self-confidence through years of being out of the work environment, guilt at neglecting home and children and the undervaluing of abilities and skills gained through full-time child care.

In the face of the groundswell of opinion that women's involvement in the workforce should be reduced, the few women to question this development in the official media have the air of voices calling in the wilderness. The implications of young women's eager acceptance of the concept of staying at home with children have received little public consideration. At a time of deepening economic crisis it seems improbable that young women will be invited to contemplate the potential effects of market forces before they are hit by them. It is to be hoped that, in their haste to avoid the fate of generations past, young women do not find themselves trapped in an even more dismal future.

Notes

1. See, for example, T. A. Gurko, 'Vliianie dobrachnogo povedeniia na stabil'nost' molodoi sem'i', *Sotsiologicheskie issledovaniia*, no. 2 (1982), pp. 88–93.
2. A. G. Khripkova and D. V. Kolesov, *Devochka – podrostok – devushka* (Moscow, 1981).
3. V. I. Cherednichenko, 'Na predele otkrovennosti', *Zdorov'e*, no. 3 (1987), p. 20; Nadezhda Shchurikova, 'Raz v nedeliu dumaiu o zhizni', *Nedelia*, no. 9 (1988), p. 21; Yurii Riurikov, 'Tri nevezhestva', *Sobesednik*, no. 10 (1987), p. 4.
4. *Sobesednik*, no. 2 (1989), p. 4.
5. Viktor Perevedentsev, 'Plach na svad'be ili pliaska na pokhoronakh', *Nedelia*, no. 2 (1988), p. 5.
6. Ibid.
7. *Sobesednik*, no. 47 (1988), p. 10.
8. Aleksandra Koroleva, 'B'em trevogu, da ne vse slyshat', *Krest'ianka*, no. 7 (1988), p. 14.
9. Masha Musina, 'Ne otrekaiutsia, liubia', *Rabotnitsa*, no. 1 (1988), pp. 26–8; Mar'iana Makarova, 'Eto my ne prokhodili', *Sobesednik*, no. 35 (1988), p. 11.
10. Makarova, 'Eto my ne prokhodili'.
11. Ibid.; V. Iumashev, 'Liubov' bez liubvi', *Komsomol'skaia pravda*, 18 May 1986, p. 2.
12. Igor Stepanov, 'Vslukh o zapretnom', *Nedelia*, no. 4 (1988), p. 15; Dmitrii Sidorov, 'Sex and us', *Moscow News*, no. 18 (1989), p. 14.
13. D. Akivis and T. Mikhailova, 'Vslukh – o tainom', *Rabotnitsa*, no. 9 (1987), pp. 28–9.
14. *Sobesednik*, no. 8 (1988), p. 11.
15. Ibid., no. 2 (1989), p. 4.
16. *Sel'skaia molodezh'*, no. 8 (1988), p. 25.
17. Ibid., no. 5 (1989), p. 13 and no. 3 (1990), p. 21.
18. T. I. Pshenichnikova, 'My igrali v romashku ...' *Zdorov'e*, no. 8 (1987), pp. 10–11.
19. Mikhail Roschin, 'Laughter through tears', *Soviet Spring*, Channel 4 and *New Statesman and Society* (London, 1990), p. 37.
20. Larisa Kuznetsova, 'Razgovor pered zerkalom?' *Rabotnitsa*, no. 3 (1990), p. 14.

200   *Sue Bridger*

21. *Moscow News*, no. 25 (1988), p. 1.
22. Masha Musina, 'Korolevskie ispytaniia', *Rabotnitsa*, no. 8 (1988), pp. 38–9.
23. Vladimir Pozner, 'Ne nado zhdat' milostei ot muzhchin', *Rabotnitsa*, no. 3 (1989), p. 23.
24. Andrei Maksimov, 'Pravo byt' razdetym', *Sobesednik*, no. 35 (1990), p. 11.
25. A. E. Kotliar and S. I. Turchaninova, *Zaniatost' zhenshchin v proizvodste* (Moscow, 1975), pp. 106–7.
26. *Izvestiia*, 1 Feb. 1987, p. 3.
27. Ibid.; N. I. Dryakhlov, I. V. Litvinova and V. V. Pavlova, 'Otsenki muzhchinami i zhenshchinami uslovii truda: sblizhenie ili differentsiatsiia?' *Sotsiologicheskie issledovaniia*, no. 4 (1987), p. 113; *Rabotnitsa*, no. 1 (1990), p. 3.
28. M. A. Lanets, 'Problemy sovershenstvovaniia, soderzhaniia, kharaktera i uslovii truda zhenshchin-rabotnits v SSSR', (Leningrad, 1986), unpublished typescript, p. 19.
29. Z. A. Khotkina, 'Problemy zaniatosti zhenshchin v usloviiakh realizatsii kursa na uskorenie sotsial'no-ekonomicheskogo razvitiia strany', in E. V. Klopov, E. B. Gruzdeva and E. S. Chertikhina (eds), *Trud i vneproizvodstvennaia zhiznedeiatel'nost' zhenshchin-rabotnits* (Moscow, 1987), p. 60; V. I. Lukina and S. B. Nekhoroshkov, *Dinamika sotsial'noi struktury naseleniia SSSR* (Moscow, 1982), pp. 125–6.
30. *Rabotnitsa*, no. 12 (1987), p. 21.
31. L. Gavriushenko, 'Pust' budet zhenshchina schastlivoi!' *Rabotnitsa*, no. 9 (1988), p. 11.
32. V. N. Zybtsev, 'Ob ispol'zovanii zhenskogo truda v metallurgicheskoi promyshlennosti', *Sotsiologicheskie issledovaniia*, no. 4 (1987), p. 110; Khotkina, 'Problemy zaniatosti', p. 69.
33. Liudmila Telen', 'Kakaia zhe ona, zhenskaia dolia?' *Sotsialisticheskaia industriia*, 22 Jan. 1988, pp. 2–3; Zybtsev, 'Ob ispol'zovanii', pp. 107–11; N. Korina, 'O traktore i o sebe', *Krest'ianka*, no. 8 (1987), pp. 14–18.
34. Driakhlov, 'Otsenki muzhchinami', p. 113.
35. Mikhail Gorbachev, *Perestroika* (London, 1988); *Izvestiia*, 29 June 1988, p. 6.
36. *Rabotnitsa*, no. 1 (1988), p. 20.
37. Gavriushenko, 'Pust' budet', p. 10.
38. Ibid.
39. Nadezhda Menitskaia, 'Ne khochu byt' bezrabotnoi!' *Rabotnitsa*, no. 7 (1989), pp. 10–12.
40. Igor Bestuzhev-Lada, 'Torzhestvennyi marsh na meste', *Nedelia*, no. 23 (1988), pp. 9–10.
41. Vladimir Gurevich, 'Free benefit', *Moscow News*, no. 27 (1989), p. 10 and 'Below the line', *Moscow News*, no. 10 (1990), pp. 8–9.
42. Irina Skliar and Nina Fedorova, 'Kak prozhit' neizvestno na chto?' *Rabotnitsa*, no. 6 (1989), pp. 10–12.
43. Ibid., p. 11; Gurevich, 'Below the line', p. 8.
44. Gurevich, 'Below the line'; *Narodnoe khoziaistvo v SSSR v 1988g* (Moscow, 1989), p. 24.
45. V. A. Sysenko, *Supruzheskie konflikty* (Moscow, 1983), p. 15; V. V. Solod-

nikov, 'Analiz predrazvodnoi situatsii v molodykh semiakh', in *Issledovaniia sem'i i praktika konsul'tatsionnoi raboty* (Moscow, 1986), p. 4.

46. Elena Tokareva, 'Eto printsipial'noe odinochestvo', *Sel'skaia molodezh'*, no. 9 (1987), p. 8.

47. I. Nasluzov, 'Sluzhba sem'i v usloviiakh krupnogo goroda', in *Molodozheny*, (Moscow, 1985), p. 69; A. A. Kostin and B. S. Pavlov, *Molodaia sem'ia: opyt i problemy* (Cheliabinsk, 1986), p. 85.

48. Igor Kon, 'Zapretnyi plod', *Nedelia*, no. 15 (1989), p. 21.

49. *Vecherniaia Moskva, reklamnoe prilozhenie*, 14 Apr. 1990, p. 5; M. Tol'ts, 'Razvod', *Pravda*, 22 Dec. 1987, p. 6.

50. P. P. Zvidrin'sh and L. P. Ezera, 'Sotsial'no-demograficheskii sostav nepolnykh semei', *Sotsiologicheskie issledovaniia*, no. 3 (1987), p. 42.

51. Menitskaia, 'Ne khochu', p. 12.

52. Tamara Ivanova, 'Roditel'skii den'', *Rabotnitsa*, no 6 (1989), p. 31.

53. Elena Tokareva, 'Ishchite zhenshchinu', *Sel'skaia molodezh'*, no. 3 (1989), p. 29.

54. Kuznetsova, 'Razgovor pered zerkalom?' p. 13.

55. *Rabotnitsa*, no. 9 (1988), p. 36; N. Boiarkina, 'Zhenshchina vybiraet', *Komsomol'skaia pravda*, 21 May 1988, p. 2; Elena Tolokina, 'Tak skol'ko dolzhna rabotat' zhenshchina?', *Rabotnitsa*, no. 9 (1989), pp. 2–5.

56. *Pravda*, 14 Apr. 1990, pp. 1–2.

57. Tolokina, 'Tak skol'ko', p. 4.

58. Larisa Kuznetsova, 'Val i Valentina', *Rabotnitsa*, no. 9 (1988), p. 23.

59. Ibid., p. 22.

60. *Izvestiia*, 1 Feb. 1987, p. 3: *Rabotnitsa*, no. 3 (1988), p. 36.

61. Gurevich, 'Free benefit'.

62. Nikolai Volynskii, 'Pochem "Klubnichka"?', *Pravda*, 11 Oct. 1989, p. 3.

63. *Argumenty i fakty*, no. 35 (1990), p. 3; A. A. Gabiani and M. A. Manuil'skii, 'Tsena "liubvi" ', *Sotsiologicheskie issledovaniia*, no. 6 (1987), pp. 61–8; 'Prostitutki', *Inside Story*, BBC 1, 25 Apr. 1990.

1–8; 'Prostitutki', *Inside Story*, BBC 1, 25 Apr. 1990.

10 Glasnost and the woman question

Mary Buckley

Glasnost was initially conceived by Gorbachev as a necessary means to the end of perestroika, and as relative to it. His heightened conviction that glasnost was integral to the reform process was reflected in the Resolution on Glasnost adopted at the 19th Party Conference in 1988. Glasnost was praised as a 'sharp weapon of perestroika' which helped people 'better to understand their past and present' and objectively 'to assess the situation in the country'. Glasnost was a vital part of 'socialist self-government' and its extension was essential for democratization and for the 'renewal of socialism'. Moreover, every citizen enjoyed 'the inalienable right to obtain complete and reliable information on any social question' that was not a state or military secret and 'the right to open and free discussion of any socially significant issue'.[1] Although by 1990 the consequences of glasnost in the republics had outstripped perestroika, Gorbachev's commitment to glasnost endured, even if he was bewildered, exasperated and provoked by some of its results. Glasnost remained crucial to his vision of socioeconomic and political change, but after 1990 with growing and contradictory qualifications.

The application of glasnost, however, has not been homogeneous across issues in content or pace. The vigour with which it was wielded in analyses of the *natsional'nyi vopros* (national question), particularly in Lithuania as early as 1987 and 1988, then with accelerated enthusiasm and confidence in 1989 and 1990, contrasts with its more hesitant application to some aspects of the *zhenskii vopros* (woman question), to more sensitive ecological issues and to the rehabilitation of erstwhile non-persons such as Trotskii. Similarly, while *novoe myshlenie* (new thinking) was flexibly adopted in foreign policy, and quickly formulated, it was more haltingly applied to domestic social problems.

The reasons behind differential patterns of the use of glasnost and the pursuit of the new thinking are several. Firstly, some topics such as economic efficiency, corruption and bureaucratization were officially approved targets early on, since the object of perestroika was to challenge them and to transform economic decision making, whereas other topics, even if legitimate, were of much lower official salience. Newspaper editors, programme directors, journalists and academics found it easier to criticize officially defined problems central to perestroika, consistent with past norms of practice, than to turn to more peripheral ones. This was especially so from 1985 to 1987, although more daring editors and journalists pushed glasnost to its perceived, or felt, limits. Secondly, themes such as the rehabilitation of Trotskii, or criticisms of involvement in Afghanistan, were much too politically sensitive for immediate analysis since they could result in unacceptably piercing attacks on past policies; editors and authors shied away from them, and censors stamped upon them. Thirdly, some issues, such as the annexation of territory in 1940, had seriously aggrieved constituents who were prepared at a time of political relaxation 'from above' to attack the status quo beyond the limits of acceptable criticism and to demand sovereignty to rectify the injustice. Other issues, such as rape, had victims too; but these women were isolated from each other, lacked a unifying movement and had no possibility of righting the perceived wrong. Fourthly, some policy areas, such as foreign policy, were more amenable to initiatives, reassessments and change since overtures were directed at potentially more flexible, and responsive arenas, which were not perceived as threatening to domestic stability. In sum, the nature of the issue, the make-up of its constituents, the interest or indifference of politicians, editors and journalists, and the institutional support available – whether official or unofficial – affected whether and how glasnost was applied to the issues and influenced the extent to which it was addressed in the media, in unofficial publications and in political action.

Such variations in the application of glasnost are evident both across *voprosy* and within them. The *zhenskii vopros* is multifaceted and composed of several aspects which span women's economic, social and political roles. Glasnost's early and easiest targets were topics which had been debated with liveliness during the Brezhnev years and which were not cloaked in silence.[2] These included working conditions, motherhood, the double burden, divorce, single parenthood and male alcoholism. Other women's issues, largely taboo since 1930, such as prostitution, high infant mortality rates, abortion, the lack of contraceptives, rape and the self-immolation of Muslim women, also came on to the agenda in 1986 and 1987 indicating that the woman question was on the move again and becoming more complex. These issues were not all analysed in depth, but their very mention broke a stern ideological silence.[3] After Gorbachev's strong call for reform at the Central Committee Plenum in January 1987 and his attack on opponents of change, the parameters of the *zhenskii vopros* noticeably broadened; they widened still further after political reform was stepped up by the 19th Party Conference. Glasnost visibly increased its strength in 1987 and 1988 because the regime permitted it and individuals responded to the opportunities provided by political relaxation. Thereafter came attacks on patriarchy and regrets that women were absent from top decision-making posts. By late 1988 arguments characteristic of Western feminism were voiced in *Sovetskaia zhenshchina* and *Soviet Weekly*, to be pursued further in 1988 and 1989 in *Kommunist* and *Rabotnitsa*. Translations of Western feminist works also appeared in the unofficial publication *Zhenskoe chtenie* compiled by Ol'ga Lipovskaia and other women in Leningrad.

The application of glasnost to the *zhenskii vopros* has had six main results: first, past debates about women's roles have been sustained, probed more deeply and extended; second, problems long evident but not officially acknowledged, such as the lack of contraceptives and the appalling conditions in abortion clinics, finally became issues and an increasing amount of information about them was imparted; third, the publication of statistics alerted journalists, academics and policy makers to the extent of particular problems, such as infant mortality and abortion; fourth, the adoption by some female academics of new concepts previously denied ideological legitimacy, such as 'man's world', 'principles of male superiority' and 'male dominated bureaucracy' began to exert a fresh influence on the way in which gender roles were analysed; fifth, democratization and glasnost combined, particularly after 1988, facilitated the emergence of a range of women-only groups; and sixth, dubbed by some as the negative side of glasnost, images of women as sex-objects began to emerge in beauty contests and in the spread of pornography.

'Old' issues revisited and extended: the example of working conditions

In a socialist state committed to furthering the interests of the working class, the topics of labour, workplace and working conditions have a central place. Criticisms of poor working conditions, however, cannot be credited to glasnost alone, and are not new to the USSR. Particularly caustic remarks about industrial accidents, dangerous conditions and high levels of dust, steam and noise were made in the 1920s, then during the Khrushchev era, and again, in more muted form, under Brezhnev. For most of the history of the Soviet state it has been acknowledged that appalling conditions existed which harmed women's health.[4]

Glasnost, nevertheless, has given greater prominence to the problem.

Observations about poor conditions for women are no longer restricted
to academic dissertations or to the reports of trade union commissions
or to occasional newspaper articles; they have been included on the
agendas of important political events and given coverage in daily
newspapers. They were criticized in 1987 at the All-Union Conference
of Women and in 1988 at the 19th Party Conference. Reported in
Izvestiia, Tereshkova's speech at the All-Union Conference of Women
regretted the high percentage of women doing manual work, some
carrying extremely heavy loads of 50–60 kilos. She also deplored the
working conditions in the textile industry.[5] Her successor as Chair of the
Soviet Women's Committee, Zoia Pukhova, stepped up criticisms at the
19th Party Conference. In the only speech which focused on women's
issues, she pointed out that textile workers suffered acutely from high
temperatures, too much noise, gas and dust, and endured pulse rates of
90 beats per minute. In fact, 'nearly three and a half million [women]
work in conditions which do not meet the norms and rules of labour
protection'. In addition, over 4 million women worked night shifts, even
though they were forbidden by law to do so except as 'temporary
measures' in 'exceptional circumstances'. This situation had persisted
unchecked for fifty years. Work in the countryside was strenuous in a
different way. Rural women laboured 'from dawn to dusk without days
off or holidays', deprived of basic social supports, modern conveniences
or appropriate medical care.[6] The transition to *khozraschet* (cost-
accounting) and *samofinansirovanie* (self-financing) and the introduction of the brigade system meant further problems for women. These hit
mothers especially hard since other workers out of a heightened concern
with efficiency, would be less keen to work with them. The 19th Party
Conference, regretted Pukhova, had 'not spoken' about this difficulty.
Perestroika not only gave rise to the spectre of unemployment for
women, but produced specific organizational problems for female
labour that economists were not examining.

Glasnost, then, has facilitated sharper criticism of 'old' issues concerning violations of labour law and entailed some criticism of the dis-
advantages of perestroika for female labour. It has also resulted in
criticisms of aspects of working life not hitherto examined. One such
topic is the treatment of female immigrant labour.

In 1990 *Rabotnitsa* pointed out that Soviet television had in the past
exposed the shocking conditions which foreign workers in capitalist
countries suffered. Indignant reporting revealed the various ways in
which foreign labour in France, Holland and the Federal Republic of
Germany was cheated and humiliated. Morever, 'such things can only
exist under capitalism, propaganda convinced us. And we believed it.

Most of us did not suspect that in our own socialist state there were already thousands of foreign workers.'[7] Now glasnost allowed the painful story of Vietnamese labour to be uncovered. *Rabotnitsa* reported that: 'The Vietnamese come to us on hard terms: women for four years, men for six . . . Most of them leave husbands, wives and children at home. According to the agreement, they cannot bring them with them to the Union. Some of them have relatives in other towns in the USSR. Only the militia can grant them permission to meet.'[8] In some detail, *Rabotnitsa* described the difficulties faced by an unemployed woman from Hanoi who ended up in a cotton factory in Krasnodar. Her initial hopes of a better life were dashed because settling in was far from easy. The food was hard to get used to and restrictions limited her movement. On days off she could not visit nearby towns without permission from the MVD. Like many other Vietnamese workers, she was unhappy and wished to return home. The only way, however, to achieve this goal was to go absent from work and be sent home for bad conduct. This was unacceptable since it brought shame on the family. But 'notwithstanding the consequences, more and more Vietnamese are reduced to this'.[9]

The general message conveyed by *Rabotnitsa* was that Vietnamese women suffer in several ways in the USSR and that the agreement signed by the Soviet and Vietnamese governments needs serious revision. It concluded: 'to be a stranger in a foreign country and not to have the opportunity to get out – what could be more terrible?'[10]

As well as providing information about previously hidden problems, like the conditions of foreign workers, glasnost has helped to undermine the often false distinction between 'bad' working conditions under capitalism and 'rosy' ones under socialism. The resulting recognition of shared drawbacks and similar blights shatters unreal images of the two economic systems propagated in ideological texts, and challenges rigid and crude distinctions. Glasnost thus forces the introduction of nuance and complexity into analyses of the workforce.

'Old' problems become 'new' issues: prostitution, abortion, contraception, rape and child abuse

Whereas some economic and social problems, or 'non-antagonistic contradictions', were recognized in the Brezhnev years, such as the female 'double burden', the low level of mechanization of jobs done by women at work and at home and the negligible contribution of men to housework and childrearing, other well-known problems were either whitewashed by ideology or not even mentioned. These included prostitution, horrendous conditions in abortion clinics, the lack of contraception, rape and child abuse. A silence hung over them all. Since the advent of glasnost they have been admitted, albeit with varying degrees of frankness and analytic rigour.

Prostitution was one of the first 'new' issues to be covered by several newspapers and journals such as *Literaturnaia gazeta, Komsomol'skaia pravda, Sovetskaia Rossiia, Nedelia, Trud, Sovetskaia Kirgizia* and *Sotsiologicheskie issledovaniia*. The tone of reporting was that of sensational exposé rather than critical analysis of why prostitution existed. In 1986 and 1987 horror stories abounded. The press revealed that family 'dynasties' of prostitutes 'worked together' including grandmothers of seventy years old down to granddaughters of just fourteen.[11] Prostitution led to syphilis, drunkenness, paralysis, freezing in snowdrifts and the amputation of hands and feet. One deranged man cut a prostitute's throat.[12] Pimps demanded 70 roubles a day protection money; if they did not get it, they turned violent. Prostitutes even fought among themselves to defend their patch and to prevent rivals moving in. Sometimes they worked for Madames who ran teams of young women whom they regularly intimidated and threatened.[13] The prostitutes daydreamed that one day a customer would become fond of them and rescue them from their loneliness, longing and self-destruction.[14] The popular film *Interdevochka* suggested that bored young girls turned to prostitution for excitement and in the hope that a foreign customer would take them to the West.

The media conveyed the message that prostitution was an expression of moral degradation and therefore a disgrace. What reporters did not account for was how prostitution arose under socialism. Previously it had been cast as a characteristic evil of capitalism, unknown and unnecessary to socialism. Now it was common to both economic systems, but the reason why was not broached. Inadequate explanations suggested that prostitution resulted from poor upbringing, single parenthood, divorce and the 'years of stagnation'.[15] Only academic work offered more serious possibilities. A study of prostitutes in Georgia, for example, showed that women sold their bodies not for want of food, but because of differences between their aspirations and the reality of their lives. Low paid jobs made it hard for women to buy boots at 120 roubles a pair. So prostitution often began as a supplement to low incomes. Although the growth of a 'consumerist mentality' reinforced this trend, many prostitutes spent their earnings on their children, housing and food as well as on clothing and cosmetics for themselves. Researchers concluded that prostitution was a 'complex phenomenon' in need of further study.[16] Glasnost makes this possible.

Glasnost has also facilitated harrowing descriptions and condemnations of the abortion system and has given rise to a proliferation of women's letters of complaint. A personal account published in *Moscow News* gave details of the numerous queues a woman has to join in order to prepare for her abortion and documented the rude way in which doctors treat their patients. Before the procedure is performed, women already feel worn down and humiliated. When the dreaded day finally comes:

At 10 in the morning the women waiting for an abortion were lined up at the door of the operating room. God save you from causing delay in this 'conveyor' by making a wrong move or asking an irrelevant question. 'What are you waiting for? Come on, don't stare!' The doctor shouted at me as he was removing his bloodstained rubber gloves, the very sight of which makes me faint. 'You must be mad to come into the operation room wearing socks. Take them off!' he said . . . What followed was the clinking of instruments and acute pain. The anaesthetic was evidently only enough to make me too weak to moan. Well, anaesthetic is expensive, I know.[17]

The writer recalls that afterwards she lay in bed with an icepack on her stomach. But the doctors 'all went home. Not one of them looked in on me or asked how I was feeling.'[18] Such hard-hitting journalism could not have been printed as recently as 1984, except in samizdat materials.[19]

Letters to the press confirm this general picture and provide more gruesome details. One woman advised: 'Most important of all, don't forget all the necessary items: a dressing gown, slippers and two sheets because in our hospital there is not enough bed linen. There were forty of us in two wards with one bed between three. In the toilet there was not even anywhere to wash our hands. There was no tap and no washbasin.'[20] Another warned that: 'they only give anaesthetic for abortions in exceptional circumstances. Of course, anaesthetic is needed more by sick people. Agreed. Woman is by nature patient. Silence tolerates any pain. But it would be better if she did not have to suffer.'[21] Anaesthetic, however, can be produced by paying 50 roubles for an *abort po blatu*. But apparently the *blat* conveyor belt in hospitals is just as busy as the official one.[22]

Due to glasnost, public recognition has finally been given not only to the appalling conditions of the abortion clinics, but also to the obvious point that 'we have not devoted the necessary attention to modern means of contraception'.[23] Just as prostitution did not officially exist after the 1920s, neither did the lack of contraceptives. Birth control was rarely discussed in public, even in the debates about female roles in the 1970s. It received extremely brief attention in 1966 and 1968 when more contraceptives were promised.[24] The topic burst into the press and immediately left it again. Glasnost has broken this silence, helped by fears about the spread of AIDS and calls for protective condoms. Although the literature on birth control has not been as abundant as that on prostitution, it is steadily growing. Glasnost has resulted in two main sorts of publications on contraception: letters of complaint that contraceptives are unobtainable and gynaeocologists unsympathetic; and advice columns in women's magazines.

Anguished letters to *Rabotnitsa, Komsomol'skaia pravda* and *Meditsinskaia gazeta* were printed in 1987 and 1988. One lamented: 'In Ufa they cannot be bought, not even the most basic ones. Not in one chemist's! There aren't enough in Moscow to go there for them.'[25] Another observed: 'We are developing complicated electronics. We sent rockets into space, but we cannot create the needed means of protection against unwanted pregnancies.'[26] Other letters point out that blackmarkets have developed, that prices have jumped one-thousandfold and 'some people are recommending using children's balloons instead of condoms'.[27]

A different sort of letter bewails the way in which gynaecologists treat women. Young girls complain that older gynaecologists respond negatively to their requests for advice.[28] One regretted: 'I have never come across the sort of doctor talked about with rapture in the press and on television. No one eases your torment, kind words do not help. They look at you as though you were a milch cow.'[29] Advice pages on sex and contraception are beginning to fill the information gap. As one doctor interviewed in *Rabotnitsa* put it: 'As a gynaecologist, I consider this conversation my sacred duty.' His stated aim was to help prevent 'the typical situation' in which an inexperienced girl does not realize she is pregnant and later is afraid to tell her mother.[30] Once her mother notices and takes her to the doctor, the pregnancy is far gone. In order to avoid this scenario, he recommends contraception as follows: 'For the first three to four months when intimate relations have only just begun, pills are the most suitable method. With adaptation, once the young people have become used to each other, they can move on to barrier methods, to condoms. Subsequently, they can alternate these methods.'[31]

Past condemnations of contraceptive pills have now been replaced with the view that lower dose pills – Trisiston produced in the former GDR and Rigevidon from Hungary – are safe. But warnings are still issued that pills 'are not vitamins' and are best taken for short spells only.[32] Journalists, however, point out that chemists often respond to requests for pills with the remark that they have not stocked them 'for a long time'.[33]

The general spirit of current advice columns is that even though

sexual activity at a young age is not to be encouraged, advice is nevertheless necessary to prevent legal and illegal abortions and to deter early
pregnancies – all of which are felt to harm health. Glasnost, then, has
contributed to franker discussions of sex life, largely stripped of
uninvited and unhelpful moralizing and disapproval. For many citizens,
however, the key issue is whether or not glasnost results in the production of more contraceptives and then guarantees their general availability. Advice without supply is vacuous. Joint ventures with foreign
firms or an increase in imports may be the fastest ways to meet the
demand for condoms and contraceptive pills. Glasnost can identify the
problems, but action is required to solve them.

Past reluctance to discuss sexual matters such as contraception cannot
be blamed totally on ideology. Sexual issues in a rather conservative
society, often prudish (despite its paradoxically relaxed attitude to
casual sex and hedonism in private), were not publicly discussed for
sociological as well as political reasons. Even with glasnost, many are
embarrassed by these topics in a somewhat Victorian sense, or hesitate
to discuss them openly in a liberal fashion with members of the opposite
sex. As one seemingly modern Leningrader put it to me in 1989, 'you
must not discuss menstruation, birth control or abortion with men.
These are for women's ears only.'

A recent article in *Sobesednik* entitled 'Sex exists here!' challenged
this sensitivity: 'For a very long time it made us ashamed, hypocritically
we carefully hid the most important area of human relations. Now we
are paying for it with ignorance about hygiene, with sexual crudity, with
disgraceful first place in the number of abortions . . . Today it is embar-
rassing to be uneducated about sex. That means uneducated morally
and aesthetically.'[34] Cultural reluctance to discuss sexual topics may
account for why issues such as rape and child abuse have been slow to
come on to agendas. Indeed, these topics were not quick to be examined
in the West. The first became visible in the 1970s and 1980s because of
the emphasis placed by radical feminism on violence against women; the
latter was not defined in Britain as a widespread 'problem' until the late-
1980s, pushed into the headlines by the Cleveland affair.[35] Cultural
factors, a predominance of male editors, and the lack of a women's
movement in the USSR, help to account for why less prominence has
been given to rape than to prostitution or drug addiction.

One article by an academic has proclaimed: 'It's time we talked
frankly about so-called sex-crimes' and argued that the 'head in the sand
attitude' of pretending that rape does not exist 'verges on connivance
with the criminals'.[36] Deploring rape and gang rape in technical col-
leges, the author calls for an analysis of their causes, arguing that 'Men

and men only are the perpetuators [but not the instigators!] of sex crimes.' Attacking myths of the past, she notes: 'It was thought that Soviet young people had no reason to commit such sordid acts. It turns out that this is not quite the case ... It's time we looked the truth squarely in the eye, no matter how bitter it may be: some of our young people have lost their moral composure.'[37] Rape, like prostitution, is seen as a moral blight. But by contrast, glasnost has barely edged 'rape' into the press and by 1990 extremely little had been said about it. Even less has been said about child abuse. At most, there have been elliptical references to violence against children. For instance, coverage of the 1987 conference of the Lenin's Children's Fund made a passing remark that in children's homes and in boarding schools, 'beating of children is the norm'.[38] Elaboration and analysis, however, are wanting.

Glasnost, then, has allowed 'new' issues to be defined. Some problems, however, such as prostitution, crime and drug addiction have been more fully described than others, such as rape and child abuse.[39] Of the issues examined here, prostitution and abortion enjoy the most widespread coverage; the former for its sensationalism, the latter for the gravity of what Kuznetsova calls the 'hell' of the 'world's cruellest abortion system.'[40] Contraception has become an intermittent, but regular, feature in women's magazines.

Newly published statistics

As well as exposing problems and creating some sensationalism, glasnost has resulted in more detailed statistics being released about a range of women's issues. Fresh data, however, are presented in a variety of ways, some extremely incomplete. And even when full tables are produced, one should not assume that an accurate picture is revealed.

Sometimes statistics are cited only in passing and in piecemeal fashion, since they are merely incidental to a more general point. For example, a discussion of abortion and contraception tosses in the fact that only two factories in the USSR produce condoms, which results in a supply of 220 million a year, roughly four for each male.[41] Similarly, reporting on the self-immolation of Muslim women reveals that in 1984 in Tadzhikistan there were thirty known cases of this form of suicide, increasing to forty in 1986.[42] Such selected information is necessary to broader reporting and its source is frequently omitted.

Highly unreliable statistics are also printed. For instance, one article on rape in Belorussia reported that this crime had 'increased by more than 50 per cent' in 1987 in comparison with 1986. Apparently these rapes were committed by over 200 men, of whom 43 per cent were

Table 10.1. *Number of abortions by republic*

	Number of abortions (in 1,000s)			Number of abortions (per 1,000 women aged 15–49)		
	1975	1980	1985	1975	1980	1985
USSR	7,135	7,003	7,034	105.7	102.3	100.3
RSFSR	4,670	4,506	4,552	126.3	122.8	123.6
Ukraine	1,146	1,197	1,179	88.3	94.1	92.2
Belorussia	195	202	201	78.7	81.1	80.0
Uzbekistan	160	161	199	51.9	43.8	46.9
Kazakhstan	391	378	367	108.7	99.2	90.7
Georgia	95	89	69	74.0	67.7	52.4
Azerbaidzhan	59	62	54	43.1	39.0	30.8
Lithuania	46	45	42	53.0	50.9	46.3
Moldavia	93	96	103	89.7	90.7	96.0
Latvia	58	60	58	91.4	92.5	88.7
Kirgizia	64	65	69	84.1	76.6	73.8
Tadzhikistan	39	40	41	53.4	45.3	39.5
Armenia	45	32	34	60.5	38.8	38.4
Turkmenia	34	34	31	60.8	51.1	40.9
Estonia	40	36	35	107.1	96.7	91.4

Source: Goskomstat SSSR, *Naselenie SSSR 1987; Statisticheskii sbornik* (Moscow, 1988), p. 319.

teenagers. More than 70 of the victims were reported to be minors, nearly half of them schoolgirls.[43] But the claim that the incidence of rape is increasing is hard to substantiate. More women may be coming forward to report the crime. As in all countries, official crime statistics result from reported incidents only, which depend upon the willingness of citizens to cooperate. So one cannot automatically accept that the reported social composition of victims is accurate.

More complete tables are also being compiled, such as the number of abortions performed per year in each republic and the urban/rural breakdown of infant mortality rates according to republic. These sorts of comparative statistics allow more thorough analysis of social problems, but are not without their problems too.

For example, in Table 10.1, one can see that in 1985 there were 100.3 abortions for every 1,000 women between the ages of 15 and 49, totalling 7,034,000 abortions. This average is exceeded only in the Russian republic, where there are 123.6 abortions per 1,000 women. Much lower averages in Uzbekistan, Azerbaidzhan, Tadzhikistan and Turkmenia of 46.9, 30.8, 39.5 and 40.9 abortions per 1,000 women respectively, can be accounted for by larger family size among Muslim populations and by the inclination to reproduce rather than to abort. Lithuania stands out among the Baltic states for its low abortion rate of 46.3 abortions per 1,000 women. This can be explained by the strength of Catholicism among Lithuanians who make up 80 per cent of the republic's population.

These statistics, however, should not be assumed to be adequate. Even if they are accurate for official abortions (which is unlikely), they definitely remain incomplete as a record of abortions performed. Although abortions are legal, many women seek illegal abortions either because they seek secrecy or because their pregnancy has gone beyond the legal term for abortion. According to one report, in some parts of the country illegal abortions account for 80 per cent of all abortions.[44] Another notes that there are millions of unregistered abortions a year and hundreds of thousands 'underground'.[45] So whilst comparative statistics suggest social patterns across republics, one should still remain sensitive to what they omit, question the extent to which they are reliable, and query whether one's initial conclusions based upon them are therefore valid.

Just as statistics on abortion were not printed in yearly handbooks in the past, neither were infant mortality rates. Now finally available, they reveal that the death rate of children up to one year of age is exceedingly high in Turkmenia, Tadzhikistan, Uzbekistan, Azerbaidzhan and Kirgizia. As Table 10.2 shows, rates peak in Turkmenia where, distinct from other republics, differences between urban and rural rates are negligible. For instance, in 1986 in Turkmenian towns there were 56.5 deaths per 1,000 births up to the age of one and 59.3 in the countryside. The urban/rural gap is more striking elsewhere. In 1986 in towns in Kirgizia, for example, 28.6 children per 1,000 births died up to one year of age, compared with 42.4 in rural areas. Longitudinal statistics show the alarming trend that infant mortality rates in some republics are not improving, but worsening. For instance, Turkmenia's urban infant mortality rate was the worst recorded since 1980.

But these statistics, too, must be approached with caution. Journalism indicates that case histories were often falsified in the past; thus infant mortality rates were previously understated.[46] If this was regularly the case, then conclusions about trends are, after all, hazardous. Moreover, if the data were not systematically compiled within and across republics according to the same criteria, then valid comparisons cannot be drawn.

So whilst glasnost has resulted in a refreshing release of statistics on problems previously not even acknowledged, the figures should not automatically be assumed to be accurate. They inevitably suffer from fabrications and omissions. Thus data pertinent to different aspects of

Table 10.2. *Infant mortality rates in selected republics (no. of children dying up to 1 year of age, per 1,000 births)*

	1975	1980	1981	1982	1983	1984	1985	1986
RSFSR								
Total population	23.7	22.1	21.5	20.4	20.1	20.9	20.7	19.3
urban	22.5	21.2	20.3	19.5	19.2	19.9	19.8	18.8
rural	26.2	24.0	24.3	22.4	22.4	23.4	22.8	20.4
Uzbekistan								
Total population	53.8	47.0	43.8	42.0	43.1	45.1	45.3	46.2
urban	53.6	44.4	42.3	40.7	40.7	40.3	38.5	40.6
rural	53.8	48.1	44.5	42.6	44.3	47.5	48.7	48.8
Georgia								
Total population	32.7	25.4	29.7	25.4	23.9	23.9	24.0	25.5
urban	29.4	24.3	25.6	24.7	24.6	25.7	27.3	27.6
rural	35.8	26.5	34.0	26.0	23.1	22.0	20.6	23.1
Lithuania								
Total population	19.6	14.5	16.6	15.1	14.1	13.4	14.2	11.6
urban	17.8	12.9	14.5	13.7	13.4	11.8	13.2	10.5
rural	22.5	17.3	20.5	17.8	15.6	16.6	16.3	13.9
Turkmenia								
Total population	56.5	53.6	55.9	52.5	53.2	51.2	52.4	58.2
urban	54.4	57.4	55.7	54.7	55.3	49.1	49.0	56.5
rural	58.0	51.0	56.1	50.9	51.8	52.6	54.7	59.3

Source: Goskomstat, *Naselenie SSSR 1987; Statisticheskii sbornik* (Moscow, 1988), pp. 345–6.

the *zhenskii vopros* may be unreliable and only a rough guide to problem solving, rather than a precise reflection of the scale of difficulties. Nevertheless, they do reveal the immensity of the problems, if only because in the case of abortion and infant mortality, the figures are extremely high, whether or not they are understated.

'New' concepts

Just as glasnost eased the publication of statistics, so it facilitated the use of new concepts in analyses of the *zhenskii vopros*. After 1988 concepts which had previously been ideologically taboo began to be used by some female academics and political actors. These included: *muzhskoi mir* (man's world); *printsipy muzhskogo prevoskhodstva* (principles of male superiority); *patriarkhal'nye predstavleniia* (patriarchal notions); *patriarkhal'noe otnoshenie muzhchiny k zhenschchine* (patriarchal relations of man to woman) and *muzhekratiia* (male dominated bureaucracy).

The adoption of these concepts heralded a significant break with the past since 'class' and 'people' have been the central analytic constructs for the entire history of the Soviet state. Now *muzhskoi mir* suggests a social and political segmentation previously denied by the centrality of class divisions or by the homogeneity of 'all peoples' state'. Similarly, *muzhekratiia* implies that policy making and bureaucracy are male dominated, despite official proclamations about the promotion of equality of the sexes. Moreover, *muzhekratiia* is perpetuated by *print-ispy muzhskogo prevoskhodstva* and *patriarkhal'nye predstavleniia* which suggests that socialist ideology on equality of the sexes has had negligible impact in breaking down stereotypes of female inferiority. In fact, patriarchal principles pervade social life, resulting in *patriarkhal'noe otnoshenie muzhchiny k zhenshchine* which, in turn, reinforces *muzhekratiia*. In sum, patriarchy in politics, economics and society means *fakticheskoe neravenstvo* (factual inequality).

Since 1930 the concept of patriarchy was ideologically acceptable only in discussions of *otstatki neravenstva* (remnants of inequality) in Muslim areas or in more religious parts of the countryside. The party line was that revolution had led to the triumph of the working class and, consequently, the new socialist state represented the interests of working men and women, which were identical. Separate women's interests did not exist, except in so far as women in the 1920s were more 'politically backward' than men and so needed special organizations to mobilize them into politics in order to eradicate the temporary difference. The Zhenotdel and its networks of delegates' meetings and women's clubs served this purpose.[47] Similarly, women's lower rate of participation in politics and economics, regretted in 1956 by Khrushchev, merely highlighted their 'differential needs' which required special social organizations, the *zhensovety*, as tame 'helpers of the CPSU' to address them.[48] These, however, were minor differences between the sexes, of no great political significance. They did not undermine or challenge the way in which politics was run and required no feminist analysis in order to be understood. Biological differences, such as pregnancy, childbirth and motherhood also required special attention in law, and by social services.

Since 1917 'feminism' had been scorned for its misconceived and misplaced analyses of society. Feminism was officially denounced as an example of bourgeois self-indulgence which served to divide the working class since it did not give central focus to class; it was counter-revolutionary since it failed to see the significant difference between working-class and middle-class women. To put the blame on men was to ignore the fact that the interests of working women were closer to those of working-class men than to those of middle-class women. Mode of production and class relations relative to it, not patriarchy, defined women's position.

Soviet condemnations of Western feminism were particularly crude in the 1970s, dismissing it as 'anti-family' and naive in holding that women and men were 'identical'.[49] A systematic reading of liberal, socialist and radical feminism, however, would have shown the diversity and nuances of feminist arguments and revealed that many Western feminists, particularly liberals, were not against the family unit *per se* and that most feminists recognized sexual differences, and some even celebrated them, as did official Soviet ideology. Although the Brezhnev era permitted heated debate about female roles, it did not give space to avowedly feminist arguments, nor allow adoption of feminist concepts.

In 1988, the philosopher Ol'ga Voronina broke this tradition. Voronina criticized the USSR for being 'basically a man's world' in which women endured a 'subjugated position' (*podchinennoe polozhenie*), particularly evident in 'the traditional division of social roles' into 'men's' and 'women's', one result of which was 'hidden fatherlessness' (*skrytaia bezottsovshchina*). Strong patriarchal ideas still pervaded social consciousness, resulting in the widespread view that 'family, house, children – are women's business'. Lenin, she noted, had warned that 'the real emancipation of women and genuine communism only begin when a mass struggle commences against petty housework, or more accurately, a widespread perestroika of it'. In short, woman's double burden denies liberation and harms emotional and spiritual life. The development of a civilized culture and humanitarian society thus 'presupposes equal opportunities and possibilities for everyone, irrespective of sex, age, skin colour and social origin'. Voronina argued that the 'spiritual progress' of Soviet society depends upon the extent to which individuals can develop their own abilities and one necessary route to this is 'the overcoming of patriarchal attitudes towards women'.[50]

Journalist Larisa Kuznetsova echoes Voronina's arguments by claiming that Soviet society has tried to construct a 'third sex' – 'the inevitable superwoman blend of job, family, domestic and maternal roles'. Soviet women are supposed to be happy doing everything, but paradoxically alongside their enormous contribution sits 'our flourishing patriarchal society' which treats women without jobs as socially inferior, discriminates against those who do work, labels those who are unmarried or childless as 'unhappy', and relates to women's sexuality with a lack of contraception and by providing 'the world's cruellest abortion system'. Not only do 'we need to abandon patriarchal habits' but 'it's high time we saw women among the country's leaders'.[51]

Until very recently, the absence of women from the Politburo, Secretariat, Council of Ministers and Central Committee was officially dismissed as insignificant. What mattered was that women's issues were defended by male politicians on these bodies. The high percentage of women on the soviets indicated that equality of the sexes was taken seriously. The fact that women were generally absent from positions of power and present only in large numbers on relatively weak institutions was never mentioned. It was a non-problem. Now women are voicing the opinion that male policy makers overlook many women's issues and that women politicians are needed not just to promote women's issues but to incorporate different values into politics.[52] Glasnost has enabled the low political representation of women to become an issue. By 1989 *Sovetskaia zhenshchina* regretted that 'The higher the echelon of power, the lower the representation of women.'[53] In *Moscow News* Inna Vasilkova maintained that 'restructuring has barely affected the situation of Soviet women. During the 1970s and 1980s, ten women have served as Prime Ministers around the world, and several hundred more have headed government ministries . . . in our country a woman very rarely holds the rank of Minister at the national level.'[54] The situation, according to Zoia Pukhova, is, in fact, worsening. In her speech to the 19th Party Conference she observed that: 'not very long ago, of fifteen ministers of social services in the republics, ten were women – but now only four'.[55] The sharp decrease in the number of women on the Supreme Soviet after the elections of March 1989 from 33 per cent to 15.6 per cent prompted the November 1989 Plenum of the Soviet Women's Committee to ask why women candidates were not being put forward.[56]

Concern about women's low profile in politics is now expressed by female academics and by 'establishment' institutions such as the Soviet Women's Committee, which in the face of female unemployment and lower women's political representation is becoming slightly radicalized. The use of new concepts such as 'patriarchy' means that 'new' questions previously denied legitimacy can be asked. Thus 'new' concepts spark 'new' issues, arguments, conclusions and strategies. Debate is currently taking place about how best women's organizations can promote, support and sustain female people's deputies. This would not be on the agenda if the man's world of *muzhekratiia* had not been identified; nor would the anachronistic persistence of traditional patterns of domestic labour. Of course, these issues are not on all agendas, nor visible in all newspapers and magazines. But they are becoming more prominent on women's agendas – official and informal.

'New' women's groups

New concepts and new arguments are sustained by new women-only groups. Although these were slow to form after democratization made informal groups independent of the CPSU possible (especially in comparison with the speed with which popular fronts were established), by 1990 a diversity of women's groups was evident. Women with different concerns formed different sorts of groups with differing analyses of society and with different strategies for action. Women began pursuing their status as active citizens in various ways.[57]

At the time of writing, three main types of informal groups can be identified. First, there are women-only groups which have formed within broader political movements, such as the women's group of Sajudis. Second, women-only groups devoted to consciousness raising have emerged which attempt to break down traditional gender-role stereotypes and to disseminate feminist literature. The Leningrad women's group which produces *Zhenskoe chtenie* and the Moscow group LOTOS organized by Ol'ga Voronina are two clear examples. Third, several women's professional groups have been established, which stem initially from specific specialisms such as literature, cinema and journalism.

The women in Sajudis formed a separate group since they felt that some women's issues could best be discussed without men. This does not mean, however, that they wished to challenge traditional gender roles or radically to redefine women's lives. They were, in fact, reacting not against Lithuanian men, but against Russian power. As one put it in an interview: 'Men in Lithuania should conduct political struggle, while women should create a beautiful home. There is no point in having an autonomous Lithuania if home life is not improved.'[58] What has to end is not the domestic division of labour but Russian rule and Soviet-style kindergartens whose political indoctrination dishes out 'monstrous information' which produces children with 'atrophied brains'. Mothers later attempt 'to normalize' them and to give the spiritual education that kindergartens lack. The vision of Sajudis women is for 'women to become women and men to become men'. Although they support improved working conditions for women in the labour force, they stress that 'we are not a feminist movement'. Their central complaint is that 'women cannot be complete women in the Soviet Union because home and family are considered insignificant'. They believe that women's identity rests in childbirth and that an independent Lithuania would allow this more fully to blossom. As another put it: 'a bright future will come through family life'.

Whereas the women's group within Sajudis is keen to have the choice to return to *Kinder, Küche, Kirche*, other women's groups take completely different directions. Ol'ga Lipovskaia in Leningrad, with the help of other women, puts out the journal *Zhenskoe chtenie* with the aim of exposing Soviet women to translations of Western feminism. These new radical ideas were previously ideologically unacceptable in the USSR. In a similar spirit, Voronina's Moscow group LOTOS sets out to promote awareness of stereotypes about women's abilities, with the intent of undermining them. Whereas Lithuanian women wish to recapture traditional values which they feel Russian power has denied, more radical Russian women in Leningrad, Moscow and elsewhere hope to challenge patriarchal aspects of Russian society and to transform gender roles. Although it is premature to talk of a broad women's movement since only small uncoordinated women's groups have formed, the institutional potential is being developed. Verbal support for the growth of a movement has also been articulated by Kuznetsova, Lipovskaia and others. A meeting of representatives of women's groups in Moscow in the Spring of 1990 declared the beginning of a women's movement.[59]

Women-only groups organized according to profession provide a narrower base. These groups include: the club of women journalists; the union of women cinematographers; the association of women scholars; the federation of women writers within the Writers' Union; Woman Messenger (*Vestnitsa*) – a Moscow club of women writers; *Femina* – a women's writers club in Irkutsk; a women's writers association in Petrozavodsk; Creativity (*Tvorchestvo*) – an umbrella association of women from different professions.[60]

Limited information is available about the activities and aims of these groups. One should not, however, automatically assume that patterns of action are similar to those of women's professional groups in the West. The founding conference of the Federation of Women Writers, for example, itemized four main goals: first, to confirm the 'feminine principle' (*zhenskoe nachalo*) in society and in literature; second, 'with the help of women to change the climate of society'; third, 'self-determination of *zhenskoe nachalo* in the literary process'; and fourth, 'establishment and strengthening of relations among women writers'.[61] The promotion of *zhenskoe nachalo* is a goal uncharacteristic of Western women's professional groups. It implies that femininity and all that is caring, gentle and sensitive must be cultivated. These writers wish to develop *zhenskoe nachalo* in their manuscripts, in their relations with colleagues and within broader society. This concern overlaps with that of women in Sajudis to develop more fully as women, but seeks to incorporate female values in broader arenas than the family unit. Literature, work and society need *zhenskoe nachalo* too.

Although women-only groups did not form immediately after the opportunity became available, they nevertheless exhibited a great diversity when they finally did sprout. Despite the fact that their memberships are small, involving an extremely tiny percentage of Soviet women, the conviction of those women who are active is strong. Glasnost harnessed to democratization made the emergence of these groups feasible; in the next decade, if democratization proceeds unhalted, many more are likely to become established, resulting in accentuated diversity. Debates within and between women's groups are likely, as are disagreements, controversies and splits.

Women as sex objects: the negative side of glasnost?

While Western feminist literature was quick to point out common patterns of women's subordination in capitalist and socialist systems, it readily praised, as well, the absence of images of women as sex objects in the USSR.[62] The ban on pornography and the lack of advertising typical of free markets, meant that women could not be packaged as sexual playthings, victims or temptresses. A relaxation of ideological controls, however, has meant that bans of the past are gradually being eroded. Although the Resolution on Glasnost states that 'Glasnost must not be used . . . [to] disseminate pornography', by 1989 soft pornography was visible in both Moscow and Leningrad.[63] In 1990 it rapidly proliferated. Earlier in 1988 beauty contests had already brought the theme of women as sex objects into social view. Despite the disapproval of conservative ideologues and more radical women, many newspapers and women's magazines voiced their approval, suggesting that such a harmless activity allowed women to be portrayed as women again.

In September 1989, poster-sized calendars for 1990 were on sale on Moscow streets and in metro stations, portraying sexy women with naked breasts. Either these were not considered 'pornographic' or the Resolution on Glasnost was not being implemented. Although these images might be interpreted by some as examples of erotic art, or at worst, as very soft pornography, the same probably cannot be said for the films shown in several *videosalony* in Leningrad and Moscow. Journalists writing for daily newspapers have not yet asked how these videos can be reconciled with the part of the Resolution on Glasnost which declares 'It is inadmissible for glasnost to be used to the detriment of the interests of the Soviet state, society or the rights of individuals.'[64]

Whether pornography compromises women's rights and harms society has yet to be widely discussed. But in 1990 its 'immorality' was noted by religious figures and by some political actors.

The topic more frequently arises in informal conversations and interviews. Many Soviet academic women view pornography as an inevitable part of democratization. They regret it, but believe that individuals must be free to reject it for themselves. As one put it in 1989, 'Rasputin says pornography is alien to our culture. But we should not shut the door on it. People must choose correctly. It will be a temporary phenomenon.'[65] For many, pornography is not the most important topic. Other issues are far more pressing, such as whether *khozraschet* will result in serious levels of female unemployment, whether famine is imminent, or civil war likely to break out. By comparison, pornography seems trivial and just a tiny part of life, peripheral to many more central concerns.

More media attention, however, has been given to beauty contests. According to the press, the competition for Miss Moscow 1988 was 'highly favoured by the majority of the male population'.[66] In response to criticisms of sexism from the International Democratic Federation of Women, *Krest'ianka* defended the contests, declaring that 'Beauty contests in the Soviet Union are a fact and the very idea of some sort of prohibition would be bizarre'.[67] Moreover, they were properly conducted: 'We did not go the way of analogous foreign competitions like Miss America or Miss Egypt', *Krest'ianka* quoted Mikhail Zlotnikov, director of Miss Moscow 1988. He added, 'The Moscow Beauty is intelligent, discovers ways out of any difficult situation, is in some ways aristocratic (in the best sense of the word) and is, of course, beautiful.[68] In short, socialist states had beautiful women too, and it was time to show them off.

In a similar vein, the monthly digest *Socialism: Principles, Practice, Prospects* reported with pride that the Muscovite Ekaterina Chilichkina had just become Miss Europe after a contest in Helsinki. The general message was that 'While helping women assert themselves at work and be public spirited, socialism wants them to enjoy every aspect of their femininity'.[69] Similarly, *Soviet Weekly* in 1989 in an article entitled 'Face in 100,000' honoured Inna Gania from Kishinev for becoming Miss Photo USSR 1989. With approval it noted: 'The twelve finalists donated their prizes to an auction, proceeds of which went to an AIDS charity organization.'[70] Some scepticism, however, is being shown. A front cover of *Ogonek* showed ten women in glossy swimming costumes competing for 'Charm-89' or 'Fascination-89' (*Ocharovanie*-89), with the caption 'Fascination – according to the regulations?'[71] One critical reader wrote, 'if it is only one step from the sublime to the ridiculous, then there is an entire abyss between beauty and fascination'. Beauty, she argued, could be measured according to 'formulas', but fascination or charm could not. The implication here is that beauty is less important than other qualities. In addition, 'fascination is priceless, but one must pay for beauty. And people paid. The entrance to the competition was 25 roubles'.[72] The disapproval here was brief, and amusing, essentially challenging the seriousness of the event and questioning why so many famous people bothered to be on the jury. In 1988 and 1989 these gentle criticisms were in the minority. This is perhaps because women's beauty is being portrayed as a neglected aspect of femininity that Stalinism and the Brezhnev years of stagnation denied a place. Bold images of socialist realist women coupled with a lack of consumer goods meant that fashionably dressed pretty women were not in the ideological spotlight. Many citizens – female and male alike – wish to see more attention devoted to physical appearance and view criticisms of it either as unnecessarily restrictive or as designed to spoil their enjoyment of aspects of life too long frowned upon or made difficult. The excitement surrounding the opening of Christian Dior and Estee Lauder salons on Gorky Street is part of the same delight that Soviet women can finally benefit from the advantages long enjoyed by Western women.[73] Commenting on Estee Lauder, *Rabotnitsa* observed: 'Estee Lauder cosmetics are used by the most beautiful women in the world.'[74] By implication, they should be available to Soviet women too.

Given Soviet history, the disapproval by some Western feminists of the fanfare surrounding the arrival of Western cosmetics in the USSR and the dismay about the consequent stress on female appearance rather than female achievement, is somewhat misplaced because it is insensitive to what Soviet women have long wanted, envied on Western visitors, and in their overworked, often drab lives, never enjoyed the freedom to use or to reject. The issue is not one of Soviet women wishing only to please, attract or seduce men; it is a question of dressing to suit themselves too. Cosmetics and beauty contests are perceived by millions of Soviet women and men as a part of reclaiming femininity.

Conclusion

The application of glasnost from 1986 to 1990 and beyond has meant that aspects of numerous problems have been exposed, regretted and deplored. Glasnost has brought a renewed dynamism to the *zhenskii vopros* and made its parameters flexible again. Old issues, such as female labour, have become more complex and multifaceted. The implications of *khozraschet* for women are even under attack. 'New' issues have appeared, some with greater prominence than others. If democratization continues, these 'new' issues are likely to be more thoroughly examined; and additional problems will be defined. By the end of the 1990s, the discussions of current issues in the transition period up to 1990 are likely to appear to be exceedingly tame, hesitant and unsystematic.

But although glasnost has helped immigrant labour, prostitution, rape and the lack of contraceptives to shift in status from non-problems and non-topics to live difficulties, it has not always resulted in thorough explanations of why these problems arose, nor suggestions about how best to address them. More critical questions need to be put by investigative journalists, academics, new women's groups and also 'establishment' institutions such as the Soviet Women's Committee before systematic answers can be given. Moreover, the ultimate success of glasnost for citizens hangs upon concrete policies being drawn up and implemented to tackle the difficulties highlighted.

These policies, however, must be both feasible in practice and financially viable. But huge budget deficits, and the failure of perestroika in the economy, mean that the necessary finances for problem solving are limited. The low priority on consumer goods for over half a century cannot be corrected overnight. A speedy availability of contraception, or a fast setting up of rape crisis centres, is unlikely (even with foreign help) since other goods and services defined as more important, such as refrigeration, roads and food supply, are also in need of investment. The history of most states illustrates that women's economic and social needs are low political priorities, best recognized and met in times of economic well-being if women exert political pressure, and also met with extreme reluctance in subsequent periods of austerity only if they have already been enshrined in law – and even then with resistance.[75] The USSR still lacks the necessary preconditions of economic success or sufficient political pressure from women. And by 1990, political chaos meant that even if new laws were adopted, they were often not implemented.

In sum, positive practical results of glasnost's exposés demand more critical analysis, money and a political willingness to act. The first is likely, but the second and third are not. The 1990s, then, may be another unsatisfactory decade for women, of more words, more women's informal groups, even embryonic women's movements, but insufficient government support to answer the problems identified. Thus the prognosis for action rather than words is bleak. Moreover, it is additionally bleak since few women are political gate-keepers or occupy key decision-making posts. The extremely low level of women's political influence means that issues such as rape, contraception and abortion will either be kept off political agendas or, at best, be accorded low salience. Nevertheless, as civil society grows, both informal women's groups and the Soviet Women's Committee are likely to increase their pressure on the state (or states, when the Union finally splinters) for scarce resources.

Notes

I am grateful to the British Academy and to the Soviet Academy of Sciences for a research trip to Moscow and Leningrad in September 1989. I should also like to thank the Rockefeller Foundation for a residency in March 1990 in the Villa Serbelloni where the first draft of this paper was written.

1. 'Rezoliutsiia "o glasnosti"', *XX Vsesoiuznaia Konferentsiia Kommunisticheskoi Partii Sovetskogo Soiuza: stenograficheskii otchet*, vol. 2 (Moscow, 1990), pp. 166–70.
2. Mary Buckley, *Women and Ideology in the Soviet Union* (Hemel Hempstead, Ann Arbor, 1989), pp. 161–90; Mary Buckley, *Soviet Social Scientists Talking: An Official Debate About Women* (London, 1986).
3. Buckley, *Women and Ideology*, pp. 191–223.
4. S. Khavno, '2,000 neschastnykh sluchaev', *Leningradskii rabochii*, no. 3 (1926); G. Zdorovets (ed.), *Khoziaika strany gor: materialy raboty 8-go s"ezda zhenshchin Dagestana* (Makhachkala, 1961); N. V. Panova, *Zhenskii trud v sotsialisticheskom proizvodstve* (candidate degree dissertation abstract, Vilnius, 1970); Z. A. Volkova, *Komissiia profkoma po voprosam truda i byta zhenshchin, okhrany materinstva i detstva* (Moscow, 1984).
5. *Izvestiia*, 1 Feb. 1987.
6. *Izvestiia*, 2 July 1988, p. 10.
7. *Rabotnitsa*, no. 2 (1990), pp. 17, 23.
8. Ibid.
9. Ibid.
10. Ibid.
11. *Sovetskaia Rossiia*, 12 Mar. 1987.
12. Ibid.
13. *Nedelia*, no. 12 (1987), p. 15.
14. *Sovetskaia Rossiia*, 19 Mar. 1987.
15. *Nedelia*, no. 12 (1987), p. 15; *Komsomol'skaia pravda*, 23 Sept. 1987, p. 4; *Literaturnaia gazeta*, 16 Sept. 1987, p. 13.
16. A. A. Gabiani and M. A. Manuil'skii, 'Tsena "liubvi"', *Sotsiologicheskie issledovaniia*, no. 6 (1987), pp. 61–8.
17. *Moscow News*, no. 4 (1989), p. 10.
18. Ibid.
19. V. Golubeva, 'The other side of the medal', in *Woman and Russia: First Feminist Samizdat*, trans. Women in Eastern Europe Group (London, 1980), pp. 51–6.

20. *Rabotnitsa*, no. 7 (1987), p. 12.
21. Ibid.
22. *Sobesednik*, no. 47 (1988), p. 11; I am grateful to Jim Riordan for this reference. *Blat* refers to influence, an exchange of favours, or sometimes to extra payment for services rendered.
23. *Nedelia*, no. 38 (1987), p. 12.
24. *Current Digest of the Soviet Press*, vol. 18, no. 9 (1966), pp. 10–12; vol. 20, no. 49, (1968), pp. 11–12.
25. *Rabotnitsa*, no. 7 (1987), p. 13.
26. Ibid.
27. *Current Digest of the Soviet Press*, vol. 40, no. 25 (1988), p. 25.
28. *Sobesednik*, no. 47 (1988), p. 10.
29. *Rabotnitsa*, no. 7 (1987), p. 12.
30. Ibid., no. 2 (1990), p. 30.
31. Ibid.
32. Ibid.
33. *Sobesednik*, no. 47 (1988), p. 11.
34. Ibid., p. 10.
35. Beatrix Campbell, *Unofficial Secrets* (London, 1988).
36. Current Digest of the Soviet Press, vol. 39, no. 50 (1987), p. 28.
37. Ibid.
38. *Izvestiia*, 15 October 1987.
39. For details of the treatment of these and other 'new' issues, refer to Mary Buckley, 'Social policies and new social issues', in Stephen White, Alex Pravda and Zvi Gitelman (eds), *Developments in Soviet Politics* (London, 1990), pp. 185–206.
40. Larisa Kuznetsova, 'What every woman wants?' *Soviet Weekly*, 26 Nov. 1988, p. 15.
41. *Pravda International*, vol. 3, no. 2 (1988), p. 11.
42. *Komsomol'skaia pravda*, 8 Aug. 1987, p. 4.
43. *Current Digest of the Soviet Press*, vol. 39, no. 50 (1987), p. 27.
44. *Nedelia*, no. 28 (1987), p. 27.
45. *Sobesednik*, no. 47 (1988), p. 11.
46. *Current Digest of the Soviet Press*, vol. 39, no. 50 (1987), p. 29.
47. Buckley, *Women and Ideology*, pp. 18–138.
48. Ibid., pp. 139–60; Genia Browning, *Women and Politics in the USSR* (Hemel Hempstead, 1987).
49. Z. A. Iankova, 'Razvitie lichnosti zhenshchiny v Sovetskom obshchestve', *Sotsiologicheskie issledovaniia*, no. 4 (1975), pp. 42–51.
50. Ol'ga Voronina, 'Muzhchiny sozdali mir dlia sebia', *Sovetskaia zhenshchina*, no. 11 (1988), pp. 14–15.
51. Kuznetsova, 'What every woman wants?' p. 15.
52. Ibid.
53. *Sovetskaia zhenshchina*, no. 1 (1989), p. 4.
54. *Moskovskie novosti*, no. 44, (1989), p. 12.
55. *Izvestiia*, 2 July 1988, p. 10.
56. *Rabotnitsa*, no. 1. (1990), pp. 18–20.
57. For fuller discussion, refer to Mary Buckley 'Gender and reform' in

Catherine Merridale and Chris Ward (eds), *Perestroika in Historical Perspective* (Dunton Green, 1991), pp. 67–80.

58. Information presented here is based upon a meeting with women in Sajudis, which took place in Vilnius in March 1989.
59. *The Guardian*, 19 March 1990.
60. Larisa Vasil'eva, 'Zhenshchina. Zhizn'. Literatura', *Literaturnaia gazeta*, 20 Dec. 1989, p. 7. I am grateful to Gerry Smith for this reference.
61. Ibid.
62. Barbara Holland (ed.), *Soviet Sisterhood* (London, 1985), p. 10.
63. 'Rezoliutsiia "o glasnosti"', p. 170.
64. Ibid.
65. Interview conducted in Moscow, Sept. 1989.
66. *Sputnik*, Dec. 1988, p. 32.
67. *Krest'ianka*, no. 2 (1989), p. 39.
68. Ibid.
69. *Socialism: Principles, Practice, Prospects*, no. 3 (1989) p. 1.
70. *Soviet Weekly*, 28 Dec 1989, p. 6.
71. *Ogonek*, no. 7 (1989), p. 29.
72. Ibid., p. 29.
73. *Moskovskie novosti*, no. 50 (1989), p. 14; *Rabotnitsa*, no. 1 (1990) p. 5.
74. *Rabotnitsa*, no. 1 (1990), p. 5.
75. Mary Buckley and Malcolm Anderson (eds), *Women, Equality and Europe* (London, 1988).

Index

abortion, 168
   discussion of, under glasnost, 204, 208, 210, 211, 217, 224
   statistics, 212–13, 214
   and young women, 182–3
Adamovich, Georgii, 151–2
age
   of beginning sexual relationships, 183
   at marriage, 194
agriculture
   women employed in, 192–3
AIDS (Acquired Immune Deficiency Syndrome), 184, 209
Aizenshtadt, Bertha, 55
Akhmadulina, Bella, 153
Akhmatova, Anna, 38, 40, 41, 42, 147, 149, 152, 156
Akker, Z.I., 51, 59, 61
alcohol abuse, 197
Alekseev-Iakovlev, A.I., 12
Alekseeva, Lidiia, 154
Alexander II, Tsar, 78, 79
Alexander III, Tsar, 49
Aliger, Margarita, 152, 153
androgynous personae
   in women's poetry, 38–9, 40
Anisimov, V.A., 113
Annenskii, I.F., 32, 40
Anstei, Ol'ga, 154
Armenia
   abortion statistics, 212
Austria–Hungary
   women pharmacists, 49
autobiography, women's, 42–3
Azerbaidzhan
   abortion statistics, 212
   infant mortality rates, 213

'back to the home' lobby, 191–3, 196–9
Bal'mont, K.D., 40
Bashkirtseva, Mariia, 34–6, 43
beauty contests, 185–7, 220, 221–2

Bebel, August, 164, 173
Belavina, Nonna, 154
Belgium
   women pharmacists, 49
Belokonskii, I.P., 106
Belorussia
   abortion statistics, 212
   rape statistics, 211–12
Belyi, Andrei, 40
Besant, Annie, 35
birth control, see contraception
birthrate, 179, 180, 190
Blok, A.A., 40, 148
Blokh, Raisa, 152
Bloody Sunday (1905), 78, 83, 85
Bobroff, Anne, 8, 9, 21, 23
Bocharnikova, Mariia, 131, 132, 140
Bochkareva, Mariia, 125, 127, 128, 129, 131, 132, 133–4, 135–7, 138, 141
Bogoslovskii, V.S., 49
Brecht, Bertolt, 21
Breshko-Breshkovskaia, E.K., 105
Brezhnev, L.I., 178, 179
Britain
   women pharmacists, 48
Briusov, Valerii, 36, 40
Broido, Eva, 53, 54, 61
Bronner, V.M., 169–70, 172
Brusilov, General, 129, 133, 141
Bryant, Louise, 124, 132, 134–5, 136, 137, 140
Buchanan, Meriel, 135
Bunin, I.A., 38, 40
Burke, Peter, 6
Burtsev, V.I., 106
Bushman, Irina, 154

Canada
   women pharmacists, 48
capitalism
   and prostitution, 160, 162, 165

227